Don't let the word 'theologian' in the title fool you. There's nothing 'ivory tower' about this book. To the contrary, Burns articulately argues that missionaries should, indeed, be out and about and engaged in God's global mission. But they may not—they must not—be driven by mere emotions. Rather, they must be masters of the Word of God, and they must be mastered by the God of the Word. They must be rooted in Christ and the Bible like Isaiah's 'oaks of righteousness, a planting of the Lord for the display of his splendor' (Isa. 61:3). Burns skillfully takes the reader on a journey 'of thought, reflection, and biblical convictions about the vocation of the missionary ... for the sake of the least reached and the sake of God's global glory.' He does so with rich and insightful doses of Scripture, history, theology, and missiology, as well as illuminating examples from his own life and others'. As both a missionary and a theologian, Burns has written with aplomb and authority; as an impassioned follower of Christ, he's written with humility and hope. Being the co-founder of a mission agency, a professor, and a cross-cultural missionary myself since 1989, I'll be utilizing this book with the missionaries and students I serve, and recommending it at every possible opportunity.

João Mordomo
Co-founder and Vice-Chair, Crossover Global
Senior Associate, Lausanne Movement
Professor of Missiology and Intercultural Studies

Timely, compelling, practical, and perceptive, *The Missionary-Theologian* reunites what many have divided—global missions and gospel doctrine. It warns us of dangerous landmines, guides us through the thicket of contemporary missions issues, and offers us a Christ-centered, biblically serious, church-minded, and grace-driven approach to missions. Missionaries—and those who teach, mobilize, send, support, and pray for them—will want to read this fresh and straightforward volume.

CHRISTOPHER W. MORGAN
Dean of Theology, California Baptist University, Riverside, California
Author/editor of more than twenty books

Should missionaries be theologians? E.D. Burns' study—a carefully reasoned and scriptural reminder that our theology should drive our missiology, including its methodology—argues that they should. It is a clarion call to rethink what we are doing, and in particular, why and how we are doing it in the light of our theology. All of us who aspire to do God's work in missions would do well to read it and seek biblical compliance in our ministries.

DAVE DEUEL
Academic Dean Emeritus, the Master's Academy International, Sun Valley, California
Senior Research Fellow, the Christian Institute on Disability
Disability Catalyst, the Lausanne Movement

This new book by E.D. Burns, focusing on the crucial fundamentals that should undergird today's mission, has been sorely needed for some time. It is refreshing to once again have available for mission practitioners a strongly biblical approach to and subsequent evaluation of, the praxis of missions. Written by a perceptive 'missionary-theologian,' Burns guides missionaries how to be theologically adept as they perform their high calling as God's global message bearers. I cannot recommend this book enough.

MARVIN J. NEWELL
Staff Missiologist, Missio Nexus

When I desire a direct and biblical answer to a complex theological question, I ask E.D. Burns. When the Lord's church needs an earnest reminder of the Christ-centered nature of missions, they should read Burns. I rejoice that he writes clearly, simply, and directly with both conviction of the soul and an irrepressible insistence that Jesus be exalted among the nations. My prediction: you will read this book twice!

MIKE ABENDROTH
Pastor of Bethlehem Bible Church, Boylston, Massachusetts
Host of No Compromise Radio

Few areas of Christian ministry have suffered mission drift as subtly and dramatically as Christian missions. The reason for this slide is simple. For far too many, missionary work has been severed from theology. This is a book I have been hoping to find for years. It is a biblical tonic for missions misunderstanding. I know E.D. Burns and have tasted the fruit of his missionary efforts; he is the right person to pen this book. This volume is for missionaries, pastors, congregants, missionaries-in-training, and anyone who wants to think more biblically about Christ's heart for the nations. It will strengthen your theological moorings, correct sentimental misconceptions, and warm your heart devotionally toward biblical missions.

RICK HOLLAND
Mission Road Bible Church, Kansas City, Kansas

Missionary life is replete with failures, distractions, and frustrations, causing many missionaries to question their effectiveness or, worse, doubt their calling. In this thought-provoking yet accessible book, Burns draws on his many years of experience as a cross-cultural practitioner and theologian to help release the missionary from this self-focused introspection and find hope, assurance, and endurance in the all-sufficient power of Christ and His Word. The result is a Gospel-driven approach to mission that is theologically rich, Spirit-empowered, and biblically informed.

JAMES A. BLUMENSTOCK
Dean & Associate Professor of Philosophical Theology,
Asia Biblical Theological Seminary, Chiang Mai, Thailand

The Missionary-Theologian provides a no-nonsense, hard-hitting resource that refuses to reduce the missionary calling to anything less than a Christocentric, Word-driven, Spirit-led, church-affirmed, theologically equipped invitation to proclaim the good news of Jesus Christ to the unreached peoples of the world. Emphasizing that methodology follows theology, Burns urges with both passion and experience how the Word of God must be central to every aspect of the missionary's life and relationships, both abroad and at home. This book is a valuable antidote to the increasing tendency to reduce missions to experiential-only encounters that fear offending man rather than fearing God.

BILLY COPPEDGE
Lausanne Movement Catalyst for Orality
Worker for Africa Gospel Church, Uganda (World Gospel Mission)

The Missionary-Theologian is a must read for all Christian leaders, even more so for those called to serve as missionaries. Since the Bible is the Word of God, it contains the self-sufficient content and strategy for missions. The missionary should know how to properly handle, proclaim, and obey it. In this book Dr. Burns makes a solid argument for this simple and powerful eternal truth in a beautifully presented and solidly supported fashion. As a product of missions myself, and now serving as a missionary among the 'least reached', I've seen the fruit of the sacrificial labor of those that follow this truth, and, sadly, the lack of fruit of those that follow their own well-intended and grandiose-sounding strategies. Either we seriously and practically make Jesus our example, work together and preach the Word, or resign ourselves to fruitless and frustrating lives with fruit that will not last. This book is a clarion call for lives that bear fruit that last.

CARLOS CALDERÓN
Vice President, Partners International

In *The Missionary-Theologian*, Dr. Burns has given the church a clear call to consider the gospel as the greatest motivation for missions, not simply as the missionary message to preach to the world, but as the sustaining joy and hope of missionary life and ministry. He reminds the reader of the centrality of the written Word while igniting a passion for the necessity of boldly, clearly, and verbally proclaiming the Word to the world.

JOE FAUTH
Senior Pastor, Calvary Bible Church, Wrightsville, Pennsylvania
Co-founder, Spread of Grace Ministries

The Missionary-Theologian cuts like a surgeon's scalpel, graciously excising the disease and bringing wholeness to form a theology and philosophy of missions that is emphatically biblical. As a pastor in the local church, this work brings great hope to my soul for the future of missions and its enduring legacy, rooted in fidelity to sound doctrine. For too long, we in the West have minimized the heart of gospel ministry as being profoundly and primarily theological. Instead we have substituted biblical truth with the temporary, pseudo-spiritual remedies of man-centered experience and emotion. Dr. Burns has written with clarity, boldness, and accuracy to call all who value the glory of God among the nations to reconsider and retool for a ministry founded upon the power of the Word of God. His writing here cannot be missed or overlooked in our churches, our seminaries, or on the field. Read it and apply!

BRIAN FAIRCHILD
Pastor, Colonial Bible Church, Midland, Texas

Tenacious. That word kept coming to mind as I read this book. I met Burns when we were students together. He was the one leading spontaneous prayer meetings for the nations and speaking about the glory of God. Neither would let him go. This work represents that happy union of theology and mission after two decades in the meat smoker of study and experience. Here is a book on the church and her mission and a theology of both; a book that holds onto the doctrine of sola scriptura and to the practice of global missions as though everything depends on it. Let this book convince you—or re-convince you—that indeed everything is at stake.

TRENT HUNTER
Pastor for Preaching and Teaching, Heritage Bible Church, Greer, South Carolina

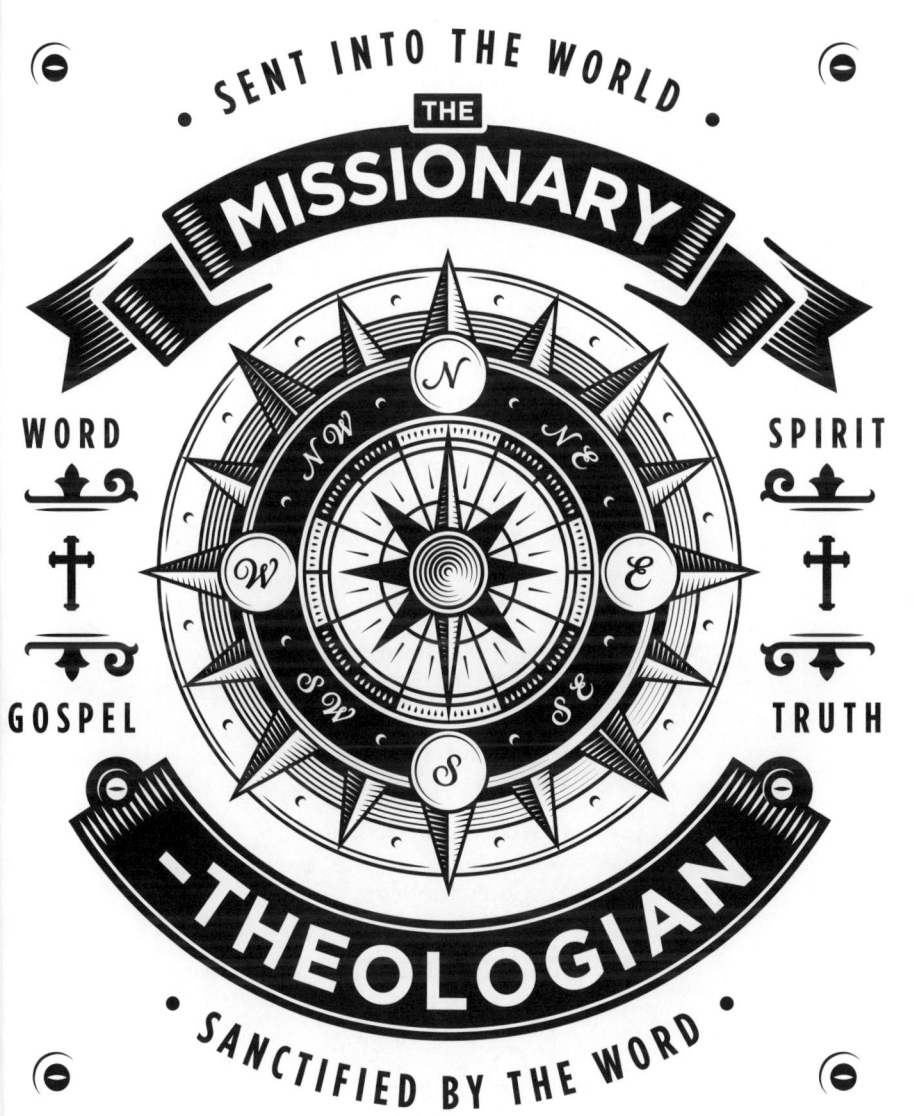

Scripture quotations are from *The Holy Bible, English Standard Version*, copyright © 2001 by Crossway Bibles, a division of Good News Publishers. Used by permission. All rights reserved.

Scripture quotations marked "NKJV" are taken from the *New King James Version*. Copyright © 1982 by Thomas Nelson, Inc. Used by permission. All rights reserved.

Scripture quotations marked "KJV" are taken from *The King James Version*.

Copyright © E.D. Burns 2020

paperback ISBN 978-1-5271-0539-3
epub ISBN 978-1-5271-0599-7
mobi ISBN 978-1-5271-0600-0

10 9 8 7 6 5 4 3 2 1

Published in 2020
by
Christian Focus Publications Ltd,
Geanies House, Fearn, Ross-shire,
IV20 1TW, Great Britain.

www.christianfocus.com

Cover design by
Pete Barnsley

Printed and bound by
Bell & Bain

All rights reserved. No part of this publication may be reproduced, stored in a retrieval system, or transmitted, in any form, by any means, electronic, mechanical, photocopying, recording or otherwise without the prior permission of the publisher or a licence permitting restricted copying. In the U.K. such licences are issued by the Copyright Licensing Agency, Saffron House, 6-10 Kirby Street, London, EC1 8TS. www.cla.co.uk

CONTENTS

Dedication 10

Foreword 13

Preface 17

Acknowledgements 19

Introduction 21

1. The Making of a Missionary-Theologian 33

2. The Missionary as Summoned from the Word 51

3. The Missionary in Prayer and Consecration with the Word 69

4. The Missionary as Servant of the Word 91

5. The Missionary as 'Sent One' of the Sending Church 119

6. The Missionary in the Global Context 143

7. The Missionary as Pastoral Model and Church-Planter 167

8. The Missionary as Apologist 191

9. Adoniram and Ann Judson as Word-Driven Missionary-Theologians 207

Conclusion 225

Appendix 1: The Missionary Life: No Shortcuts, by E.D. Burns 229

Appendix 2: Advice to Missionary Candidates, by Adoniram Judson 233

Appendix 3: The Missionaries' Charge and Charter, by C.H. Spurgeon 237

Sources 255

Dedicated to:
My father, the man who taught me both courage for the Word of Christ and compassion for the unreached and afflicted.

'All that I am I owe to Jesus Christ, revealed to me in His divine Book.'

– DAVID LIVINGSTONE

FOREWORD

IT is now a commonplace to separate missions from theology, Christian action from Christian doctrine. More than we know, we live in a post-truth culture. In such a setting, deeds trump thinking. Thinking, in fact, gets in the way of deeds. Better to put the books back on the shelf, sing some soaring anthems, and get out into the world in order to 'love on people.'

This is a tragic and unbiblical divorce. In Scripture, there is no tension between truth and truth-telling, between adoration of God and proclamation of God. The two work together. The study of God fuels the pursuit of God. Zeal for the Father in our devotional life yields zeal in everyday life. The preaching of sound doctrine creates sound men who lead sound churches as elders, whether 'at home' or in the missionary fields that are white for harvest (John 4:34).

E.D. Burns makes this critical connection in this very helpful book. He shows that the missionary must be a theologian. In his understanding, theological work is not high, lofty, and above the clouds. Theology is made for the street, for the bazaar, for the difficult evangelistic challenges missionaries face, for apologetics, for needy people in the local congregation, for husbands and wives tackling the challenges of marriage in the setting of cross-cultural missions. Theology—the truth of God—is not a luxury. Theology is a necessity.

This conviction infuses the pages that follow. Burns issues a call in this text for missionaries to return to a robustly doctrinal conception of their work. His call has first reference, rightly so, to men, for men must form the backbone of the local church on the mission field. This is an important point. We sometimes seem to send missionaries out on their own with little ecclesiological strategy other than to meet whomever they can and win lost souls however they're able. There are doubtless good motives at play here, but problems quickly proliferate. As one example, what happens when people get genuinely saved, and the disciples made through faithful evangelism need a shepherd and a pastor and—over time, as men are trained up—a body of elders to lead them? Suffice it to say that Burns' text will help us reenvision the way we structure the teams we send to the mission field. We need to do so with ecclesiology not as an afterthought, but as a pressing concern.

In the precise ordering of church polity, Burns is more flexible than some. Nonetheless his call is a valuable one. He rightly sees men and women working together in the great endeavor of missions, but he has the mark of leadership where Scripture has it, where the apostles had it. We need pastoral shepherding no less in cross-cultural contexts than our own. This book makes a link that is often nowhere to be found: it builds the case for sound doctrine creating sound men who lead sound churches on the field, to restate the matter. Praise God for this estimable recovery, unfolded with eloquence and dogged biblical fidelity in these pages.

Burns does not shy away from hard topics and difficult experiences. He writes not only as a theologian, but as a missionary, and one who has navigated hardships in past days. This is not a theoretical text, and readers must not draw that conclusion: 'Well, he's a theology geek, so of course he's going to say that doctrine matters!' No, Burns has suffered for Christ. He and his family have labored in the name of Jesus to advance the glory of that name. There are distant echoes of Paul's experience to be found in these pages; the same Paul who is dismissed as 'Western' in his ideas (but was a Middle-Eastern Jew by background, we note!) and airily theological in his platform was actually a ruggedly tough, ferociously committed, nearly-broken-by-stress-and-pain missionary. His catalogue of woes suffered on the field is nothing less than breathtaking (see 2 Cor. 11:21-29). We get some of that taste of missions work in this book, and much frank, spirited, and profitable discussion of how to handle seemingly small—but quite important—matters like coordination with sending churches, giving, visits, and so on.

This is a book worthy of study. For all who are thinking through the call to missions, this is a sturdy, sobering, and insightful text. Right after a student, for example, hears a stirring challenge to go and share the gospel to unreached peoples, they should read this book. They should, in other words, count the cost. Both elements, the inspiring call and the careful consideration, are needed. But we must think more about the fact that we are in a feelings-driven age, and it is now easier than ever to surf the wave of an experience all the way to a faraway place, only to find that once the feeling subsides, so too does the zeal for gospel promotion. Feelings are not bad; God gave them to us, and God wants them channeled heavenward (read Psalm 119 afresh). But we need something stronger than feelings to make missionaries and to advance the gospel by the power of the Spirit. We need truth. We need doctrine. We need gospel conviction pulsing in our blood. We need toughness born of a reverential vision of the Almighty. We need hope that is theocentric, and so cannot be blown away by the severe attacks of the devil who hates us and seeks our ruin, temporally and eternally.

We need also to remember the faithful example of past heroes like Adoniram Judson, no stranger to the upcoming chapters. After a missionary career of great trials and brutal costs, Judson did not lament the toll taken by his exertions. He did not gripe. He did not look downward at all, but lifted his gaze—and ours—by remembering the kindness of the Lord: 'If I had not felt certain that every additional trial was ordered by infinite love and mercy, I could not have survived my accumulated sufferings.'

It was not feelings or church acclaim or 'can do' spirit that put a banner over all Judson's work. It was the fact that a holy and loving God had ordered every detail of his ministry and existence. Did Judson need sound doctrine? Yes, he did. Was Judson a missionary-theologian? Yes, he was. Should we go and do likewise in our time, facing many threats and difficulties? Yes, we should.

This faithful book is a summons to that glorious end.

Dr Owen Strachan
Associate Professor of Christian Theology,
Midwestern Baptist Theological Seminary

PREFACE

THIS book is truly comprised of many little books that I have written throughout my missionary career. It is a compilation of many years, even decades, of thought, reflection, and biblical convictions about the vocation of the missionary. I am always learning more and growing in this area myself, so as with any book, I have made hard decisions about what to emphasize to the omission of other pertinent topics. Realizing that there is much more I could have said and maybe should have said, my prayer is that this book will not just inform the mind of missionaries and missions-minded people, but that it will ultimately leave an impression on their souls to be doggedly determined to rest in Christ as their righteousness, to joyfully surrender to the Word of God, to wholeheartedly trust Christ to build His global church, and to be bold in liberally disseminating the gospel, knowing that the power is in the seed.

Regarding language, spelling and conventions follow U.S. style, and unless otherwise noted, all quotations maintain the original spelling and all Scriptural references derive from the English Standard Version.[1] I have consciously chosen to use the generic 'he' unless speaking of a particular person or group of people, mainly because of how clunky it is to always say 'he/she' and 'him/her'. The audience I have in mind is generally the Western-educated graduate student and missionary-in-training, the missionary-sending pastor, the mission agency leader, and ultimately the missionary on the field. Additionally, it is my assumption that the missionaries who might benefit most from

---

1. Holy Bible, *English Standard Version* (Wheaton: Crossway, 2011).

this book will typically be men occupying positions of leadership, training pastors/leaders, and planting churches. However, I do hope female missionaries will benefit from this book as well. I am so thankful for the many godly women on the mission field who are great evangelists, teachers, helpers, administrators, counselors, disciple-makers, wives, and mothers. Half of the adult population around the world are women, and there are many more children. There are billions of unreached women and children whom female missionaries reach much more easily—due to cultural customs and taboos—than male missionaries ever could. To their credit, there are approximately twice as many women as men on the mission field. It is difficult to imagine how tiny the missionary force would be without the strong, devout, and proven women serving in ways that very few would desire.

ACKNOWLEDGEMENTS

I AM indebted to many friends and mentors over the years who have invested in me and influenced my thinking and spiritual growth. This book is an outgrowth of many years of meditating on the Bible, serving internationally as a missionary, studying church history and theology, and learning from Christian servants much godlier and more qualified than me.

First, I wish to thank my friend, Mike Abendroth, for reminding me to rest in Jesus and His sufficient work for me. Mike has encouraged me in writing this book, and having scrutinized the early manuscript, he provided invaluable sage-like feedback, as that of a model pastor-theologian.

I wish to thank my students and alumni who have encouraged me to write this book over the years. I wrote this book for my students and those around the world whom they will influence. I am thankful for my many missionary friends, pastors, and colleagues who have challenged my thinking and sharpened my ideas.

I am grateful to my mother and father for their undying support and love for me; to my mother who models a caring affection for people, and to my father who is a man of courage, love, and soul-earnest devotion to the gospel of God. I can't imagine better parents.

I am thankful for my sister, her humor and undying love, and to the rest of my family and extended family, thank you for standing with me in the gospel.

Most of all, I am indebted to my sweet, faithful, encouraging wife, Kristie. The sacrifices she has made in enabling me to take two short writing leaves to finish this book were an immeasurable blessing. She has affirmed and supported the passion for this book. She is a better helpmate than I ever knew to pray for. And for our sons, Elijah and Isaiah, I am so proud to see their personal love for the God of the Bible, their deep-seated concern for the plight of the unreached, and their commitment to the missionary calling at such a young age. I am truly undeserving and blessed beyond description to be their father.

I give thanks to the triune God for saving me, sanctifying me by the Word, and sending me into the world for the gospel of Christ. I feel both humbled and honored.

INTRODUCTION

TRUTH matters for eternity. Words have meaning, and ideas have consequences. I care deeply about the eternal state of souls, both the lost and the redeemed. I ache over the plight of the unreached perishing apart from any knowledge of Christ, but I am also saddened for those big-hearted Christians who lack discernment and go from one waterless cloud to another, seeking refreshment and fruitfulness, but in the end feeling weary and unsure that their lives and ministries are actually producing fruit at all. This book is for you.

Hopefully you will see this book not as a strident criticism of the state of missions and the thankless work of missionaries, but rather as a brotherly and friendly plea that we rest in Christ's work and abide in His Word. For the sake of the least reached and for the sake of God's global glory, my prayer is that together we seek to be found faithful to the Pioneer of our faith and to His final commission.

Addressing common observations

As I have traveled the world and worked alongside numerous mission agencies and have seen varying styles of church leadership and missions philosophy, I have come to realize that most people, whether senders or goers, make emotional, experience-based, and reactionary decisions about missions. They care deeply and are whole-heartedly invested; often they just lack the cultural, historical, and theological perspective needed to make wise, discerning, long-range decisions that are biblically faithful, theologically consistent, and culturally wise. Furthermore, many are not theologically trained and not competent to teach the whole counsel of God.

In this age, fewer and fewer missionaries ground their missionary conviction and call in the Scriptures, and increasingly they cite compelling experiences, dreams, leading signs, open doors, and actual words from the Lord. I have also seen a handful of missionaries who, after going through dark seasons on the field, return to their sending country and sometimes leave the faith altogether. Often one of the main reasons given is because they cannot hear the voice of God telling them what to do, and they are paralyzed in fear that they will miss God's perfect will. I realize this is evidence of a larger problem they already had that was just squeezed out by the meat grinder of missionary living, but a common denominator in each of their lives that I have witnessed is that they inadequately handle the Bible, they do not hide it in their hearts and store it up like gold, they do not trust it to do its work in their ministries, and they find their strength from popular books about hearing God's voice and from conferences and prayer times where people share 'words from the Lord' with them. They are far more fascinated with the mystical than the biblical, with the pragmatic than the propositional.

Considering current trends

The twentieth century saw an explosion of missions involvement, but in contrast to those who went before, this last generation has been woefully untrained theologically. Most missionaries in church history have, in preparation for the field, committed themselves to rigorous study and extraordinary theological training that, compared to our educational standards today, seem draconian and excessive. However, increasingly the sentiment is that the less you are theologically trained, the closer you are to Jesus; the logic goes that knowledge quenches the Spirit and puts God in a theological box, which is blamed as the fruit of European rationalism and American fundamentalism.

How did we get to this place? Many factors have contributed, probably even some undetected ones, but to name a few dominant factors that missiologists and historians have shared with me over the last twenty years: the short-term missions boom and the subsequent reduction of interest in long-term commitment, the rise of egalitarianism and the consequent flattening of roles and duties, the death of expertise, anti-authoritarian movements, the gutting of inerrancy from flagship seminaries for global mission, the ease of jet travel, unprecedented affluence, the globalization of pop culture, the information age explosion, the syncretizing of soft evangelicalism with the latest cultural fads, the mainstreaming of anti-dogmatic liberal theology, and the overall juvenilization of evangelicalism that has abandoned the doctrinal and textual for the experiential and emotional.

No coordinated conspiracy to dumb down missions exists; there can sometimes be just a lack of thoughtfulness, discernment, care, and wise long-term planning. The principles of this book could be applied to most ministry leaders anywhere in the global church, but I have written most directly and naturally to those from historically missionary-sending nations. I believe there are innumerable unknown courageous acts of Christian sacrifice accomplished around the world for the gospel; I look forward to hearing those marvelous stories upon arriving at our heavenly country. I hope this book helps those at the beginning and in the middle of their missionary story to think biblically, discern theologically, and work faithfully for the rest of their earthly chapters.

Seeing the scope of the book

The main point of this book is this: Because of our righteous standing and union with Christ and because of His reign over the nations, when the Holy Spirit propels Bible-centrality that mobilizes the heart, instructs the mind, and consecrates the life of the missionary to Christ, fruit-bearing in mission will result. Out of a trusting gratitude to Christ for His substitutionary, redeeming grace alone, received by faith alone, *to the degree that missionaries lead with the Christ-centered Word, are directed by the Christ-centered Word, experience God through the Christ-centered Word, and impress upon people the sufficiency of the Christ-centered Word, to that degree are they faithfully following Christ as He establishes His church among all the nations. Jesus is the true Missionary; proclaiming His Word is the method, through the means of His Spirit.*

The first chapter contends that gospel doctrine is the lifeblood of a missionary-theologian; the second chapter grounds the missionary mandate and subjective/objective missionary call in the Word of God; the third chapter outlines the centrality of prayer and the pursuit of Word-centered godliness for the missionary; the fourth chapter argues that the missionary should devoutly immerse himself in the biblical text so that his ministry philosophy and methods are theologically sound; the fifth chapter highlights how to theologically consider the challenges and opportunities of partnering with sending churches; the sixth chapter makes a case for leading, serving, and partnering with the global church in a way that is biblically faithful, theologically helpful, and relationally sensitive; the seventh chapter discusses how a missionary-theologian should consider modeling the role of a humble Bible-centered shepherd and not overstepping his delegated authority; the eighth chapter demonstrates how the missionary should and can be a courageous apologist that neither compromises the gospel nor unnecessarily accommodates the worldviews of the target culture; and the ninth chapter is a historical and academic synthesis of the Word-centered strategies of the first American missionaries to Burma—Adoniram Jr. (1788–1850) and Ann Judson (1789–1826).

Hearing the heart of the book

I have consciously written this book with varied styles—polemical, devotional, popular, exegetical, theological, and academic—seeking to model various perspectives a missionary-theologian might want to consider. Moreover, my general writing style aims at those in the middle of their missionary career and the generations following them, since they are the future of global missions and will most likely be the ones reading this. With the culture of that audience in mind, without apology, my argumentation style is punchy and to the point. This persuasive style of writing is intentional, especially since so much best-selling evangelical publications and popular Christian radio exhibit levity more than gravity, plastic more than granite. At times these chapters might seem like a round-table debate with like-minded colleagues, and in other places it might seem like auditing a seminary classroom lecture. Though I could have written strictly for the academic guild as I have done with other publications, I chose, rather, to write for the practitioner who is passionate for God's name to be

INTRODUCTION

worshiped around the world, who likes to ponder deep consequential matters, and yet maybe who has rarely been stirred up to think of these subjects much before. I have prioritized and consciously included some themes to the exclusion of others. And none of my chapters purport to exhaustively cover their topics. Hopefully they will at least jumpstart dialogue, debate, and deep thinking. I have aimed to sensitively examine some issues that are allegedly politically incorrect or incongruent with our twenty-first-century cultural sensibilities. I realize it would be ideal to communicate the contents of this book along with non-verbal language, voice intonation, and in a class setting with question-and-answer and group discussion. This book grew out of numerous class lectures and discussions that my students found helpful for encouraging fresh thinking.

I have heard from booksellers that Millennials tend to be cause-driven and in need of constant praise, and consequently books not substantially incorporating those elements do not popularly sell. This assertion precisely proves my point: we need less cause-driven missionaries and more truth-driven missionaries. Indeed, it is true that mobilizing missionaries today based upon a noble cause is most motivationally effective, but what happens when they discover what feels like a greater cause? A more exciting and well-admired initiative? What happens when the emotions run dry and when all optimism for kingdom impact, as genuine and noble as it might be, seems shattered? What then when the heart is sick with dashed hopes and when feelings of triumph languish like a fading dream? If there is no one standing on Scripture alone now, then no one will remain standing.

This book will have its limitations and faults, which are entirely my own. I am aware that my experience and education limit my perspective, and I frequently feel humbled and even embarrassed by my own myopic perspectives and what I have yet to learn. Moreover, I realize that I do not see, explain, and prioritize the same issues as brothers and sisters would in other parts of the world, such as in Myanmar, Chile, South Africa, Palestine, Romania, or Australia. I am always growing and in need of improvement. No two missionaries are equal; everyone has their own experiences, personalities, temperaments, gifts, vocations, and influences. My way of saying these things and the particular issues

I have highlighted to the exclusion of other worthy topics will greatly differ from other godlier, sharper, and wiser missionaries. And to be sure, the missionary I am today in the middle of my missionary 'career' is not the same person I will be in thirty more years, and if I were to write this book then, hopefully I would be markedly humbler, wiser, and more biblical.

A missionary-theologian is not necessarily someone who has a doctorate, who publishes, and who operates at an academic level; very few will endeavor to attain that threshold. Not many will have opportunity or ability to train theologically at an advanced level. Some missionaries can thrive by mere self-study, whereas some would benefit more from formal, face-to-face interaction with professors and colleagues. Most are doers more than they are thinkers. There is nothing wrong with that, but with the immense amount of popular literature that focuses on methods and techniques, slowing down to contemplate the theology and implications of fundamental ideas is always a beneficial exercise. Most of us missions-minded folk are productivity-driven activists and legalists at heart. And it takes a work of the Holy Spirit to drive our roots down deep into the Word, where we meditate and take refuge in Christ's work and wait on Him to accomplish His purposes in His way and in His time.

Paul the missionary

It is my conviction that the Apostle Paul was the exemplary missionary-theologian. Many pastors like to describe Paul as the exemplary pastor, but when comparing the two, he functioned much more like a missionary than a pastor. True, pastors can and should learn from Paul's pastoral theology, but if anyone should be looking to Paul for cues and instruction, it should be missionaries.

This book is a clarion call to stir up a new breed of Pauline missionary-theologians, who rest in Christ's work alone, standing on *sola scriptura* in the face of any new missions methods that supposedly 'really work this time' and of any new spiritual experience that promises real power, inner-healing, and freedom from brokenness, and of any Christian leaders who claim to speak on behalf of God and know God's secret will. My prayer is that this book will awaken missionaries and missionary-senders to cling for their lives to Christ and His sacred text with this steadfast resolve: 'To the teaching and to the testimony! If they will not speak according to this word, it is because they have no dawn. They will pass through the land, greatly distressed and hungry' (Isa. 8:20-21).

The Great Commission is inevitably theological work; to make disciples of Christ is to make students of Christ, which means the teacher must first be a student of Christ Himself. Being a student requires studying, which is textual and theological work. It is hard, slow, and often feels inglorious and not as flashy as ministries that produce immediate 'results' that so many people love to support. But if the awards ceremony decided by the Judge at the end of our marathon is our goal, then why preoccupy ourselves with the latest passing fads? Why not fix our eyes on the long-distance prize, training and competing according to the rules?

The Church's mission

The famous social justice maxim, 'go into the world and preach the gospel, and if necessary, use words,'[1] reveals our woeful ignorance of the biblically prescribed act of preaching Christ, which is indispensable to both evangelism and discipleship. Missiologist and professor, David Hesselgrave's (1924–2018) definition of the mission of the church helpfully combines evangelism and discipleship with the chief action being the proclamation of Christ: 'The primary mission of the church, and, therefore, of the churches is to proclaim the gospel of Christ and gather believers into local churches where they can be built up in the faith and made effective in service.'[2] Additionally, the definition of

---

1. Though Francis of Assisi (1182–1226) is commonly credited with saying this, it is just a legend. Francis was actually a powerful street preacher. The closest statement comes from his Rule of 1221, Chapter XII on how the Franciscans should practice their preaching: 'No brother should preach contrary to the form and regulations of the holy Church nor unless he has been permitted by his minister ... All the Friars ... should preach by their deeds.' See: Joe Carter, 'Factchecker: Misquoting Francis of Assisi', The Gospel Coalition Blog, entry posted 11 July 2012, http://thegospelcoalition.org/blogs/tgc/2012/07/11/factchecker-misquoting-francis-of-assisi/ (accessed 17 May 2013).

2. David J. Hesselgrave, *Planting Churches Cross-Culturally: North America and Beyond*, 2nd ed. (Grand Rapids: Baker Academic, 2000), p. 17.

the church's mission from pastors Kevin DeYoung and Greg Gilbert brings some clarity:

> Essentially, the mission of the church is summarized in the Great Commission passages—the climactic marching orders Jesus issues at the ends of the Gospels and at the beginning of Acts. We believe the church is sent into the world to witness to Jesus by proclaiming the gospel and making disciples of all nations. This is our task. This is our unique and central calling.[3]

Similarly, DeYoung and Gilbert wisely make a pastoral and theological case for not conflating social work and evangelism:

> Though we do not believe that the mission of the church is to build the kingdom or to partner with God in remaking the world, this does not mean we are against cultural engagement. Our point is simply that we must understand these endeavors in the right theological categories and embrace them without sacrificing more explicit priorities. We should not cheapen good deeds by making them only a means to some other end (evangelism), but neither do we want to exaggerate our responsibility by thinking it is our duty to build the kingdom through our good deeds. Similarly, we should not overspiritualize social action by making it equivalent to God's shalom. As the church loves the world so loved by God, we will work to relieve suffering wherever we can, but especially eternal suffering.[4]

Majority-world theologian, Ajith Fernando, likewise asserts: 'The tendency among some evangelicals to downplay verbal proclamation—including persuading people to receive Christ's salvation—demands a fresh call for evangelicals to emphasize the urgency of proactive evangelism. And if talk of priority will help the church to a fresh commitment, then so be it.'[5]

---

3. Kevin DeYoung and Greg Gilbert, *What is the Mission of the Church?: Making Sense of Social Justice, Shalom, and the Great Commission* (Wheaton: Crossway, 2011), p. 63.

4. DeYoung and Gilbert, *What is the Mission of the Church?*, p. 27.

5. Ajith Fernando, 'Getting Back on Course', *Christianity Today* (November 2007), 51:44.

The Apostolic Model

The apostolic *philosophy* of missions is that sinners are saved and believers are sanctified through the Word of Christ, and the apostolic *method* is proclamation; the *message* is the Christ-centered Word; the *center of the message* is the crucifixion, resurrection, and kingship of Christ; the *effect* is aroused religious affections for obeying Christ the King. Or to say it in a different way: the apostolic philosophy of missions combines reaching the unevangelized with the Word of Christ and teaching the undiscipled to keep the Word of Christ; and, the apostolic methodology of missions employs proclaiming the Christ-centered Word in such a way that arouses religious affections for submission to Christ the King among the church and the unreached.

Numerous missions-oriented strategies use the biblical phrase, 'preach the gospel', and it seems that there is no universal definition of 'preaching' assumed by all. Historian Stephen Neill (1900–1984) aptly said, 'if everything is mission, nothing is mission.'[6] Similarly, if in missions everything is preaching the gospel, then nothing is preaching the gospel. Just as there is a danger of not biblically defining mission, which leads to viewing every Christian activity as mission, there is a similar danger of not biblically defining proclamation. Missions debates and discussions rarely deal with the apostolic understanding of preaching, and we defer that discussion to professional pulpiteers or homileticians. Eckhard Schnabel, theologian and professor of New Testament, helpfully explains:

> Missionary proclamation is never 'effective' in the sense that it produces the conditions in which conversions occur, let alone the event of conversion itself. Missionaries, evangelists and teachers who have understood both the scandal of the cross and the irreplaceable and foundational significance of the news of Jesus the crucified and risen Messiah and Savior will not rely on strategies, models, methods or techniques. They rely on the presence of God when they proclaim Jesus Christ, and on the effective power of the Holy Spirit. This dependence on God rather than on methods liberates them from following every new fad, from using only one particular method, from using always the same techniques, and from copying methods and techniques

---

6. Quoted in DeYoung and Gilbert, *What is the Mission of the Church?*, p. 15.

from others whose ministry is deemed successful. Preachers of the gospel ... are authentically flexible because they are motivated not by the pressure of demonstrating the 'effectiveness' of their methods or the 'success' of their ministry but by their commitment to God and by their commitment to the people they seek to reach with the news of Jesus.[7]

The Gospel for the reached and unreached

Proclaiming Christ is fundamental for both evangelism *and* discipleship, reaching *and* teaching, and this is made clear by the bookends of the epistle to the Romans. Paul stated his ministry philosophy in Romans, which is essentially a missionary support letter that must be read both theologically and missiologically. In the first bookend of Romans, Paul says:

> Paul, a servant of Christ Jesus, *called to be an apostle*, set apart for the *gospel* of God, which he promised beforehand through his prophets in the holy Scriptures, concerning his Son, who was descended from David according to the flesh and was declared to be the Son of God in power according to the Spirit of holiness by his resurrection from the dead, Jesus Christ our Lord, through whom we have received grace and *apostleship to bring about the obedience of faith for the sake of his name among all the nations, including you who are called to belong to Jesus Christ.* ... For I long to see you, that I may impart to you some spiritual gift *to strengthen you*—that is, that we may be mutually encouraged by each other's faith, both yours and mine. I do not want you to be unaware brothers, that I have often intended to come to you (but thus far have been prevented), in order that I may reap some harvest among you as well as among the rest of the Gentiles. *I am under obligation* both to Greeks and to barbarians, both to the wise and to the foolish. *So I am eager to preach the gospel to you also* who are in Rome. For I am not ashamed of the gospel, *for it is the power of God for salvation to everyone who believes*, to the Jew first and also to the Greek (Rom. 1:1-6, 11-16, emphasis added).

Paul is under obligation to preach Christ, period. So he preaches it *evangelistically* to unbelieving Greeks, barbarians, wise, and foolish;

---

7. Eckhard Schnabel, *Paul the Missionary: Realities, Strategies and Methods* (Downers Grove, IL: InterVarsity Press, 2008), p. 404.

likewise, he is under obligation to preach Christ *evangelically* as a means of sanctifying and building the faith of the Christians. He employs both of these modes of preaching—to convert unbelievers and to disciple believers—as a well-studied, text-driven, *evangel*-motivated theologian.

At the end of Romans, in the second bookend, Paul restates the same idea as Romans 1:11-16 to form a missiological-theological *inclusio*. In his doxology he says:

> Now to him who is able to *strengthen you according to my gospel and the preaching of Jesus Christ,* according to the revelation of the mystery that was kept secret for long ages but has now been disclosed and through the prophetic writings has been *made known to all nations, according to the command of the eternal God, to bring about the obedience of faith*—to the only wise God be glory forevermore through Jesus Christ! Amen (Rom. 16:25-27, emphasis added).

From the bookends of this letter written by the missionary-theologian extraordinaire, clearly Paul's philosophy and methodology of missions includes proclaiming the Word of Christ as a theologian for the evangelism of the nations *and* the discipleship of the church. 'Paul's description of his missionary task focuses on the preaching of the gospel as the primary goal. ... Paul understood his primary task as an apostle who has been called and sent by God to preach the gospel.'[8]

Preaching Christ is our Pauline legacy; we must not forfeit our apostolic vocation. Often, discussions of missions strategies deal with degrees of contextualization, cultural relevance, sociological research, intercultural communication, and dynamic equivalence, which are all very valuable issues, yet if such discussions *assume* the place of gospel proclamation, the core method of our missionary calling is in danger of being eclipsed altogether. Therefore, for the sake of clarifying this Pauline missionary-theologian *ethos*, we must reconsider what we are doing in the name of missions today and how we can reclaim the apostolic craft of proclaiming the Word of Christ as missionary-theologians, as pioneer-apologists.

---

8. Schnabel, *Paul the Missionary*, p. 210.

CHAPTER 1

THE MAKING OF A MISSIONARY-THEOLOGIAN

'For I am not ashamed of the gospel, for it is the power of God for salvation to everyone who believes, first to the Jew, and also to the Greek. For in it the righteousness of God is revealed from faith for faith, just as it is written: The righteous will live by faith.'

—Paul the Missionary

WE had only been stationed at our first assignment in the Middle East for less than a year, and my wife and I were overwhelmed, depressed, and spiritually exhausted. Part of it was fear induced by the culture's suspicion and disdain for foreigners; part of it was the palpable spiritual darkness of Islam; part of it was the heavy burden of learning a very difficult language among an unfriendly people; and part of our struggle, which we later learned was the locus of our struggle, was rooted in underdeveloped theology. We needed to pull some unbiblical weeds, separate our minds from some poisonous theology, and plant fresh gospel seeds in our souls.

Missionaries are a strange breed of Christian servants. Who would decide that they want to risk their lives, careers, and health, moving their family around the world to live in obscurity in politically hostile environments, willingly succumbing to foreign fevers and illnesses at the mercy of physicians who speak another language, spending the first four years of their service in language study, feeling like children trying to babble their way through a new grammatical and alphabetic system, attempting the most creative platforms (of which they are often not qualified) in order to secure a visa for their family, and living in fear that their children will become socially odd in both their passport country and their visa-holding country? And to top it off, they regularly need to travel around their passport country, explaining to churches and individuals why their work is worthy of any donation, with churches pledging as little as twenty-five dollars per month and individuals as little as five dollars per month, amounting to countless visits, potluck presentations, and follow-up phone calls and newsletters. Who in the world would do that? Few. And even fewer for longer than two years.

During my first year as a missionary, I learned very quickly that missionaries were rarely on the field for theological and truth-oriented reasons. Many were there because of an experience they had, from which they concluded that God was telling them to go. Many wanted to devote their young lives to some worthwhile cause, which was even more romantic if it included adventure and the adrenaline rush of cross-cultural living. Truthfully, I could relate to these passionate aspirations; these are normal feelings for most young missionaries.

I also observed that many missionary leaders spoke and acted like they had a direct line to heaven, God speaking to them regularly through dreams and inner impressions. Many took comfort in how well they were performing at their Spirit-directed mission tasks, assured that God was blessing them; and yet others felt a silent sinister discouragement that they were underperforming and that if any of their churches found out how miniscule their ministries were, they would surely be removed from the field. There is a haunting emptiness in the gut of most missionaries, worried that they are not doing enough, which affects how they view their relationship with God. Is He pleased with me? Will He ever bless my work? Am I doing enough? Does He care? Why am I struggling? Am I even a Christian?

I quickly became convinced that the main thing that could hold back the flood of missionary attrition was neither another mystical experience confirming that the missionary had indeed heard God's secret whisper nor another supportive retreat where missionaries could share their struggles and discover effective methods based upon the new thing God is doing today. Those might seem to help sedate the ache temporarily, but they typically fade away. The ground into which a missionary's roots must go down deep is the fertile soil of the Word of God. Gospel truth is not just the message missionaries should promote; it is the heart that pulses blood through their veins. I came to see that resting in the work of Christ and His loving promises was essential for persevering in the lonesome wasteland that is the mission field.

How justification saves a missionary

Missionaries are often very concerned to please the Lord. They shudder at the thought of God, their churches, and their colleagues inspecting their lives and work and being ashamed of them. Do you want God to be unashamed to be called your God? What must you do? Be a better missionary, like the biographies we all celebrate? Create a life-changing humanitarian platform—caring for orphans, rescuing trafficked women, promoting creation care, or building a kingdom-impacting business? Surely such good works would make God proud of you, right? Jesus said, 'Many will say to me in that day and say, "Lord, Lord, did we not prophesy in your name, and cast out demons in your name, and do many mighty works in your name?" And then I will declare to them, "I never knew you; depart from me"' (Matt. 7:22). Trusting in your hard work in addition to trusting in Christ will send you to hell, which is why the Protestant Reformation turned on the word, 'alone'. We must trust in Christ *alone*, not in addition.

When you stand before the judgment seat of Christ, if He were to look into your heart with His eyes blazing, shining light into the dark cobwebs of your soul, and assert, 'You do not deserve to be here. Why should my Father not be ashamed of you and let you in to His presence?', how would you respond? Defend yourself? Would you protest, 'Lord, Lord, did I not preach the gospel in your name, rescue enslaved children in your name, risk my life and my family on the mission field in your name, translate the Bible in your name, create transformational culture in your name, defend social justice in your name, train pastors in your name?' If you were to feel anxiety by such probing questions and answer this way by defending yourself based on what you have done, you would actually reveal what you had been trusting in all along. And He would say to you, 'I never knew you. Depart from me.'

However, if you were to say, 'You are right, I don't deserve to be here. The only reason your Father shouldn't be ashamed of me is because you took away my shame and guilt on the cross and credited me with your God-honoring righteousness instead. I myself bring nothing worthy of the Father's approval. Jesus, you only are my hope.' To that response, Jesus would say, 'Enter into the joy of your Master. You are my Father's legally adopted child. All that is mine is yours.'

Any attempt to serve the Lord in the pressure cooker of the mission field that is not solely resting in Jesus and His victorious work can easily devolve into a form of works-righteousness. Missionaries need to remember and remind each other that the gospel both saves *and* sanctifies. God is neither more pleased with them for how hard they work and how effective they are, nor is He displeased with them for how they struggle and underperform. The Father equally loves and accepts all Christians, and even hard-charging type-A missionaries, only because Christ earned their righteousness and absorbed their condemnation. The Father loves you with the delight with which He views His Son. Truly pleasing. Truly honorable.

When you are forgiven, God treats you as innocent, as having never broken the law. But, being forgiven is only half of the good news; that means you have not done anything wrong in God's eyes. You are innocent. But when you are justified, God treats you as He does Christ—as having obeyed Him and His law perfectly; that means, though you are a sinner, you have legally done everything right in God's eyes. Though a sinner, you are legally credited with Christ's righteousness. You are a justified sinner.

Forgiveness takes away your guilt; it gets you out of your sinful debt and brings you to debt-free standing, but you are still at zero. However, justification fully credits you with Christ's Father-pleasing perfection, and gets you from debt-free standing at zero to perfect righteous standing at 100 per cent.

When Christ was on the cross, the Bible says it was the will of the Father to crush Him (Isa. 53:10). Christ's passive obedience on the cross was the climax of His life's active obedience. Jesus sweat blood, as it were, in anxiety because of His final act of obedience—He was about to drink the cup of the fury of the eternal wrath of God, as though a mountain-sized tsunami of the lava of God's judgment were charging faster than a jet plane, devastating everything in its way. And Jesus stands in front of anyone who would trust in Him and swallows the crushing wave. Downed the very last drop. Dry. Jesus absorbed an eternity of His Father's wrath there on the cross—infinite time compressed into three hours, holy justice being served and holy love being displayed. Essentially the Father looked at His righteous Son and then looked at God-hating, hostile sinners and took the weight of our curse, our Adamic guilt, and our eternal punishment and crushed His Son, saying, 'condemned!' And He took Christ's perfect obedience and love for the Father and ascribed it to all who would believe and lovingly said, 'justified!' Our judgment and Christ's righteousness were exchanged on the cross. 'For our sake he made him to be sin who knew no sin, so that in him we might become the righteousness of God' (2 Cor. 5:21).

If God the Father lived in a magnificent palace, and you were to walk up to the door, knock and say, 'God, please forgive me, for I am a sinner,' He would open the door to you. That is what forgiveness does; it takes away our guilt and the barrier between us and God. And upon declaring, 'I trust that you killed your only Son in my place for my trespasses,' He would step through the doorway, embrace you, and say, 'Jesus lived the perfect life you should have lived, and He satisfied my just punishment that you should have suffered forever. I have raised Him up as Savior and Anointed King, and because you trust alone in His obedience, death, and resurrection, I will credit and honor you with His righteousness. You are now loved and secure as part of my family. I will delight in you with the same love I have for my Son. I am your Father, and I will never leave you. Welcome home. Enjoy my rest.' Safe. Adopted. Adored.

That is the doctrine that Martin Luther (1483–1546) rediscovered in the Bible. *Justification by grace alone through faith alone in Christ alone.* Imagine how that truth alone could radically enhance your missionary labor, disciple-making, counseling, spiritual disciplines, ministry training, and leadership development! Imagine leaning forward in a counseling session or an accountability meeting and not just saying, 'you are forgiven,' but saying, 'you are justified … God is as pleased with you as He is with Jesus, as though you had done everything right.' Such a rock would indelibly reinforce your endurance through the onslaught of dejection and affliction.

Luther as spiritual mentor for missionaries

More than any other theologian, Martin Luther and his teaching on Christian righteousness have helped me and many other missionaries stay the course and abide in the unwavering love of God in Christ. Martin Luther challenged many aberrant doctrines in his day, but the one doctrine that he argued for most vehemently was that of Christian righteousness. Christian righteousness is the exchange of our sin for Christ's righteousness. It is free, permanent, and undeserved. This doctrine is unique in that it fundamentally rebukes those who can intellectually affirm the creedal statements of Christ and the Trinity but who are trusting in their works, even if they are in addition to the grace of God.

We have an unrelenting propensity to try to earn God's favor, even after conversion. It is a fight to trust in Christ's work alone, not just once for salvation but daily until we see Him face to face. We cannot be declared righteous through faith and then sanctified through our effort, ministry, and good works. It is out of imputed righteousness that the fruit of righteousness grows. Professing Christians may not reject the doctrines of the Trinity and of Christ's Person, but they may prove to be unregenerate if they unrepentantly rely on their own works to secure God's approval, demonstrating they reject the doctrine of Christ's work. This doctrine was the eye of the storm for Luther. His theological arguments are exegetically established and relevant for those today, like missionaries, who are active in the Lord's service.

Luther took no prisoners in his theological assertions. It seems futile to describe Luther's passion for the doctrine of Christian righteousness. It is better to just hear it from the source. The following excerpts from his commentary on Galatians exemplify his zeal for the doctrine of Christian righteousness:

- There is a clear and present danger that the devil may take away from us the pure doctrine of faith and may substitute for it the doctrines of works and of human traditions. It is very necessary, therefore, that this doctrine of faith be continually read and heard in public.... This doctrine can never be discussed and taught enough. If it is lost and perishes, the whole knowledge of truth, life, and salvation is lost and perishes at the same time. But if it flourishes, everything good flourishes.[1]

- If the doctrine of justification is lost, the whole of Christian doctrine is lost.... For between these two kinds of righteousness, the active righteousness of the Law and the passive righteousness of Christ, there is no middle ground. Therefore he who has strayed away from this Christian righteousness will necessarily relapse into the active righteousness; that is, when he has lost Christ, he must fall into a trust in his own works.[2]

- Therefore we always repeat, urge, and inculcate this doctrine of faith or Christian righteousness, so that it may be observed by continuous use and may be precisely distinguished from the active righteousness of the Law. (For by this doctrine alone and through it alone is the church built, and in this it consists).[3]

- The second kind of righteousness is our proper righteousness, not because we alone work it, but because we work with that first and alien righteousness. This is that matter of life spent profitably in good works, in the first place, in slaying the flesh and crucifying the desires with respect to the self.[4]

For Luther, eternal joy and eternal punishment were at stake in this doctrine. He would argue that the Christian servant ought to be fervent and constant in teaching this doctrine. One cannot be casual and lackadaisical in proclaiming Christian righteousness. As Luther said, there is no middle ground. This doctrine is essential for salvation.

---

1. Timothy Lull, *Martin Luther's Basic Theological Writings,* 2nd ed. (Minneapolis: Fortress Press, 2005), p. 18.

2. Lull, *Martin Luther's Basic Theological Writings,* p. 22.

3. Lull, *Martin Luther's Basic Theological Writings,* p. 22.

4. Lull, *Martin Luther's Basic Theological Writings,* p. 136.

The two kinds of righteousness

In order to begin understanding the doctrine of Christian righteousness and why it is essential for missionaries to rest in Christ, it is helpful to distinguish Luther's elucidation of two kinds of righteousness.[5] According to Luther, Paul's argument underlines faith, grace, and forgiveness, which are all a part of Christian righteousness. Righteousness is that which makes us right. There is a moral righteousness—the righteousness of following the commands of God. But this is not a saving righteousness. And there is a saving, passive righteousness that God gives to us by faith. It is the righteousness of being an adopted son of God.

In the first category of righteousness, it is external, measurable, and active righteousness of human performance. To understand Luther correctly, we must focus on where the burden falls. The chief result of focusing on horizontal righteousness results in being burdened by the law. Out of his experience, Luther said Satan aggravates feelings of inability to be righteous, to perform satisfactorily. The law is good but under sin it crushes the sinner.

The second category of righteousness is passive righteousness. Our vertical righteousness is a product of God's love. This love of God evokes in us trust and faith; trust itself is a gift and we cannot muster it on our own. This is a righteousness of relationship and not of performance; this is not a measurable righteousness but a status of sonship. The burden falls on God; it is God who gives life and birth and new birth. The highest focus of the Christian is to ignore his own active righteousness and simply to rest in imputed righteousness. Luther warned that every Christian's inclination is to pursue active righteousness through working for God's approval and thus neglect resting in passive righteousness. This vertical righteousness is the root and sap, and in the Christian's life, horizontal righteousness is the fruit of that life-giving sap.[6]

---

5. This content section on 'two kinds of righteousness' largely derives from Robert Kolb, *The Theology of Martin Luther*, 'Lecture Notes 6' (Grand Rapids: The Institute of Theological Studies), 1994.

6. Lull, *Martin Luther's Basic Theological Writings*, p. 136.

Law and gospel

Luther saw the law and gospel as essentially complementary to one another in Eden but now opposed to one another. Though they pitted against one another, law and gospel are effective when both are used.[7] The law condemns us because it points out that we have failed. Luther said the sinner needs to hear the law as a command to active righteousness and when he is terrified by his own works, then the sinner needs to hear the good news of passive righteousness. A person must tremble under the law before the gospel comes. First the law wounds, then the gospel heals.

For Luther the answer to the key question of how the Christian becomes and stays righteous is through the continual mediation of the Great High Priest. For the Christian, the law tells him how to live a fruitful life. So, the gospel comes and takes that burden and puts it on Christ. The Christian lives a fruitful life in obedience to the law because trust is ultimately in Christ for righteousness. The use of the law for the Christian, then, comes out of motivation from the gospel.

Inseparable to Luther's doctrine of the two categories of righteousness was his theme of 'the joyous exchange'.[8] This helped explain what Christ did in order to provide us with passive righteousness. Jesus was righteous; the sinner was sinful. Jesus the righteous took the sinner's sin upon Himself and credited the sinner with His life of perfect active righteousness. God came to terms with His own wrath against the disobedient. Christ went obediently to the cross and received the wrath of God. Christ's obedience to the Father is imputed to Christians, which grants us legal adoptive sonship in the family of God. The Father looked down on the spotless Son and saw Him extinguish the curse of the law as He stood before the Father with all of His people's sins on Him. Christ did not merely mask or remove the accusation of the law; rather, He exhausted the condemnation of the law. Now, the sinner no longer lives as a sinner but as a pleasing son of God. This is the joyous exchange.

---

7. For more details on 'law and gospel', see Kolb, 'Lecture Notes 6'.

8. See Kolb, 'Lecture Notes 11'.

This joyous exchange has impregnable power to sustain a missionary when all else is falling around him and when all he has to show for his unnoticed labors are embarrassing failures, burned relationships, a worn out body, shameful secret sins, language skills that never seem to improve, and a few fledgling indigenous believers who cannot even get along. Conversely, for the missionaries who experience the blessing of manifest fruitfulness, conversions, churches planted, miraculous providences, and great deliverances, resting in Christ's imputed righteousness is the antidote to sipping the poison of boasting and trusting in those biography-worthy accomplishments. For the weary missionary struggling against the stiff gusts of those nagging, intrusive thoughts of discouragement and self-ridicule for every failed attempt, and then for the assured missionary relishing the warm spotlight of notoriety among churches and colleagues for achieving textbook successes, Luther would say, hide yourself in Christ. Jesus has you covered. It is His work. He will perform what He has purposed. He has overcome the world. Nothing you do can diminish or improve the love of God for you in Christ.

The Gospel saves and sanctifies

In Luther's commentary on Galatians, he often explains how Paul argues for the value of embracing Christian righteousness throughout the Christian life, even after conversion. The following three verses from Galatians help demonstrate Luther's theological and pastoral concern for Christians to grow in and through the gospel: 'Let me ask you only this: Did you receive the Spirit by works of the law or by hearing with faith? Are you so foolish? Having begun by the Spirit, are you now being perfected by the flesh? Did you suffer so many things in vain—if indeed it was in vain?' (Gal. 3:2-4).

When I first studied this text as a missionary in Asia, I was thunderstruck at the centrality of the gospel for Christian living. This is certainly not the only biblical passage that highlights this, but it is potent, nonetheless. Missionaries need to get their minds around Paul's argument here in order to grasp the danger of seeking spiritual growth and seeking to please God by their own faithfulness. Do more, work harder, be better, pray longer—Paul would strongly caution against such gritty dutifulness, and maybe even *anathematize* it if done out of anything but trusting in Jesus and gratitude to the Father for His sovereign saving grace.

- *(3:2) Let me ask you only this: Did you receive the Spirit by works of the law or by hearing with faith?*

Paul here is referring to when the Galatians became Christians. The gift of the Spirit is central for living a gospel-lifestyle. *Only this* suggests there is one thing necessary for making his case. In asking this question, Paul is pushing them to start contemplating not only their doctrine but their experience of that doctrine. Paul is calling them to examine the basis of their conversion experience. The purpose of the question here in verse 2 is similar to that of verse 5. They both utilize the same antithesis: *by works of the law* or *by hearing with faith*. He confidently asks the question knowing that the answer would make a decisive argument. His question brings into sharp contrast two different ways the Galatians could interpret their reception of the Spirit—either by works or by faith alone. They would understand what he is saying if they would remember what the Spirit did in their lives at their conversion, before they had been bewitched by the Judaizers into keeping the Law (3:1).[9] Not to mention, true believers have the Spirit indwelling them (Rom. 8:9, 14-15) because the Spirit has been poured out into their hearts (Rom. 5:5), whereas unregenerate people are not indwelt with the Spirit (1 Cor. 2:14).

In Galatians 2 Paul contrasts *faith* with *works of the law*, but now he brings in *Spirit*, which sets up a broader redemptive-historical framework. 'For the apostle, the Holy Spirit is the clearest evidence that the time of fulfillment, the new aeon, has arrived. ... Their movement away from the gospel of freedom signifies a return to the old aeon, that is, the present evil age (1:4), the age of the flesh (3:3).'[10] He says that the Judaizers' message is a product of a bygone era. They are

---

9. F.F. Bruce, *The Epistle to the Galatians: A Commentary on the Greek Text*, The New International Greek Testament Commentary (Grand Rapids: Eerdmans, 1982), p. 149.

10. Moises Silva, *Interpreting Galatians*, 2nd ed. (Grand Rapids: Baker Academic, 2001), p. 176.

simply outdated. 'The mode of existence based on works of the law is eschatologically obsolete.'[11] Not only does the Spirit testify to their spirits that they are adopted into the family of God (4:6), the Spirit bears witness to them that they are a new creation (6:15).

There are two key words in Paul's question that highlight the theology of grace characterized in his doctrine of the Spirit. The first is the verb, *received*, which occurs later again in 3:14 to refer to receiving by faith with gratitude the promise of the Spirit.[12] This idea of receiving has nowhere in it the idea of receiving through first striving or exertion. It is a gift of grace, unearned kindness from God.

So, the question begs to be asked, 'how does one receive the Spirit?' The answer is found in the second key word Paul employs in reference to the theology of grace—*hearing*. Reception of the Spirit (conversion) comes via hearing. Justification (2:16) and the gift of the Spirit are equally received not *by works of the law* but *by faith*. 'The gift of the Spirit and justification are two sides of the one coin.'[13] Paul's point is that the gospel is heard, and the Spirit is received freely by hearing with belief that trusts God.

Now on the other hand, it helps to clarify what *works of the law* does and does not mean. Augustine (354–430) argues that the works of the law were twofold; for they reside partly in ceremonial ordinances and partly in morals. The ordinances would include things like circumcision, Sabbaths, festivals, etc. And the morals would include basic commands related to the Ten Commandments.[14] Luther picks up Augustine's interpretation and elaborates even further:

> Here again I warn you, that Paul speaketh not only of the ceremonial law, but of the whole law. ... All that is not the Holy Ghost or the

---

11. Silva, *Interpreting Galatians*, p. 176.

12. 'This verse had a powerful effect on Augustine in opening up for him the mystery of God's grace; later it was a crucial weapon in his struggle against the Pelagians.' Timothy George, *Galatians*, The New American Commentary, vol. 30, ed. E. Ray Clendenen (Nashville: Broadman Holman, 1994), p. 211.

13. Bruce, *The Epistle to the Galatians*, p. 149.

14. Augustine, *Galatians, Ephesians, Philippians, Ancient Christian Commentary on Scripture, NT,* vol. 8, ed. Mark J. Edwards (Downers Grove, IL: Inter Varsity Press, 1999), p. 36.

preaching of faith, is the law.... To attain justification, there is no other way but either the voice of the gospel, or the voice of the law. Wherefore the law is here taken generally as wholly separate from the gospel. But it is not the ceremonial law only that is separate from the gospel, but also the moral law, or the law of the ten commandments.[15]

Clearly Paul is not arguing against Jewish ethnocentric exclusion of Gentiles based on ceremonial rites, contrary to the New Perspective on Paul. Never in the history of Israel did they receive the Holy Spirit as believers have since Pentecost. How then did the Galatians receive the Spirit? They could have only received it by faith. Luther rightly argues, 'The accomplishment of the law never brought the Holy Ghost: much less could the only hearing of the law do it.'[16] The *works of the law* cannot refer only to ceremonial rituals and ethnic boundary markers. In 3:10 Paul teaches that the curse of the law affects all people, not just Jews, since all people rebel against God's commands. In 2:16, Paul explains that the works of the law are powerless to justify anyone. He makes an allusion to Psalm 143:2, which says: 'Enter not into judgment with your servant, for no one living is righteous before you.' Plainly the law was never meant for sinners to keep unto salvation.

Basically, anything that you trust in apart from or in addition to the gospel is considered works of the law, or in other words, a false gospel. You receive the Spirit through trusting alone in the message of the cross. It is not the gospel plus doing acts of love and justice, plus avoiding immorality, plus casting off ethnocentric xenophobia, plus spiritual disciplines, plus spiritual experiences, plus showing kindness, plus performance. It is the gospel alone.

- *(3:3) Are you so foolish? Having begun by the Spirit, are you now being perfected by the flesh?*

There is a twofold contrast in the second question: 'beginning/completing and spirit/flesh'.[17] Paul told the Philippians that 'he who

---

15. Martin Luther, *A Commentary on St Paul's Epistle to the Galatians* (Philadelphia: Quaker City Publishing, 1872), p. 295.

16. Luther, *Galatians*, p. 295.

17. George, *Galatians*, p. 212.

began a good work in you will carry it on to completion' (Phil. 1:6). The Galatians, on the other hand, were being tempted to turn back to those enslaving principles in which they walked before they were converted, even though they began their Christian life so well in the Spirit. They had lapsed back into the works of the flesh. Though some commentators suggest the *flesh* is a reference to circumcision, its wider meaning is that of the seat of evil desires. Luther says: 'Flesh therefore is here taken for the very righteousness and wisdom of the flesh, and judgment of reason, which seeketh to be justified by the law.'[18]

In context with the previous verse, *begun by the Spirit* would correspond to *receiving the Spirit by hearing with faith,* and *flesh* corresponds to *works of the law.* Somebody in Galatia came along and essentially said, 'Yes, you are saved by grace, but you must now do something more to grow in holiness and be perfected.' Paul basically says, 'Your means of seeking to maintain God's approval and become more godly is wrong. You think that if only you were more disciplined, if you were more educated, if you were more tolerant, if you read the right books or listened to the right music, if you avoided certain sins, employed the most effective missions methods, learned to discern the voice of God in listening prayer, then you will grow in God's approval; the gospel which you now profess is not the same as the gospel in which you were saved. But it is resting in the gospel alone that saves and sanctifies.' Paul is saying between these two verses that the Galatians received the Spirit at conversion and started off strong, dependent on the Spirit. They did not receive the Spirit by perfectly keeping the law, since that is clearly impossible. But then in their bewitched state (3:1), they reverted back to depending on the works of the law for spiritual growth and neglected the gospel. They 'got saved' and then they attempted to 'stay saved' through perfectionism.

How about you? Are you trying to keep God's approval through uncommon sacrifices on the mission field and radical risk-taking for the unreached? There are many Galatian-like servants in missions today. At our peril we forget that it is grace from start to finish. This is a *grace race.* This does not mean that we do not seek to grow in godliness,

---

18. Luther, *Galatians,* p. 296.

nor is this a promotion of cheap grace that says we can indulge in sin as we wish. Rather, we must trust God for His saving grace from start to finish, and that grace empowers us to live like Christ.

Paul says later in Galatians, 'if we live by the Spirit, let us also walk by the Spirit' (5:25). The holy imperative to walk by the Spirit (sanctification) is grounded in the gospel indicative that we received new life in the Spirit (justification/regeneration). Progressive sanctification is just as dependent on the gospel as positional sanctification; or, horizontal righteousness is just as dependent on the gospel as is vertical righteousness. Christians do not receive the Spirit at justification through faith and then press on to maturity independent of resting in Christ. It is empowering grace from start to finish—taking refuge in Christ, freely, fully, and forever.

- *(3:4) Did you suffer so many things in vain—if indeed it was in vain?*

Paul speaks as if he is despairing and even rightfully angry, especially considering his expressive disgust and merciless condemnation of false teaching (1:8-9; 5:12). Paul is appealing to the Galatians' suffering and experience. It seems that if the Galatians were truly on the verge of committing apostasy, what would be truly vain in their Christian 'experience' would not be the blessings of miracles and ecstasies but the suffering they would have experienced for calling themselves Christians. Enduring persecution and affliction for something one ends up recanting or abandoning would be a waste.

Nevertheless, the word *suffer* is not the main point of this verse. Paul is gravely concerned that though it appears that they had started off in the Spirit, they are now showing signs of making a shipwreck of their faith. They cannot lose their salvation, but they can prove that they never had it. Even though Paul saw evidence that many of the Galatian converts had embraced legalistic error, he cannot believe that all their experiences, both pleasant and painful, had been in vain. 'He leaves open the possibility that what he has written may be a trifle too strong, as he has striven to make clear the danger of inherent legalism.'[19]

---

19. Leon Morris, *Galatians* (Downers Grove, IL: Inter Varsity Press, 1996), p. 97.

It appears that Paul genuinely believes that the Galatians are mostly true believers. However, that does not give him reason to falsely assure them with mushy sentimentality. He uses a stiff warning and threat to call them back to the gospel. He threatens them as if they were all on the verge of committing apostasy. Essentially, he says to them, 'See where this kind of theology will lead you! If salvation is not the work of God from first to last, then the preaching of the gospel is vanity, the cross of Christ was a farce, and the gift of the Holy Spirit means nothing!'[20] Paul calls them to an obedient, Spirit-led lifestyle, because their lack of active growth in the grace of the gospel shows the object of their trust—law, self-righteousness, performance.

Paul's argument here unfolds thoroughly in Luther's appeals for growing in and through the gospel and the doctrine of Christian righteousness. If missionaries attempt to grow in godliness and serve God in their own way with their own strength, they might be striving in vain. Trusting in Christ's imputed alien righteousness is of monumental importance for those who spend their lives in the Master's service, especially for those who have minimal fruit to show.

Practical effects

In my years on the mission field, I have seen a handful of missionaries fall away from the faith because they became tired of working so hard for so little return on investment, because they sadly surrendered to sexual sin, because they grew socially embarrassed by an exclusivistic message, and because the pangs of the mission field revealed in them what they were truly trusting in, hoping in, and loving.

Luther was absolutely right to contend so strongly for the doctrine of the imputation of Christ's righteousness. It is a shame if this doctrine is relegated to an outdated chapter in church history, abandoned to the theological musings of the academy. This doctrine of Christian righteousness is not optional, and especially for the missionary. It must be rejoiced in, sung about, treasured, and proclaimed, again and again. It is a rock for those who struggle with depression and melancholy. It saves marriages and broken-hearted parents. It obliterates self-esteem

---

20. George, *Galatians*, p. 214.

psychobabble, setting our hearts on Christ's worth. The doctrine of Christ's imputed righteousness is the ground for joyful contentment in gain and in loss, the root for humility in all success and failure, and the foundation for gratitude in poverty and in wealth, in sickness and in health. Though there is nothing we can do to earn God's approval and pleasure, even sacrificially laying our lives down for the unreached, Christ has perfectly obeyed His Father and credited to us His righteous standing. And, Jesus took our sin on the cross, securing irrevocable peace with God.

Only when this truth sinks deep into our souls will we be freed of our never-ending rule-keeping to make and keep God happy with us. Holding firm to this truth is the only way to fight the temptations of proving self-worth and maintaining God's love. The sweet subjective experience of God's love always emerges from knowing the objective truth of His love in Christ, and so, any claims of experiencing His love apart from worshiping the person and work of Christ should be treated with suspicion.

It is not enough to preach the gospel to unbelievers. The gospel must be preached to believers as well. And missionaries need to be trained theologians who know how to preach the gospel to themselves and one another, because they often labor in places where there are no churches and no Christians, which is obviously why they are there in the first place. But by going to the unreached, they set themselves up for immense opposition. The adrenal glands of global travel will dry up and the passionate emotions of chasing a great cause will cool. What then? Where will your thirsty soul be slaked? We can never declare the doctrine of Christ's imputed righteousness enough. We must never assume it lest we lose it. It is relevant for the endurance of faith, growing in the Spirit, and for hope of glorification. As Luther would contend, there is no middle ground. The fight of faith is to *not* work, but to rest in Jesus as the ground, growth, and goal of your missionary life.

'For by grace you have been saved through faith. And this is not your own doing; it is the gift of God, not a result of works, so that no one may boast. For we are his workmanship, created in Christ Jesus for good works, which God prepared beforehand, that we should walk in them' (Eph. 2:8-10).

CHAPTER 2

THE MISSIONARY AS SUMMONED FROM THE WORD

'Why do you need a voice when you have a verse?'
—JIM ELLIOT

'I DISAGREE with Spurgeon!' I blurted out in a voice that started out confidently, yet my brief assertion diminished with hesitancy and reservation. Who in their right mind would have the audacity to publicly admit disagreement with the Prince of Preachers—Charles Spurgeon (1834–1892)—in a Ph.D. seminar at The Southern Baptist Theological Seminary of all places? Well, I did. The quote that the professor used was, 'Either every Christian is a missionary or an imposter.'[1] As liberally as we quote Spurgeon in evangelical circles, it is probably safe to assume that we frequently quote him out of context, which was indeed the case in this situation.[2] But the quote

---

1. Charles H. Spurgeon, 'A Sermon and a Reminiscence', *Sword and the Trowel* (March 1873), as cited on http://www.spurgeon.org/s_and_t/srmn1873.htm

2. The full context of Spurgeon's quote indicates that if Spurgeon would have spoken in contemporary terms, he would have likely maintained that every Christian is an *evangelist* or an imposter. Consider the immediate context: 'Every Christian here is either a missionary or an impostor. Recollect that. You either try to spread abroad the kingdom of Christ, or else you do not love Him at all. It cannot be that there is a high appreciation of Jesus and a totally silent tongue about Him. Of course I do not mean by that, that those who use the pen are silent: they are not. And those who help others to use the tongue, or spread that which others have written, are doing their part well: but that man who says, 'I believe in Jesus,' but does not think enough of Jesus

from Spurgeon reflected a popular sentiment today that claims every Christian is indeed a missionary. Such a statement demonstrates a naive view of the missionary calling.

Defining terms and seeking direction

In my formative ministry-training years, a close colleague and friend would often remind me that words have meaning, and ideas have consequences.[3] This concept has proven true repeatedly in my experience. The sloppy use of 'missionary' in evangelicalism is likely because we are increasingly uncritical thinkers and consequently quick to sanction any Christian-sounding emotion that inspires and mobilizes evangelical activism. Words indeed have meaning, and ideas truly have consequences. In evangelicalism, we are good at speaking common evangelical vocabulary, but the dictionary definitions we assume are often as diverse as each individual. Based on the broad semantic range of how we use evangelical terminology, consider how diverse our individual definitions would be of the following examples: *kingdom, redemption, preach, love, gospel, church, mission*, and even *Jesus*.

Calling every Christian a missionary makes almost as much sense as calling every Christian a pastor or a preacher. Pastors who sense an inexplicable compulsion to proclaim the Word month after month, year after year, would likely argue that in addition to Christ-like character and Scriptural competence, any pastor who wishes to endure to the end in ministry must carry some internal, weighty burden of a God-wrought calling to preach the Word. The same is true for those whom God truly calls to be missionaries.

We may assume too much when the sense of calling that a would-be missionary describes is mainly an interest in some foreign culture/country. A bleeding heart and a world map are not enough. There are differing philosophies about what exactly the missionary call is supposed to be. We should equally consider and examine these

---

ever to tell another about Him, by mouth, or pen, or tract, is an impostor.' Spurgeon, 'A Sermon and a Reminiscence.'

3. Many thanks to Dave Butler who has encouraged me to think critically about my words and speak wisely.

various beliefs about the missionary call. And, the Scriptures must have the final say.

What is a missionary?

First, we should admit that God does not call all Christians to be missionaries. Every Christian cannot be a missionary, nor should be. Christians can dismiss the urgency and global vision of the Great Commission by saying we are all missionaries in our neighborhood and to be such is the extent of their part in the church's missionary mandate. Indeed, being a witness in one's neighborhood is part of being evangelistic, but it does not fill up the missionary mandate. So, what is an acceptable definition of a *missionary*? Missiologist J. Herbert Kane has suggested a helpful definition:

> In the traditional sense the term *missionary* has been reserved for those who have been called by God to full-time ministry of the Word and prayer (Acts 6:4), and who have crossed geographical and/or cultural boundaries (Acts 22:21) to preach the gospel in those areas of the world where Jesus Christ is largely, if not entirely, unknown (Rom. 15:20).[4]

According to Kane, missionaries go to different cultures or cross geographical boundaries in order to preach the gospel. Similarly, some contemporary missionary-theologians have helpfully defined a missionary as:

> Someone who intentionally crosses boundaries for the purpose of communicating the gospel to win people to Christ, discipling new believers, planting churches, training biblically qualified leaders, and ministering to the whole body of Christ in holistic ways. The boundaries that must be crossed may be linguistic, religious worldview, geopolitical frontiers, socioeconomic, and so on. Most of the time we mean that this individual must go from one culture to another.[5]

These scholars also, for the sake of clarity of terms, differentiate between *mission* and *missions*, which this book presupposes:

---

4. J. Herbert Kane, *Understanding Christian Missions* (Grand Rapids: Baker, 1974), p. 28.

5. Zane Pratt, et al, *Introduction to Global Missions* (Nashville: B&H Publishing Group, 2014), pp. 3-4.

> *Mission* (singular) is meant to be broader in its scope to refer to the intentional and overall purpose and goal of the church. Thus, discussions or debates about *the mission of the church* concern that which Christ has charged his church to do in the world. *Missions* (plural) refers to all the many ways that churches see to carry out their mission in the world in actual missions efforts to reach and teach the peoples of the world for Christ's sake.[6]

In his magisterial synthesis and analysis of Paul's missionary labor, *Paul the Missionary: Realities, Strategies and Methods,* Eckhard Schnabel classifies mission as necessarily requiring intentionality and movement. Missions activity is not just going somewhere, but going somewhere with a sense of calling, direction, and support from those behind who have sent the missionary. Schnabel points out that the threefold reality of missionary work includes communicating the news of Jesus the Messiah and Savior, communicating a new way of life, and integrating new believers into a new community. According to Schnabel, the goals of missionary work include five things: (1) preaching the message of Jesus Christ; (2) preaching that gospel to the Gentiles; (3) reaching as many people as possible; (4) leading individual people to believe in the one true God and in Jesus Christ, the Messiah, Savior, and Lord; and (5) establishing new churches of diverse communities of Christians where they hear the preached Word of God and the significance of the gospel for everyday living. Schnabel explains that missionary methods require proclaiming the gospel alone as the message, and proclamation as the means. They require missionaries to learn how to communicate to people of various backgrounds, cultures, and languages, and to travel to people in various cities and villages in locations and on occasions wherein the target people are likely to hear and listen. Because the Apostle Paul wanted to reach all people in each location, matters of ethnic identity, class, culture, or gender did not control his missionary focus. A high degree of flexibility characterized the *modus operandi* of Paul's missionary work.[7]

---

6. Pratt, et al., *Introduction to Global Missions*, p. 3.
7. See Schnabel, *Paul the Missionary*, pp. 209-55 and pp. 374-458.

Schnabel argues that Paul's desire was to preach to Jews and Gentiles living in cities between Jerusalem, Illyricum, and Spain so that he could establish local communities of new converts in these regions. Conversion was not the only goal of Paul's work. He clearly saw the establishment of churches as part of his missionary calling—communities where people would worship together in light of Christ's salvation and learn together the whole counsel of God. Schnabel also believes that Paul's intent was for these small communities to have a missionary mindset of their own for individual members to share their faith with others. By way of application, he states:

> Missionaries establish contact with non-Christians, they proclaim the news of Jesus the Messiah and Savior (proclamation, preaching, teaching, instruction), they lead people to faith in Jesus Christ (conversion, baptism), and they integrate the new believers into the local community of the followers of Jesus (Lord's Supper, transformation of social and moral behavior, charity).[8]

What was the content of Paul's gospel? The message centered on 'Jesus as the Messiah of the Jewish people and the *Kyrios* of the world.'[9] This gospel permeated the life and work of Paul, not merely as the content of his message, but also the shaper of his mission. Schnabel helpfully argues, 'Missionary work and theological reflection about the gospel depend on one another.'[10] Likewise, 'The crucified and risen Jesus Christ is the content of missionary preaching and thus the foundation, the criterion and the measure of church planting and church growth.'[11]

A missionary, then, is clearly not a person who just reaches out to his neighbor in his homogenous neighborhood. Such a person is

---

8. Schnabel, *Paul the Missionary*, p. 29. Schnabel presents his own definition of mission: 'The term "mission" or "missions" refers to the activity of a community of faith that distinguishes itself from its environment in terms of both religious beliefs (theology) and social behavior (ethics), that is convinced of the truth claims of its faith, and that actively works to win other people to the content of faith and the way of life of whose truth and necessity the members of that community are convinced.' Schnabel, *Paul the Missionary*, p. 22.

9. Schnabel, *Paul the Missionary*, p. 183.

10. Schnabel, *Paul the Missionary*, p. 140.

11. Schnabel, *Paul the Missionary*, p. 151.

obediently witnessing to their immediate surroundings for Christ, which should be part of the evangelistic ministry of any local church. But being a witness and being a missionary are two different categories—the former being the general responsibility of all Christians, and the latter being the special charge of a 'sent one'.

What is the missionary call?

It is helpful to make distinctions between full-time missionaries and lay-leaders. We must distinguish between a general practice in a church and a unique, specific gift that God gives to a select few. For example, all Christians should evangelize and witness in some way or another, but only some have the gift of evangelism. All Christians are supposed to give financially, but there are some whom God has entrusted with a special gift of giving. Likewise, Christ gave the Great Commission mandate to the local church so Christians would bear witness to the gospel, but God calls and sends only some specifically as missionaries to make disciples of all nations. 'The verb *apostello* has the idea of being sent, and from it comes the word for "apostle" (*apostolos*), which means "sent one".'[12] Our English word, 'missionary', comes from the Latin *missionem,* meaning 'mission' or 'act of sending', and *mittere* meaning 'to send'. Not all Christians can be 'sent ones' since the term requires some who are responsible for the sending.[13] We cannot all leave with no one staying behind to support. When Christians claim that all believers are missionaries, this can create excuses for people not to go to the mission field or not to send those with the genuine missionary call. Why prioritize one over another if we all bear the same title and role?

How do you discern the call?

What separates a missionary from the common Christian? What does it mean to be called? So many young people have wondered, 'What

---

12. C. Gordon Olson, *What in the World is God Doing?* (Cedar Knolls, NJ: Global Gospel Publishers, 2003), p. 10.

13. Consider what Olson aptly states: 'All Christians are to be missionary-minded in obedience to the Great Commission, but not all Christians can be missionaries in the proper biblical sense of the word.' Olson, *What in the World is God Doing?*, p. 12.

exactly is a missionary call and how can I know I have that call?' Kane says that some people claim the missionary must have a 'Macedonian call' like Paul in Acts 16:9-10. Kane claims that such a call often derives from visions, dreams, voices, and the like. According to this viewpoint, without the existential experience it is impossible to receive a missionary call. Thus, every Christian should seek out such an experience and wait until it comes.[14]

The second common viewpoint, according to Kane, is similar to the above-mentioned claim. It says that all Christians are missionaries, so no call of any kind is required. Missionary work is no different from any other Christian service. An adherent to the first position may wait around too long, waiting for a vision. An adherent to the second position may go overseas and then return home disillusioned and discouraged. These two common approaches are foreign to the matter-of-fact style of bygone eras, such as the blunt reasoning of the Scottish missionary to the Mongols, James Gilmour (1843–1891):

> I thought it reasonable that I should seek the work where the work was the most abundant and the workers fewest. ... I go out as a missionary ... that I may obey the command of Christ, 'Go into all the world and preach.' ... My going forth is a matter of obedience to a plain command; and in that place of seeking to assign a reason for going abroad, I would prefer to say that I have failed to discover any reason why I should stay at home.[15]

Consider the Apostle Paul and how he appealed to his burden to take the gospel to Spain. After preaching the gospel from Jerusalem all the way to Illyricum,[16] Paul claimed, 'I have fulfilled the ministry of the gospel of Christ' (Rom. 15:19). Paul apparently interpreted his ministry of sowing gospel seeds and planting gospel churches as fulfilling his missionary calling. He went on to describe the impulse of his unique missionary calling, 'And thus [after fulfilling the ministry

---

14. J. Herbert Kane, *Life and Work on the Mission Field* (Grand Rapids: Baker, 1990), p. 1.

15. Richard Lovett, *James Gilmour of Mongolia* (London: Religious Tract Society, 1892), pp. 42-3.

16. Modern-day Dalmatia on the eastern shore of the Adriatic Sea in Croatia.

of the gospel of Christ all the way from Jerusalem to Illyricum] I make it my ambition to preach the gospel, not where Christ has already been named, lest I build on someone else's foundation'' (Rom. 15:20). Clearly, Paul saw his missionary function as that of a pioneer. His heart burned to bring the gospel to the unreached, and in his worldview, the remotest part of the known world was Spain, to which he endeavored ultimately to go (cf. Rom. 15:24, 28).

However, there is a short yet essential verse in the middle of Paul's description of his ambition to take the gospel to Spain, not wishing to preach where Christ had already been named. After highlighting his consuming ambition, to what does he finally appeal? His spectacular experience on the road to Damascus? A prophetic word? A vision of heaven? Wanderlust and adventure? Colorful Spanish culture and tapas cuisine? No. He appeals to sacred print. An ancient scroll, 'As it is written, "Those who have never been told of him will see, and those who have never heard will understand"' (Rom. 15:21). Paul contended that the text of Isaiah 52:15 was the ground for his controlling ambition to take the gospel to the unreached. Do not skim over the inherent conviction of Paul's short transitional phrase from describing his gospel ambition in verses 18-20 to quoting Isaiah's prophecy: *But as it is written*. Of all missionaries, Paul could have legitimately cited a vision from Jesus Himself. He could have easily referenced his encounter with Christ on the Damascus road or his heavenly vision. Yet the roots of Paul's missionary impulse emerged out of the written Word as sufficient, compelling, and authoritative. It was the Scripture alone that commanded Paul's missionary allegiance.

A biblical model

We often overlook and/or misunderstand the New Testament model. From the outset, we must remember that Acts is a transitional book in the history of the church, and the Holy Spirit inspired Luke to record many events in the book to highlight historical and theological themes that are significant for understanding the establishment of the New Testament church after Christ's ascension. In other words, the narrative of Acts is primarily descriptive, but in some ways the narrative can serve as a timeless model to which we can look for wisdom.

In Acts 11:22, the church in Jerusalem sent out Barnabas when they heard that certain men from Cyprus and Cyrene were evangelizing Greeks in Syrian Antioch. There is no mention of calls for volunteers, nothing of Barnabas' own personal subjective call. It does not mean he had no subjective call, but we should notice that the church took initiative to send him. He was a Cypriot Jewish Christian and therefore known to the Antioch evangelists (Acts 11:20), many of whom were Cypriots. He was full of the Holy Spirit, and he was a good man. His name meant, 'Son of Encouragement' (Acts 4:36), and he was probably a soul-mender, apparently selected according to his suitability. Sent by the Holy Spirit through the church, he was the best man for the job. Indeed, though he could have had an internal compulsion, it seemed necessary to the Holy Spirit to inspire Luke to record only these factors of Barnabas' commission.

A year later Paul and Barnabas set out on their first missionary endeavor, which was not an individualistic decision. Acts 13:1-3 clearly says that the Lord guided the whole group of leaders in the Antioch church. It was a group decision. Later Paul chose Silas (Acts 15:40) who was a leader among the brethren (Acts 15:22), a prophet himself (15:32), and he was therefore qualified to aid Paul on his mission.

When they returned to Galatia, they met Timothy, 'well spoken of by the brethren in Lystra and Iconium' (Acts 16:2). The text says Paul wanted to take him. It does not say what Timothy felt or wanted but only that Paul took the initiative and called Timothy.

In all three examples, (sending of Barnabas, Silas, and Timothy) the Bible neither emphasizes the individual initiative, nor the subjective sense of a call. Rather, it always shows the initiative of others, either of a congregation or of other Christians already active in such work. This does not eliminate the value of a personal, subjective call altogether. But it at least demonstrates the biblical priority for how to discern whom churches should send. Moreover, Acts does not define how involved the initial sending church was with the missionaries after their departure. What is clear is that once the churches initially sent out the missionaries, they were on mission to serve and preach wherever the Holy Spirit enabled them to go. The church indeed approved and launched them, but the Holy Spirit guided and directed them. There were no ongoing emails and conference calls to collaborate on new ventures and field transitions.

So, how in the world do we know if what we are discerning is a true call? Is it only an invitation by a second party, or is it the individual's initiative? The missionary call seems to be both an individual/subjective conviction and a corporate/objective confirmation. A potential missionary must have a subjective call – an unwavering, resolute conviction that is truly from God Himself. However, at the same time the individual must be careful not to confuse the 'shiver in his liver' with the voice of God. It is astounding how often we declare that we are called to cross a culture for the gospel's sake and the reason we give is because we 'love the people of that culture'. But what is more revealing is that usually those cultures that we initially profess to love and feel specifically called to reach are often very fun, polite, interesting, and hospitable; and for those cultures that rub us wrongly, ironically very few of us profess an equal enthusiasm.

A solution to this vacillating and uncertainty is objective confirmation of one's own genuine subjective call. One author proposes two steps in hearing this objective call. First, he says that the congregation that knows the candidate best must objectively recognize his strengths. Such people know his gifts and usefulness. Secondly, those involved already in some distant work of cross-cultural ministry, who, on recommendation of the church, could also confirm the readiness of that missionary candidate for that global context. Therefore, with the subjective sense of the call of God ('It seems that the Lord is calling me'), there is the objective confirmation of the sending church ('It seems to us that the Lord has set you apart to go and that He wants us to send you'), and of the receiving team of missionaries on the field awaiting more workers ('We know there is a need, and we believe that you are the kind of person the Lord could use with us').[17] This model from Acts is not only individual, but it is also corporate. This is how God so often works with us. He uses the Body of Christ to accomplish His tasks.

---

17. Michael Griffiths, *Give Up Your Small Ambitions* (Nashville: Accelerated Christian Education, 1993), p. 17.

Why does it matter?

We should celebrate the fact that there are many avenues and means for participating in missions, especially as the world is becoming a very complex place for missionaries. One note of caution that we must beware of is the tendency to innovate and improvise with sacred tasks that God has not permitted. This is exactly what happened in the account of Nadab and Abihu, the sons of Aaron the High Priest:

> Now Nadab and Abihu, the sons of Aaron, each took his censer and put fire in it and laid incense on it and offered unauthorized fire before the LORD, which he had not commanded them. And fire came out from before the LORD and consumed them, and they died before the LORD. Then Moses said to Aaron, 'This is what the LORD has said: "Among those who are near me I will be sanctified, and before all the people I will be glorified."' And Aaron held his peace (Lev. 10:1-3).

Notice carefully what the text says and does not say. Did Nadab and Abihu offer specific fire that the Lord explicitly told them not to offer? In Exodus 30:8-9 the Lord certainly instructs Aaron to offer regular incense over against some other unauthorized incense. But this record in Leviticus 10:1-3 does not emphasize the fact that they offered fire that God unambiguously *prohibited*; it underscores, rather, that they offered unauthorized fire that God *had not commanded them*. In other words, Moses is recording that Nadab and Abihu exceeded what God had mandated. The Lord had told them what to offer. They relaxed, innovated, and improvised. They erred by going beyond the bounds of the Word and not holding fast to the instructions. Jealous for the church to not esteem the Apostles higher than they ought, but rather as trustworthy stewards of the Word, Paul issues a similar New Testament instruction in 1 Corinthians 4:5-6:

> Therefore do not pronounce judgment before the time, before the Lord comes, who will bring to light the things now hidden in darkness and will disclose the purposes of the heart. Then each one will receive his commendation from God. I have applied all these things to myself and Apollos for your benefit, brothers, that you may learn by us not to go beyond what is written, that none of you may be puffed up in favor of one against another.

Wisdom applications of this theology of Christian service can apply to missions. This does not mean that we must retrofit our missionary endeavors to imitate exactly the precise descriptions of Paul's methods, and it does not mean that we cannot develop creative platforms to access hard-to-reach peoples in countries politically and religiously hostile to Christianity. It does mean, however, that we should fearfully heed and faithfully hold fast to the Great Commission passages that mandate the transcultural and timeless requirements of the church's mission as senders and sent ones. Would that missionary-theologians devote themselves to keeping the missionary commands of Scripture, not going beyond what is written by creatively making biblical imperatives out of theological implications, inferences, or indicatives. Not to overstate the case, it helps to remember that we should avoid what Scripture forbids and obey what it commands. And where it does not speak, we have freedom within the bounds of Scriptural wisdom and theological discernment. Kevin DeYoung and Greg Gilbert make a helpful point:

> We are concerned that in our newfound missional zeal we sometimes put hard 'oughts' on Christians where there should be inviting 'cans'. You ought to do something about human trafficking. You ought to do something about AIDS. You ought to do something about lack of good public education. When you say 'ought', you imply that if the church does not tackle these problems, we are being disobedient. We think it would be better to invite individual Christians, in keeping with their gifts and calling, to try to solve these problems rather than indicting the church for 'not caring'.[18]

In missions, creativity is good but not ultimate. We should be thankful that we are not all clones of one single personality, temperament, and background. Frankly, that would be as bland as all having the same voice, accent, and rhythm of speaking. All missionaries uniquely contribute to the Great Commission in ways that God has specially designed. Yet, at times the focus on discovering and using one's passion internationally for God can get a bit bizarre: 'I have a passion for surfing; the Lord told me to reach Hindu surfers in Bali. ... I am

---

18. DeYoung and Gilbert, *What is the Mission of the Church?*, p. 21.

passionate for mountain climbing; God has called me to start a mountain climbing business in Nepal. ... I love horses; God wants me to teach animal husbandry to Mongolians.' These are just a sampling of what I have heard as evidence of God's call to the mission field. These statements could be improved with more theologically careful and precise language, not confidently claiming that God has said more than what He has said in the Bible and by just describing how He seems to have providentially led.

Lest we overemphasize and confuse individuality with ministry philosophy specifics, we must remember that methodology of missions is never neutral. We will lose the message of Christ crucified as we innovate our methods and standards insofar as they are incompatible with the honor and truth of the message. Casual, pragmatic, and light-hearted methods and standards cheapen an otherworldly, profound message. No king or president on the eve of war or on the morning after the country's decisive victory would address his nation in a costume, entertaining with levity and originality. The gravity and the good news of taking refuge in his authority would dwindle under the weightlessness of his frivolous methods of delivery.

We all recognize that titles, offices, and ranks matter. An on-duty police officer wields the force of the law by nature of his appointed office. A common citizen cannot claim to be a servant of justice and an enforcer of the law without earning the official approval of the duties and privileges of that office. The same is true for nearly any other duty and office: military special forces, cardiologists, NASA scientists, and university presidents. Though a well-meaning person might claim a certain office, it does not mean they are qualified for that role. Noble aspirations, persistent interest, and unique experiences never qualify anyone to perform brain surgery, establish new laws, judge a criminal, or engage in battle with a foreign enemy. If these are true for temporal offices and duties that pertain only to this life, why do we permit anyone and everyone to 'do missions' based upon merely an express interest and compelling desire?

To be sure, people who volunteer for missions mean well and want to make a difference, and this is an admirable desire. And truly, the modern missionary movement of the nineteenth and twentieth centuries, fueled by volunteerism, is one of the most influential movements in world history. As much as we should celebrate the many who willingly made great sacrifices, we must remember that desire for ministry does not equal calling. Paul makes this clear: 'Certain persons, by swerving from these, have wandered away into vain discussion, desiring to be teachers of the law, without understanding either what they are saying or the things about which they make confident assertions' (1 Tim. 1:6-7). In principle, desire to cross a culture and proclaim the gospel for the goal of making disciples does not equal competence to do so. Desire indeed inspires discipline to attain the necessary competence, but they are not equal. If your loved one had a brain tumor, though you had a desire to remove it, you would surely seek out a qualified neurosurgeon. Moreover, even if you were a credentialed massage therapist, you would never pretend that a scalp massage would fix the tumor. If this is the common logic we use in every other sphere of our temporal existence in this world, why do we settle for less when it comes to matters of eternal damnation and eternal life? To do so borders on cruel, unloving, and ministerial malpractice.

Do not let the priesthood of all believers devolve into the missionary-hood of all believers. They are not one and the same; ask any biblically grounded pastor—they all know they have an office to uphold, and such sacred duties they do not share and relinquish easily. The same should be true for biblically grounded and truly called missionaries. Those of you who support missionaries, please use discernment. Ask yourself, 'Is this person qualified to be an elder or a deacon? Would this person be suitably serving in one of those offices and/or in a leadership position?' Many churches squander much money and time supporting people with whom they should never entrust the mantle of 'missionary', and many of those whom God has genuinely called/equipped struggle to raise support because many who should never be on the front lines soak up so much energy and resources from their sending/supporting churches.

Pastors, how would you feel if churchgoers often claimed that 'everyone is a pastor', and if every summer there were groups from churches all over the country that came and preached for you, did pastoral counseling in your place, announced to their social media followers that they were on summer pastor-trips, and spent in travel and accommodations approximately the same amount of money that you make in one year? Though these people who go and those people who support them might mean well, would this not cheapen the office of pastor? Is your calling merely a task that anyone could really do? Is everyone a pastor? We all know the answer.

Pastor and author Bruce Thielemann said about the pastoral office: 'There is no special honor in preaching, there is only special pain. The pulpit calls those anointed to it as the sea calls its sailors; and like the sea, it batters and bruises, and does not rest. To preach, to really preach, is to die naked a little at a time and to know each time you do it that you must do it again.'[19] In a similar way, the unremitting calling of a missionary can pound and strip the missionary of all sense of security, dignity, and confidence. Every year of willful self-denial on the mission field is a slow bleed—death by a thousand paper cuts:

- That financial supporter who knew you since you first became a Christian and has redirected much-needed donations to another ministry, whether for specified or unspecified reasons, can erode the missionary's resolve to go on, leaving him to wonder in soul-searching emptiness what he said or left unsaid that compelled that long-time supporter to invest in a better 'product';

- That mind-consuming stress over impulsive nationalistic laws that make it increasingly problematic to obtain visas, not knowing if, when you leave the host country, they will let you back in upon returning;

- That impossibly busy weekly schedule where many missionaries must juggle full-time language learning, often a non-salaried job of thirty-sixty hours a week to secure a visa, home-schooling their children, maintaining a healthy lifestyle for ministry longevity and fruitfulness, and seeking opportunities to do the

---

19. Quoted in Ben Patterson, 'Heart and Soul', *Leadership Journal* (Winter 2000), p. 122.

work of missions where there is no formal platform and where all gospel conversations must be covert and secretive;

- Those daily occasions of rife humility when locals smirk, laugh, or poke fun at missionaries for trying their best to put together a well-accented, tone-perfect, and grammatically correct sentence to describe an item they need to buy at the market or a medication they desperately need in order to help alleviate their child's mysterious fever, and sometimes all the missionary can understand are the locals smirking in amusement and murmuring amongst themselves, 'he's just a foreigner... he talks funny... tell him that we don't have whatever he is looking for and to go somewhere else';

- Those inflexible expectations from churches and supporters to come back to your home country regularly in order to be part of their church life, and then also to equally let them fly around the world with a large team to 'partner' with you, spending monetarily in one trip what you need for one year, leaving you exhausted and sometimes discouraged, knowing that they will never know what it is like to deny themselves longer than two weeks the comforts and conveniences of their wealthy home country; and yet they promote themselves as 'doing missions' to friends and supporters.

Conclusion

If you think I am being nitpicky and splitting hairs, ask yourself this, 'Those who serve to protect and promote national interests and freedom, do they all deserve the same honor? Is every duty created equal?' We all know that, though worthy of public honor, there is a chasm of difference between the ascribed honor of a newly elected senator and the achieved honor of a purple-heart-clad Marine.

So why does it matter whom we call 'missionary'? It matters because the glory of God and the good of the nations are at stake; it matters because the lifelong, fruit-bearing missionary office will fade into silence behind the adventurous buzz of what sometimes appears to be a short-term Christian vacation, just long enough to get over jet lag, have indigestion, post some altruistic looking pictures on social media, and then return home. If there is no definition of the historical office and biblical responsibilities of a 'sent one', when indescribable adversity and soul-crushing loneliness plunge the supposed missionary into depression, why would he have the resolve to persevere if it is just a voluntary endeavor that he is only trying out? If anyone can be a missionary, then nobody truly will be. Few will go for life. Fewer will commit to sending for life. This might sound harsh, but it is the truth. This is not a game. This is not a hobby. The glory of God is at stake. Eternal hell and heaven are on the line. In our age of entitlements and participation awards, combined with an egalitarian reaction to titles, ranks, and roles, it makes sense that the general populace seems more cynical and suspicious than honoring and respectful of established roles and offices. Moreover, with the Protestant value of the priesthood of all believers, many Christians, though intending well, do not doubt that they can be and indeed are missionaries.

The missionary call is a lifelong and relentless calling that we must not trivialize, lest we lose its sacredness like a rare heirloom surrounded by unwanted, dusty trinkets in a dilapidated thrift store. The missionary call is a potent and unyielding impulse that consumes your all, demanding no less than a bloody, burning sacrifice. It is a sacred summons from the King, not a volunteer venture; it is a holy enlistment that the 'sent ones' cannot deny. In the war for souls, draft dodgers like Jonah are swallowed up by big fish, as it were, and spat upon the very ground where they must preach. The missionary call, as an irrefutable conscription from the King, is truly an honor. It is a privilege. It is a joy.

CHAPTER 3

THE MISSIONARY IN PRAYER AND CONSECRATION WITH THE WORD

*'Only a life of prayer and meditation will render a
vessel ready for the Master's use.'*
—George Müller

'IT'S amazing what American Christians can do without prayer to God,' one Asian Christian leader once told me after visiting a Western evangelical conference that boasted of some of the best expositors and gospel-centered scholars in the West who were promoting cutting-edge ideas for successful church planting. His observation was penetrating. In his experience, it was impossible to see sinners converted and disciples made, let alone churches planted, without long, desperate seasons of persevering prayer. That desperate prayer is not an ordinary expression of contemporary Western evangelicalism should be no surprise to most.

We rightly devote time and resources to constructing church buildings, organizing ministries, and perfecting our sermonic craft, but a tepid timidity pervades our praying. Our prayers are short, sweet, and to the point, not extended, fervent, and perseverant. Could it be that our lack of devotion to prayer is because we do not feel desperate for God? Could our lack of crying out to God indicate that we lack a regular experience of communion with Him?

The missionary and desperation for God

Where desire for God is weak and desperation for His power is weak, prayer will be weak. Lack of hunger for God, lack of heat in prayer. And too often any sort of praying to God is solely contingent on felt needs, all for which we rightly should pray; nevertheless, how much of our praying is out of a burning desire to know God better? To glorify Him in fruit-bearing? How much of our praying is for those things which would honor His name and not ours? When we say we want God to use us, do we mean that we want to use God so that we feel useful and successful?

Too often prayers for usefulness could easily become requests for self-promoting attention. In a narcissistic age, where a young person is more motivated to be a reality-TV star or a viral video sensation, is it any wonder that all talk of seeking the face of God seems overly pious and old-fashioned? Imagine having never seen a portrait or image of yourself for most of your life. The clear, pristine mirror as we know it was a nineteenth-century invention. Granted, ancient cultures had dim reflective glass, but nothing flawless like our mirrors today. Most people in the history of the world have never had access to a perfect self-reflection. Neither was the camera developed until the nineteenth century. Imagine having never seen a picture of your face unless you looked in still water on a bright day. In today's selfie generation, we consume hours each day considering and promoting our appearances and impressions, and self-forgetfulness and sustained godly affections are rare virtues.

Those brothers and sisters of generations past who so passionately cried out to God, not for their own self-fulfilling usefulness, exemplify what desperation for God looks like. Much more, in this easily distracted and self-consuming age, we must put to death our selfie impulses and seek God for God. God is our *telos*. Our chief end. He is not a means to our self-actualizing end. Theologian J.I. Packer contrasts how Puritans differ from today's evangelicals:

> Communion with God was a *great* thing, to evangelicals today it is a comparatively *small* thing. The Puritans were concerned about communion with God in a way that we are not. The measure of our unconcern is the little that we say about it. When Christians meet, they talk to each other about their Christian work and Christian interests, their Christian acquaintances, the state of the churches, and the problems of theology—but rarely of their daily experience of God.[1]

---

1. J.I. Packer, *A Quest for Godliness: The Puritan vision of the Christian Life*, reprint ed. (Wheaton: Crossway, 2010), p. 215. Emphasis in original.

Prayer is evidence of an extraordinary dependence upon the Spirit. It recognizes and applies the belief that the Holy Spirit is the true driving force of awakening. When God desires to bring about a renewal, He initiates Spirit-prompted praying among His people. Such was the case at Brown University early in the nineteenth century when the Spirit, prior to visiting that particular campus with an awakening, prompted three students to form a 'College Praying Society'. Coinciding with various awakenings at Yale, Williams, Harvard, and Middlebury Colleges, groups of students likewise hosted gatherings of prayer.[2] Gatherings to pray specifically for revival—known as concerts of prayer—registered at the four colleges mentioned above. 'The fruit of such prayers were eight powerful revivals within a twenty-six-year period at Williams College.'[3] These revivals were instrumental in launching the first wave of the modern missionary movement from America. When God is preparing a missionary, He often uses some sort of personal or corporate renewal to stir up affections for Him and a desire to take His gospel to the unreached.

There is no biblical or historical formula for God to spark a personal or corporate revival. Packer makes three helpful observations about the history of revival: First, 'spiritual movements are partly shaped by preexisting needs, which in their turn reflect all sorts of non-recurring cultural and economic factors.' In other words, given the variations in time and culture, revival in China in the twentieth century may be far different from revival in America in the eighteenth century. Second, Packer says: 'the spiritual experiences of Christians are determined in part by temperament, by atmosphere, and by pressure groups, all of which are variables.' And then Packer observes, 'God the Lord appears to delight in variety and never quite repeats himself.'[4]

As mentioned, there is no special formula that will guarantee personal or corporate revival. Author and minister Robert Davis Smart

---

2. Michael F. Gleason, *When God Walked on Campus* (Dundas, Ontario: Joshua Press, 2002), pp. 121-2.

3. Gleason, *When God Walked*, p. 30.

4. J.I. Packer, *God in Our Midst: Seeking and Receiving Ongoing Revival* (UK: Authentic Publishing, 1987), p. 25.

aptly explains, 'Revival is a sovereign gift from God in which, for a special season, His normal and true work of advancing His kingdom is sped up or quickened so that more is accomplished through His servants in a shorter period of time. Revivals cannot be merited by us but have been secured by another—Jesus Christ.'[5] There are, however, signs that either commonly precede or follow a revival: *a burden for prayer, conviction and confession of sin, Word-centeredness, and missions fervor.* But much more than the rest, prayer is the one spiritual practice that most often precedes and sustains an awakening. Though the particular timing of any revival is known and governed by God alone, in His marvelous kindness He calls the Christian community to express their yearnings freely, deliberately, and persistently for future outpourings.

When the Spirit compels earnest believers to steadfast intercession, Christians should take heart, because history has demonstrated the fact that when God desires to bring about an awakening, He moves His people to prayer. When revival and reformation are at their brightest and hottest, God often moves His people to the nations.[6] Author and minister David Bryant explains, 'When God awakens us to Himself He awakens us to the whole earth. As He shows us Christ, He also shows us His worldwide purpose in Christ, the world full of possibilities for fulfilling that purpose through Christ and a world full of people without Christ who are currently beyond the reach of the gospel.'[7] Moreover, in the past as God birthed revivals in prayer, He frequently fueled them with Word-centeredness and missions fervor. Historian Iain Murray also states:

> The more living experience there is of Christ, and the stronger the faith of believers in the truth of his word, the greater will be their concern for the conversion of others. It is when sense of debt to Christ and awareness of his love are at their height that the church has ever made the swiftest advances in the world.[8]

---

5. Robert Davis Smart, 'Introduction', in *Pentecostal Outpourings: Revival and the Reformed Tradition* (Grand Rapids: Reformation Heritage Books, 2016), p. ix.

6. Gleason, *When God Walked*, p. 122.

7. David Bryant, *Concerts of Prayer: For Spiritual Awakening and World Evangelization* (Grand Rapids: Baker Publishing Group, 1988), pp. 88-9.

8. Iain H. Murray, *Pentecost—Today?: The Biblical Basis for Understanding Revival* reprint ed. (Carlisle, PA: Banner of Truth Trust, 2015), p. 180.

The missionary and persevering prayer

The eminent missionary to the Islamic world, Samuel M. Zwemer (1887–1952), famously contended, 'The history of missions is the history of answered prayer. It is the key to the whole mission problem. All human means are secondary.'[9] The task of global proclamation demands persevering prayer, which is crucial for overcoming the hard-hearted resistance of the lost. Immediately following the Lord's Prayer in Luke 11:5-9, Jesus teaches a critical lesson about the role of perseverance in prayer.

To teach us persevering prayer, Jesus uses a peculiar parable about a man who persistently asks for bread from a friend. The friend gives the man the bread, not on the basis of their friendship, but because of his persistence: 'I say to you, though he will not rise and give to him because he is his friend, yet because of his persistence he will rise and give him as many as he needs' (Luke 11:8 NKJV). If persistence affects an earthly friend, imagine how much more it will accomplish with our heavenly Friend.

It is interesting to read the rest of the passage in light of the immediately surrounding context. In verse 8, Jesus just finished emphasizing that persistence in prayer is what often determines the outcome. And then in the following verse, Jesus continues: 'So I say to you, ask [*aiteō*], and it will be given to you; seek [*zēteō*], and you will find; knock [*krouō*], and it will be opened to you (NKJV). Each of the Greek verbs (ask, seek, knock) are present, active, imperatives.[10] The nuance can imply continuous action. Since the surrounding context clearly emphasizes persistence in prayer, which is continuous prayer, it would make sense to translate the verbs in verse 9 as such: *keep asking, keep seeking, keep knocking*, which in some versions, such as the NASB, the footnotes suggest this alternative translation. This continuous nuance emphasizes the idea of persistence in prayer that the parable is stressing so heavily.

---

9. Patrick O. Cate, *Through God's Eyes* (Pasadena, CA: William Carey Library, 2003), p. 86.

10. 'Ask': αἰτεῖτε verb imperative present active 2nd person plural from αἰτέω; 'Seek': ζητεῖτε verb imperative present active 2nd person plural from ζητέω; 'Knock': κρούετε verb imperative present active 2nd person plural from κρούω.

There are a few fundamental lessons about prayer in this parable. First, notice what Jesus says about their relationship: Even though they are friends, the one friend will not get up and fetch a loaf, implying that our relationship with God does not finally determine whether we get what we ask. Granted, our relationship with God is the *basis* upon which He listens to our prayers at all, but that is not always the final reason for why He answers them. (Be careful not to overapply this as the only reason for answered or unanswered prayer). Often, God will answer our prayers based on our persistence.

Persevering prayer is faith breathing and living. The resolve of our perseverance demonstrates our faith and hope in God. *In prayer, faith does not necessarily determine how soon our answers will come; rather, faith often determines how long we will persevere until those answers come.* Faith and perseverance are companions. The persevering prayer life of George Müller (1805–1898), nineteenth-century Prussian missionary to Bristol, England, illustrates this truth. Müller famously prayed for the needs of orphans and saw God answer regularly, and he prayed daily for the conversion of eight friends. In his lifetime, Müller saw all but one of those friends convert to Christ. Müller prayed for over sixty-three years for this friend's salvation, and his friend finally trusted in Christ at Müller's funeral, kneeling beside his casket. Müller's trust in God to save sinners and answer prayer was so resolute (not wavering) that he could persevere in prayer for over sixty-three years, go to the grave, and still not see the answer to his intercession this side of eternity. But he prayed to the end, nonetheless, stubbornly trusting that the Father is a benevolent, prayer-hearing God.[11]

Persevering prayer is essential for overcoming the resistance of lost peoples. We must keep banging on the door of heaven, hounding God to blow apart the daunting resistance of the hostile peoples. We must not tire; we must not relent; we must continually fight on our knees. We must confront resistance of the heart head-on with resistance in prayer to never give up.

---

11. For helpful sources on the life and piety of George Müller, see A.T. Pierson, *George Müller of Bristol and His Witness to a Prayer-Hearing God* (New York: Fleming H. Revell, 1899); Roger Steer, *George Müller: Delighted in God* (Scotland, UK: Christian Focus Publications, 1997).

Prayer wields the Word

In the Gospel of John, Jesus often speaks synonymously of His words and Himself.[12] In the Upper Room Discourse (John 13-17), *after* Jesus identifies Himself as the truth (14:6) and *before* He identifies the Word of God as the truth (17:17), He draws a fascinating connection to His words, Himself, and fruit-bearing. In John 15:4-8, Jesus says:

> Abide in me, and I in you. As the branch cannot bear fruit by itself, unless it abides in the vine, neither can you, unless you abide in me. I am the vine; you are the branches. Whoever abides in me and I in him, he it is that bears much fruit, for apart from me you can do nothing. If anyone does not abide in me he is thrown away like a branch and withers; and the branches are gathered, thrown into the fire, and burned. If you abide in me, and my words abide in you, ask whatever you wish, and it will be done for you. By this my Father is glorified, that you bear much fruit and so prove to be my disciples.

Jesus commands His disciples in verse 4 to abide in Him and He in them, and without such abiding, there can be no fruit-bearing. And then verse 8 indicates that this fruit-bearing both glorifies the Father and demonstrates who the true disciples really are. So, how do we abide in Christ and He in us so that we can bear fruit that both glorifies the Father and proves that we are His true disciples? Jesus clarifies how all this works in verse 7: 'If you abide in me, and my words abide in you, ask whatever you wish, and it will be done for you.' So, here abiding in Christ and He in us looks like letting His *words* abide in us. Of course, Jesus is physically ascendant and reigning from heaven, but we experience His sanctifying presence by the Spirit through His speaking.

When we seek Jesus by letting His Word dominate our minds, affections, and wills, we then know experientially His life-giving power. To the degree that the Christ-centered Word of God dwells richly in us, to the same degree we know the empowering, life-giving

---

12. For a fascinating study on the use of the Word of God as the person of God in the Old Testament and John's adoption of the Jewish concept of the λόγος, see Daniel Boyarin, *The Jewish Gospels: The Story of the Jewish Christ* (New York: The New Press, 2012).

presence of Christ. Just as the sap is what transfers life from the vine to a grafted branch enabling it to blossom and bear fruit, so the Word of Christ is the lifeblood of our souls and enables us to mature and make disciples. Moreover, as if the blessing of having the life-giving, fruit-bearing words of Christ were not enough grace, the experience of this abiding in Christ is the joyful abiding in His love: 'As the Father has loved me, so have I loved you. Abide in my love. If you keep my commandments, you will abide in my love, just as I have kept my Father's commandments and abide in His love. These things I have spoken to you, that my joy may be in you, and that your joy may be full' (15:9-11). The Christ-centered Word is for joy—enjoyment in the abiding love of Jesus. The doctrine of Christ should not eradicate joy; rather, it should enhance joy.

There is one more indispensable aspect of Jesus' theology of missiocentric, bibliocentric, and Christocentric sanctification: prayer. Fruit-bearing comes through answered prayer. John provides the condition in 15:7— 'if you abide in me and my words abide in you'—followed by the result— '[then] ask whatever you wish, and it will be done for you.' When the Word of Christ—Scripture's commands, priorities, thoughts, worldview, promises—control our affections, we will then pray with power and effectiveness because our desires will conform to Christ's. We will yearn for His desires. We will esteem and value His purposes and His mission for us over and against our own goals and ambitions. God designs prayer so that we would bear fruit. God is honored in our asking and in our bearing much fruit, not just some fruit. Much. And this proves that we are His disciples (cf. vv. 7-8). Our fruit-bearing is a product of our praying. And the effectiveness of our praying is contingent upon the abiding words of Christ, indeed, the abiding Christ Himself.

Additionally, a few verses later in John 15:16, Jesus explicitly says that fruit-bearing is directly connected to asking the Father to bear fruit: 'You did not choose me, but I chose you and appointed you that you should go and bear fruit and that your fruit should abide, so that whatever you ask the Father in my name, He may give it to you.' Some might assume that this fruit is surely only talking about spiritual virtues, like the fruit of the Spirit—love, joy, peace, patience, kindness, goodness, gentleness, faithfulness, and self-control—as mentioned in Galatians 5:22-23. Though very important, fruit-bearing as Christian character and virtue is not what Jesus is mainly referring to here, and that is not how John primarily uses the idea of fruit-bearing throughout his Gospel. Theologian and professor of New Testament D.A. Carson helpfully explains the identity of this fruit:

> The verb [*ethēka*: 'appointed'] commonly occurs, with a personal object, in contexts where people are being 'set apart' for particular ministry (e.g., Acts 13:47 [citing Isa. 49:6]; 1 Tim. 1:12). This fact, and the emphasis on *going* and bearing fruit, have suggested to many commentators, probably rightly, that the fruit primarily in view in this verse is the fruit that emerges from mission, from specific ministry to which the disciples have been sent. The fruit, in short, is new converts.... However comprehensive the nature of the fruit that Christians bear, the focus on evangelism and mission is truly central.... The union of love that joins believers with Jesus can never become a comfortable, exclusivistic huddle that only they can share. Doubtless it is a unique union, an extension of the union of the Godhead; but by its very nature, it is a union, an intimacy, which, by the necessity of its own constitution, seeks to bring others into its orb.[13]

Jesus has designed a fruit-bearing mission for us so that we would see the answers to our prayers. Theologian John Piper aptly comments on verse 16:

> The logical connection between the two parts of this verse are tremendously important. Jesus says that he chose and appointed the disciples that they should go and bear fruit that remains ... 'that [in order that] whatever you ask of the Father in my name, he may give it to you.' Shortened down it says, 'I have given you a fruit-bearing mission in order that your prayers might be answered!' This only makes sense if prayer is for fruit-bearing. You would expect the verse to be just the reverse: God will give you what you ask in order that you might have a fruit-bearing mission. But Jesus says it the other way around: I give you a fruit-bearing mission in order that the Father might

---

13. D.A. Carson, *The Gospel of John*, The Pillar New Testament Commentary (Grand Rapids: Eerdmans, 1991), pp. 523-4. Emphasis in original.

> answer your prayers. The point: prayer malfunctions when it is not used in fruit-bearing. Prayer is for fruit-bearing. Therefore, since I want you to pray and to get answers to your prayers, I chose you and I appointed you to go and bear fruit. Because prayer is for fruit-bearing. If you do not devote yourself to fruit-bearing, you have no warrant for expecting answers to prayer.[14]

Prayerfulness is a higher level of work for those whom God has called to ministry (Acts 6:4), just as Jesus devoted Himself to prayer (Luke 5:12-16). God answering our prayer renders gospel proclamation effective (Eph. 6:19-20), and it opens doors for the Word (Col. 4:2-4). If missionaries do not set aside daily time to meditate on and abide in the Word of Christ—which should be considered part of missionary-labor—then missionaries are not guaranteed any fruitfulness, according to John 15:16. True, we might be busy doing good things, but busyness is not equivalent to fruitfulness. Just as prayer was the background noise throughout the book of Acts, so prayerful abiding in Christ must be the constant hum in the background of our methodology and philosophy of missions.[15] And this practice of prayer and meditation is not only for ministry effectiveness; it is for communion with Christ. He is our chief end. David Brainerd (1718-1747), the famous eighteenth-century missionary to the Delaware Indians, once said, 'When you cease from labour, fill up your time in reading, meditation, and prayer: and while your hands are labouring, let your heart be employed, as much as possible, in divine thoughts.'[16] And George Müller said it this way:

> I saw more clearly than ever that the first great and primary business to which I ought to attend every day was to have my soul happy in the Lord. The first thing to be concerned about was not how much I might serve the Lord, how I might glorify the Lord; but how I might get my soul

---

14. Sermon preached on January 10, 1993: John Piper, 'Ask Whatever You Wish', *www.desiringGod.org* (Minneapolis: Desiring God Foundation, 1993), http://www.desiringgod.org/messages/ask-whatever-you-wish (accessed: 31 July 2017).

15. Consider some texts that demonstrate how normative prayer was in the spirituality and mission of the New Testament church: Acts 1:14; 2;42; 4:31; 6:4; 12:5, 12; 13:3; 14:23.

16. David Brainerd, *The Life and Diary of David Brainerd: With Notes and Reflections*, ed. Jonathan Edwards (ReadaClassic.com, 2010), 264.

into a happy state, and how my inner man might be nourished. ... Now that God has taught me this point, it is as plain to me as anything that the first thing the child of God has to do morning by morning is to obtain food for the inner man. As the outward man is not fit for work for any length of time, except we take food, and as this is one of the first things we do in the morning, so it should be with the inner man. We should take food for that, as everyone must allow. Now what is the food for the inner man? Not prayer, but the word of God; and here again, not the simple reading of the word of God, so that it only passes through our minds, just as water runs through a pipe, but considering what we read, pondering over it, and applying it to our hearts. ... How different when the soul is refreshed and made happy early in the morning, from what it is when, without spiritual preparation, the service, the trials, and the temptations of the day come upon one![17]

It is no wonder that when revival and reformation grip a Christian community, their affections are reawakened to the kingship of Christ over all of life, under the proclamation of the Christ-centered Word. Moreover, when such renewal occurs, the Holy Spirit often mobilizes many to go to the nations as missionaries, which is a result of praying that asks for God to honor His name among the peoples through the proclamation of the gospel.

Devoted to godliness

For both full-time missionaries and missionaries-in-training, there may be no issue more critical for increase of character and competency than that of disciplines of godliness. Many young people who claim they sense a divine call to take the gospel across the globe fail to endure in their supposed call because they fail in this one area. Digital natives (those who have grown up not knowing life without the Internet), who are distracted more than previous generations, easily neglect to accomplish tasks and thus flounder in achieving long-range goals—the tyranny of the 'now'. Social media invades every corner of our lives, and it is difficult to discern what is best now—replying quickly

---

17. George Müller, *A Narrative of Some of the Lord's Dealing with George Müller, Written by Himself, Jehovah Magnified. Addresses by George Müller Complete and Unabridged*, 2 vols (Muskegon, MI: Dust and Ashes, 2003), 1:272-3.

to a post, commenting on a thread, or finishing our Bible reading and prayer time. Little by little, the missionary's devotion to God gets crowded with all the alerts and pings of our digital-infiltrated age. Not only does this interrupt us from doing those good things that God has called us to do as missionaries—prayer, Bible meditation, study, language acquisition, evangelism/discipleship—but it can desensitize us to what is ultimately important. Is it more important to reply to an inconsequential post or to focus your soul on weightier matters such as the Word, the state of the unevangelized and undiscipled, and the tasks at hand to bring the Word to such people? Considering social media and the eternal consequences of our mission, we should positively view social media more as a tool than a toy; and conversely, we should negatively view it more as an invasion from the spirit of the age into every moment of our lives than as merely a pesky distracting habit of which we only need to be mindful.

We must remember that our small daily routines—time management, scheduled prayer/meditation, financial spending, task completion—all serve our larger long-term goals of evangelizing that unreached group, teaching those untrained village pastors, communicating in that perplexing tonal dialect, preparing theologically to handle the Word competently, etc. We accomplish every major responsibility by minor concentrated routines; we meet every big goal by small faithful steps. For a non-committal, attention-deficient age, this talk of discipline, routine, and duty seems puritanical and spartan. But it is, nevertheless, part of the training for our sacred calling. Author Peter Lewis describes Puritan piety as 'iron discipline', in a way that contrasts the casual approach to godliness of our contemporary evangelical subculture:

> Puritanism was not merely a set of rules or a larger creed, but a lifeforce: a vision and a compulsion which saw the beauty of a holy life and moved towards it, marveling at the possibilities and thrilling to the satisfaction of a God-centered life. Moreover, the Puritans combined iron discipline with fervent devotion, saving the Puritan from a fitful mysticism on the one hand, and a mere worldly religion. ... Every area of life came under the influence of God and the guidance of the Word.[18]

---

18. Peter Lewis, *The Genius of Puritanism* (Morgan, PA: Soli Deo Gloria, 1995), p. 11.

Writer and philosopher C.S. Lewis (1898–1963) candidly remarked:

> If you read history, you will find that the Christians who did the most for the present world were just those who thought most of the next... [They] all left their mark on Earth, precisely because their minds were occupied with heaven. It is since Christians have largely ceased to think of the other world that they have become so ineffective in this one. Aim at heaven and you will get earth 'thrown in.' Aim at earth and you will get neither.[19]

Adoniram Judson said in a letter about screening missionary candidates:

> I feel, however, more and more the inadequacy and comparative significance of all human accomplishments whether in a minister or a missionary, and the unspeakable, overwhelming importance of spiritual graces—humility, patience, meekness, and love—the habitual enjoyment of closet religion, a soul abstracted from this world, and much occupied in the contemplation of heavenly glories.[20]

Doctrinal teaching for the sake of godliness

The true crisis in missions today is not that too few are going out as missionaries but that even fewer seek to make disciples, and an even smaller amount seek to make godly disciples with the written Word. Paul, once he established a church in Ephesus, commissioned Timothy as a pastor he had trained up to shepherd the flock. In his first letter to Timothy, Paul says: 'For there is one God, and there is one mediator between God and men, the man Christ Jesus, who gave himself as a ransom for all, which is the testimony given at the proper time. For this I was appointed a preacher and an apostle (I am telling the truth, I am not lying), a teacher of the Gentiles in faith and truth' (1 Tim. 2:5-7). Paul tells Timothy that the message of Christ giving Himself as a ransom for sinners is the testimony for which the Lord set him apart as a preacher and apostle. Then he goes on to further

---

19. C.S. Lewis, *Mere Christianity* (San Francisco: Harper, 2001), p. 118.

20. Francis Wayland, *A Memoir of the Life and Labors of the Rev. Adoniram Judson, D.D.* 2 vols (Boston: Phillips, Samson and Company, 1853), 1:211.

clarify what that looks like: teaching the Gentiles in faith and truth. In other words, the outworking of Paul's missionary vocation was largely through *teaching*.

As a teacher of the Gentiles, Paul admonishes Timothy to be a good servant of Christ. Later Paul says: 'If you put these things before the brothers, you will be a good servant of Christ Jesus, being trained in the words of the faith and of the good doctrine that you have followed' (1 Tim. 4:6). The antecedent to 'these things' here (and in verses 11 and 15) likely refers to the content of the whole letter but at least to the preceding literary context. In the preceding paragraphs, Paul unpacks the 'mystery of godliness' (1 Tim. 3:16)—namely, the gospel message, and he issues a warning of those who will defect from the faith (1 Tim. 4:1-5). Paul argues that Timothy will demonstrate he is a faithful servant of Christ when he continually teaches these gospel truths and admonitions to the Christians under Timothy's care. And Paul goes on to identify how Timothy can ensure that he is a good servant of Christ who routinely teaches gospel truths and issues warnings: 'being trained in the words of the faith and of the good doctrine you have followed' (1 Tim. 4:6). Paul's burden is that Timothy's training would be not by technique or style but by sound doctrinal teaching.

Timothy's process of preparation for that which Paul, as a missionary, has handed off to him, is the pursuit of sound doctrinal teaching. In his second letter, Paul is even more explicit: 'Follow the pattern of sound words that you have heard from me' (2 Tim. 1:13). Paul is not only concerned for promoting general ideas of theology; he focuses on even the pattern of words he uses, much like a catechism, confession, or creed. In his first letter, Paul instructs Timothy: 'Have nothing to do with irreverent, silly myths. Rather train yourself for godliness; for while bodily training is of some value, godliness is of value in every way, as it holds promise for the present life and also for the life to come' (1 Tim. 4:7-8). Paul's burden is for Timothy to take up the mantle that he has passed on to him as a shepherd of the young church in Ephesus. Paul knows from experience as a church-planter that personal godliness does not come easily. It requires disciplined training, comparable to the intense routine devotion one gives to bodily training.

In the next paragraph, Paul again revisits the theme of personal godliness and the importance of protecting good doctrine: 'Keep a close watch on yourself and on the teaching. Persist in this, for by so doing you will save both yourself and your hearers' (1 Tim. 4:16). Paul, as a devout missionary, knows the power of a disciplined life. Paul tells us that guarding our souls and training ourselves in godliness in addition to guarding the gospel and receiving training in its words will not only preserve and sanctify ourselves, but such personal and doctrinal devotion will do the same for those whom we evangelize and disciple.

Notice that Paul does not endorse casual Christian living, nor does he allow for an unintentional and unpremeditated spirit. Training requires discipline and hard work. Training requires planning and discipline to execute those plans. A failure to plan is essentially a plan to fail. The missionary calling requires growth in godliness, which necessitates disciplined and devoted training

Making disciples in the pursuit of godliness

In his second letter to Timothy, Paul revisits this theme of discipline and devotion for ministry. This passage of Scripture is an example of Paul's missionary heart; he longed for his mission in Ephesus to continue to bear fruit and for the church to be reproducing and self-propagating:

> You then, my child, be strengthened by the grace that is in Christ Jesus, and what you have heard from me in the presence of many witnesses, entrust to faithful men who will be able to teach others also. Share in suffering as a good soldier of Christ Jesus. No soldier gets entangled in civilian pursuits, since his aim is to please the one who enlisted him. An athlete is not crowned unless he competes according to the rules. It is the hard-working farmer who ought to have the first share of the crops. Think over what I say, for the Lord will give you understanding in everything. Remember Jesus Christ, risen from the dead, the offspring of David, as preached in my gospel, for which I am suffering, bound with chains as a criminal. But the word of God is not bound! Therefore I endure everything for the sake of the elect, that they also may obtain the salvation that is in Christ Jesus with eternal glory (2 Tim. 2:1-10).

Verses 1-2 well outline the Pauline Great Commission. The content of Timothy's charge here is the grace that is in Christ Jesus. He is to equip and train in the grace of the good news of Christ's obedient life, atoning death, resurrection, and ascension. And with this gospel in which Timothy immerses himself, his method is then to imitate Paul's missionary example and train other faithful men to do the same, and so on. Handing off his missionary burden to Timothy, Paul wants him to train trainers and teach teachers who will keep a close watch on their souls and on their gospel doctrine and thus preserve themselves and their hearers.

Timothy's ministry will not go without spiritual confrontation and challenge. Paul commands Timothy, as part of his training as a trainer of trainers, to put on a disciplined mindset. As Paul soberly addresses Timothy, he likewise instructs us.

First, we must be ready for suffering and opposition as strong-hearted soldiers of Christ. Paying close attention to his calling and duty, a soldier must make tough decisions to focus on pleasing his master; such decisions are neither comfortable nor always understandable by those whom God has not conscripted to such frontline warfare. Like soldiers, missionaries must not feel crippled by the reality that friends and family do not always endorse or agree with the decisions that they must make for the sake of Christ and His cause. In other words, do not be a missionary if your aim is to please people, even those who love you most.

Second, a devoted missionary mindset requires Olympian endurance and energy. It is amazing how much an athlete's aggressive edge requires self-denial, routine grueling exercise, and mental concentration. This kind of mental and physical training is all-consuming. The conditioned athlete meticulously accounts for every meal, tracks every mile, and records every minute. Competitive athletes are not just born; they are made. Equally, missionaries do not just receive a call; they train through desire, discipline, and devotion.

Third, the missionary should consider the roles and responsibilities of a fruit-bearing, hard-working farmer. No farmer reaps a harvest without first carefully planning and executing all the mundane, tedious steps necessary in the weeks and months prior—year after year. If there are no steps of initiative-taking, no time management, no planning, and no follow-through in the hot, laborious hours, then there will be no harvesting a crop later and certainly no food to eat. Similarly, doing the hard work of missions requires a disciplined farmer mindset.

Fourth, the missionary mindset requires the mental discipline of a student. Paul admonishes Timothy to think hard over what he says, and in so doing, the Lord would illumine Timothy's mind (2 Tim. 2:7). The missionary mindset requires focused thinking and meditation. Eight verses later, in verse 15, Paul charges Timothy: 'Do your best to present yourself to God as one approved, a worker who has no need to be ashamed, rightly handling the word of truth.' Timothy must do his best to present himself to God (or as the King James Version says: 'Study to shew thyself approved unto God') as a shameless and approved worker who rightly handles the Scripture. The missionary must have the mind of a scrutinizing, thorough, and attentive-to-detail student.

Fifth, though what seems to be the beginning of a new thought, Paul commands Timothy to remember Jesus, the Anointed One, the resurrected One, the final Davidic king—the focus of Paul's gospel proclamation modeled for Timothy. In other words, these above-mentioned mindsets of being a soldier, an athlete, a farmer, and a student are all part of being a faithful 'sent one', but if the missionary does not remember and rest in the true Sent One, he will slowly slip away from trusting in the grace that alone can strengthen him. The ground of Paul's imperatives does not reside in the faithfulness of the missionary; rather, the missionary is *only* able to faithfully employ his calling because of what Christ has done (past tense) for him in uniting the missionary to Himself through faith alone, because of what Christ does (present tense) for him in supplying sovereign grace to strengthen and uphold him, and because of what Christ will do (future tense) through the sufficient and infallible Word in saving the elect unto eternal glory. The missionary can rest in the sovereign King who supplies strengthening grace to endure affliction and to labor in spreading the gospel in order to gather those upon whom the King has laid claim. From start to finish, it is all grace. It is all Jesus.

All these examples that Paul uses to prepare Timothy for the challenges ahead are instructive for missionaries. We, who seek to train trainers, must contend for the gospel like a single-minded soldier, focusing on pleasing Christ over and against the opinions of others. We must consider the cost of training as a competitive athlete who secures a gold medal. We must plan and follow through with tasks as would a hard-working farmer who seeks a harvest. And we must employ our minds to think hard to rightly handle the Scripture, as any student would seeking to master his subject. These analogies all highlight the disciplined missionary mindset.

Conclusion

There are numerous ways a missionary or a missionary-in-training can pray for training in godliness. Because the immediate, pressing issues in the missionary's life can sometimes feel more urgent and take mental precedent over simple Bible meditation and Scripture-based praying, we must remind ourselves and one another that praying from God's Word is always valuable and applicable in every season and place. Here are seven simple ways missionaries can pray for themselves and each other from Paul's charge to Timothy (see 2 Tim. 2:1 7):[21]

- **To be strengthened in Christ.** Pray that the grace of Christ would strengthen you; pray that you would stand on the promises of God and derive your confidence from the past, present, and future triumph of Christ (2 Tim. 2:1; cf. Rom. 16:25; Eph. 3:14-20).

- **To make disciples.** Pray that you would be actively making disciples. There are many good, helpful services that a missionary can do on the mission field, but he fails to obey Christ if he is not actively seeking to make disciples. Making disciples does not happen passively; it requires actively pursuing people, planning what to teach, and raising up nationals to lead and serve the local church. Essentially, missionaries should always

---

21. Some of these points were taken from the author's blog post, 'Seven Things to Pray for Missionaries', Southern Equip, http://equip.sbts.edu/article/7-things-to-pray-for-missionaries/.

be looking for ways to work themselves out of a job (2 Tim. 2:2; cf. Matt. 28:18-20; Titus 1:5; 1 Tim. 4:16).

- **To suffer well.** Pray that you would be ready to suffer with Christ. There is a heightened level of adversity and affliction that missionaries experience due to the spiritual darkness of the host culture, the overall stress of living cross-culturally and its physiological effects, the mental exhaustion of learning to operate in a foreign language, the emotional challenges that can result from isolation, strained relationships, and overall discouragement in the ministry. And, there are many other unique factors that contribute to the suffering of missionaries. The missionary needs to pray for Spirit-filled perseverance and heavenly-minded perspective (2 Tim. 2:3; cf. Eph. 6:17-20; 1 Cor. 15:58; 2 Cor. 12:1-10; Phil. 3:7-10).

- **To stay focused on the mission.** Pray that you do not fall into legitimate distractions. In our globalized culture, there are many ways to stay connected. For some missionaries, the host culture can be so difficult and daunting that they slip into anesthetizing habits and seek to escape to their friends back home through social media. They unduly waste much time simply trying to stay connected to everyone and stay up to date on the latest entertainment, news, and trends of the home culture. They spend too little time in prayer, intercession, and meditation, which can result in disheartened evangelistic efforts, undisciplined language learning, indifference to disciple-making, and overall spiritual anemia (2 Tim. 2:4; cf. 1 Tim. 1:18; 6:12; 2 Cor. 5:9-11; 10:4).

- **To keep the Word.** Pray that you would carefully keep the Word of God. There are many pragmatic ways to create a platform, fund a project, or start a church, ways that Scripture might never prescribe. There is a temptation to call every good activity 'preaching the gospel' or 'missions,' when in fact there might be no gospel preaching at all. There are many good deeds done in the name of love, hope, and peace; just as words that have no works are empty, so are good works without good news

(2 Tim. 2:5; cf. John 15:4-11; 1 Cor. 9:25; 1 Tim. 6:12; 2 Tim. 4:7; Isa. 8:20; Josh. 1:6-9).

- **To work hard.** Pray for a hard-work ethic. As in any ministry where there is sometimes little accountability, idleness and slothfulness can become big temptations for missionaries. Because of the stress and exhaustion of living cross-culturally and in hostile countries, unconscious discouragement can lead to resignation and apathy. Sometimes the hardest thing is merely to survive a normal day. So, we can weaken in our efforts to evangelize, make disciples, and pray. Because of the daily sacrifices and the relentless spiritual battle, the gospel labor of a missionary is indeed by the power of Christ alone working effectively through the missionary. No one has the strength in himself to proclaim the gospel, let alone in a foreign language and hostile culture (2 Tim. 2:6; cf. 1 Cor. 15:10; Col. 1:29; 1 Pet. 4:11; Rom. 15:18).

- **To meditate on the Word.** Pray for illumination from the Word. Pray that you would do the work of Bible memory and meditation. One of the greatest ways to fall into despondency, to slacken in evangelistic zeal, to neglect prayer, and to abandon Bible-driven ministry for other more tolerable and socially acceptable ventures is to lose confidence in the supremacy and sufficiency of the Word of God. This happens when the missionary does not regularly recalibrate and immerse his mind in the Scriptures. Missionaries will lose perspective and hope if they only read the Bible briefly and occasionally but do not take time to absorb it and think hard about the Spirit-intended meaning (2 Tim. 2:7; cf. Ps. 19:7-11; Ps. 119:9-11, 18, 41-47, 129-131; Prov. 6:23; John 14:23-24; 15:4-11).

- **Remember Jesus.** Pray for grace to rest in Jesus. We are all little legalists at heart. We are prone to impress God, pay back God, help God, and do better for God. Just as laziness and indifference are dangers for a missionary, maybe the more deadly danger is guilt-based activism—do more, work harder, be better, pray longer, and then, God might finally be pleased enough to reward our labor with noticeable fruit. True, we must work hard, soldier on, and train like Olympians, but pray that your labor and endurance emerge out of abiding in the Vine, resting in Jesus, and remembering what He has decisively accomplished for you in securing your full forgiveness, imputed righteousness, legal adoption, peace-filled reconciliation, Spirit-indwelling, future resurrection, and every other glorious gospel blessing and promise. The main challenge is neither to avoid burn out from overactivity nor to avoid black out from inactivity; the challenge is to rest in and find strength in Jesus alone.

As God prepares missionaries, He often brings them to despair of their own usefulness and strength. The best thing for the missionary is to be confident not in themselves but in God. It starts with a desperation for God, leading to communion with God and perseverance in prayer for the gospel goals that God has promised. A soul dominated by a vision of a glorious God must apply Himself to the Word of God, training for godliness. Iron discipline, emerging out of and empowered by Christ Himself, is indeed necessary for readiness and usefulness in the hands of God.

CHAPTER 4

THE MISSIONARY AS SERVANT OF THE WORD

> 'There are three great truths: 1st, That there is a God; 2nd, That he has spoken to us in the Bible; 3rd, That he means what he says.'
> —Hudson Taylor

IN contemporary culinary circles, business is booming. The consumer's fascination in the creative blending of flavors and transforming cuisines shows no sign of slowing. In similar fashion, there is no shortage of innovative missional philosophies. Missional connoisseurs can sample the latest flavors cooked up by renowned innovators. Many virtuously promote kingdom-building, orphan-care, micro-enterprising, rapid church-planting, prayer-walking, artistic flourishing, culture-creation, and so much more. Consider some modified mission statements I have heard over the years, from big-hearted short-term volunteers, passionate for their new venture:

- We exist to love on hurting and abandoned people, effectively bridging a gap between the kingdom of God and the broken world.

- We are a community that builds God's kingdom through redeeming the city by initiating loving relationships and effective cultural change-agents.

- Our mission is committed to initiating hundreds of church-planting movements in each major urban center in [anonymous country].

- Our mission is to establish houses of prayer in urban centers that usher in shalom, healing, and justice to all segments of society.

- God cares for the unloved and so do we; we seek to partner with God's mission of love and incarnate authentic relationships with the forgotten of society.

No doubt such mission statements reflect genuine, heart-felt enthusiasm of Christians seeking to help those in need. I am so thankful for the changed lives affected through these self-sacrificing saints. The question for constructive reflection is: What do all these have in common? Among many things, they all betray a lack of definition and acumen in theological thinking. To be sure, our methodology (strategies, initiatives, tasks, etc.) of missions always demonstrates our philosophy of missions (aims, goals, objectives, etc.), but beneath all that, our theology guides our philosophy and consequent methodology. These above mission statements do not demonstrate lack of passion, praise the Lord for that; but they do manifest a theological imprecision and carelessness.

It is nonsense to relegate the theologian to the seminary and the activist to the mission field. If scholars are so academically enamored that they have no desire to work towards the reaching of the unevangelized and the teaching of the undiscipled, then they are living out of sync with the gospel they profess to study and articulate in their research and lectures. And what is more, they may not even delight in it themselves. If missionaries have no desire to study hard the deep truths of Scripture and thus derive no spiritual heat from theological light, they demonstrate a defective or immature view of Scripture, God, Christ, and the gospel.

Your doctrine affects your methods

If the Bible is not the driving force behind missionary endeavors, then what is? Of course, there is surely an element of compassion and kindhearted emotion that plays out in the urgency missionaries feel toward the marginalized. But deeper than that is theology, albeit not from Scripture, but it is a theological system nonetheless. As the Reformed theologian, R.C. Sproul (1939–2017) aptly observed: 'No Christian can avoid theology. Every Christian is a theologian. Perhaps not a theologian in the technical or professional sense, but a theologian nevertheless. The issue for Christians is not whether we are going to be theologians but whether we are going to be good theologians or bad ones.'[1] We all believe something about the triune God, mankind, sin, salvation, and the Bible.

Many mission endeavors are intent on helping and essentially changing people through meeting their physical needs and improving their overall life quality and environment, without addressing sin as the Bible describes it—guilty in Adam and living in defiance of God through not conforming to or transgressing His righteous laws and thus dishonoring His name. Such missionary efforts betray a view of human sinfulness as environmentally conditioned and a result of broken systems, under which the marginalized are suffering the consequences of the sin of injustice. God becomes a social liberator that saves peoples' lives by changing society's structures to create a heaven-on-earth experience. And Jesus' life serves as our mandate for carrying out His earthly mission to heal the broken and to build His kingdom on earth where peace and justice reign, effectively transforming culture. The cross becomes the emblem of Christ identifying as a pacifistic martyr-revolutionary and a victim of bigotry, intolerance, and violence perpetrated by the power-brokers of society and the Satanic influences behind such systems. The Bible then becomes a guide for living the way of Jesus, which is chiefly marked by peace, love, and justice. And the Gospels become a canon within the canon in that they promote imitating the way of Jesus, which includes practicing simplicity, contemplation, justice, and community-oriented ways of life; proponents of this Anabaptist-influenced interpretive grid promote these practices as essential to the gospel because they provide a taste of eternal life now through peaceful and anxiety-less rhythms of living in this frenetic era. And the gospel becomes the living reality of heaven breaking into earth as God brings His kingdom shalom through the lives of Christ-following revolutionaries.

---

1. R.C. Sproul, *Knowing Scripture* (Downers Grove, IL: InterVarsity Press, 2009), p. 25.

Moreover, such mission efforts are considered to be most strategically launched in the urban centers from which cultural, educational, and political systems penetrate the masses. Essentially, the gospel functions no longer as a good news announcement of Christ's past, present, and future work for His people that merely requires our repentance and trust alone; rather, it functions as an ancient sage-like story, promoting heaven's wisest counsel about devoutly emulating Christ's life-giving piety, which, if a critical mass of Christ followers would adopt, then social transformation would inevitably follow. With all the positive benefits that Christ-imitating piety produces, this actually reflects the spirit of the non-confessional and pietistic evangelical age; this imitation-of-Christ activism is a far cry from the chief purpose of Christ's incarnation to fulfill all righteousness and to be the atoning sacrifice for those who would believe in Him.

These doctrineless, egalitarian, and emotive movements, though surging with noble intentions, have distracted evangelicals from remembering and teaching the historic creeds and confessions of the faith, passed down through the ages from the early church. Instead, we often modify the doctrine of *sola scriptura* to promote a me-and-my-Bible-only approach to the Christian life. Modern evangelicalism has famously championed a least-common-doctrinal-denominator, emotions-based, Jesus-is-my-buddy, theology-quenches-the-Spirit approach to spirituality that bases its assurance subjectively on listening for God's soft whisper for direction in decision-making and responding obediently to promptings of the heart. Some popular expressions of evangelicalism demonstrate a mystical spirituality foreign to the Bible, emphasizing a utilitarian relationship with God, treating His Word like a horoscope, His Spirit like a force or a cheap buzz, His power like a magic genie, His gospel like an echo of our self-esteem, His kingdom like a community organizing agenda for culture change, His grace like a licence to sin, and His church like a day at the mall and the theater.

Possibly one of the most obvious examples of this utilitarian vision of being a 'follower of Christ' is seen in how preoccupied we are with 'finding God's will'. Is it any wonder that in the history of the church, there is a deafening silence among written sermons, letters, and treatises on what we today consider to be a normal part of the Christian life—

hearing God's voice, seeing a sign, sensing a prompt from the Spirit, interpreting a dream, and having a worship experience that helps us discover God's perfect plan for us. Professor of Old Testament Bruce Waltke aptly explains:

> When we seek to 'find' God's will, we are attempting to discover hidden knowledge by supernatural activity. If we are going to find His will on one specific choice, we will have to penetrate the divine mind to get His decision. 'Finding' in this sense is really a form of divination. This idea was common in pagan religions. As a matter of fact, it was the preoccupation of pagan kings. ... The king would never act in something as important as going into battle until he had the mind of the god as to whether he should or should not go to war. Many Christians follow this same path in seeking the divine mind in decisions. ... There isn't a magic formula offered Christians that will open some mysterious door of wonder, allowing us to get a glimpse of the mind of the Almighty. The Bible forbids pagan divination (Deuteronomy 18:10) and invokes severe penalties for those who resort to magic for determining the will of God in this way.[2]

Just as theologian J. Gresham Machen (1881–1937) argued that modernism threatened Christianity by emphasizing what is useful and productive,[3] so the post-modernism of our therapeutic age threatens

---

2. Bruce Waltke, *Finding the Will of God: A Pagan Notion?* (Grand Rapids: Eerdmans, 1995), pp. 11-12. For sources that discuss the contemporary implications of evangelicalism's historical and theological roots, see Thomas Bergler, *The Juvenilization of American Christianity* (Grand Rapids: Eerdmans, 2012); Brian Stanley, *The Global Diffusion of Evangelicalism: The Age of Billy Graham and John Stott* (Downers Grove, IL: 2018); George M. Marsden, *Fundamentalism and American Culture* (Oxford University, 2006); Mark A. Noll, *The Rise of Evangelicalism: The Age of Edwards, Whitefield, and the Wesleys* (Downers Grove, IL: IVP Academic, 2018); Douglas A. Sweeney, *The American Evangelical Story: A History of the Movement* (Grand Rapids: Baker Academic, 2005); David W. Bebbington, *Evangelicalism in Modern Britain: A History from the 1730s to the 1980s* (Oxfordshire, UK: Routledge, 1989); Mark A. Noll, David W. Bebbington, and George M. Marsden, *Evangelicals: Who They Have Been, Are Now, and Could Be* (Grand Rapids: Eerdmans, 2019); R. Scott Clark, *Recovering the Reformed Confession: Our Theology, Piety, and Practice* (Phillipsburg, NJ: P&R Publishing, 2008); Carl R. Trueman, *The Creedal Imperative* (Wheaton: Crossway, 2012).

3. See J. Gresham Machen, *Christianity and Liberalism* (Grand Rapids: Eerdmans, 2009), pp. 3-6.

to quietly dilute and stealthily replace biblical evangelicalism by promoting what is useful in helping us feel better through self-discovery, whole-person well-being, and the maximum enjoyment of the good things in this life. Not that those things are evil in themselves, but it is evil to emphasize them as essential to, in place of, or equal to the gospel message. Doubtful that Polycarp (69–156), Perpetua (182–203), Ramon Lull (1232–1315), Jan Hus (1370–1415), William Tyndale (1495–1536), and today's unknown thousands of martyrs would promote the gospel as useful for modeling kingdom rhythms for living so that God-rejecting sinners could be empowered, achieve wholeness, feel at peace, and live life to the full. In C.S. Lewis' *Screwtape Letters*, to entice Christians into mission drift, Screwtape devises a distraction:

> On the other hand we do want, and want very much, to make men treat Christianity as a means; preferably, of course, as a means to their own advancement, but, failing that, as a means to anything—even to social justice. The thing to do is to get a man at first to value social justice as a thing which the Enemy demands, and then work him on to the stage at which he values Christianity because it may produce social justice. For the Enemy will not be used as a convenience. Men or nations who think they can revive the Faith in order to make a good society might just as well think they can use the stairs of Heaven as a short cut to the nearest chemist's shop. Fortunately it is quite easy to coax humans round this little corner. ... You see the little rift? 'Believe this, not because it is true, but for some other reason.' That's the game.[4]

Furthermore, when we describe and limit injustice mainly to social ills such as economic and ethnocentric injustices (which in many cultures is truly a heart-breaking, chronic problem where lower castes and shunned minorities are blatantly abused, manipulated, and poorly tolerated at best), we then easily overlook the greatest vertical injustice in the world—the fact that all of Adam's descendants, made in the image of God, defy their Creator by loving and following what is right in their own eyes. Secondly, strictly in terms of horizontal injustice among people, is there any greater human injustice in the world than the fact that approximately one-third of the world's population

---

4. C.S. Lewis, *The Screwtape Letters* (San Francisco: HarperOne, 2017), pp. 126-7.

consists of lost souls who have no access to a Christian, the gospel, or a Bible in their language and who do not even have a word for Jesus Christ in their mother tongue? Those are billions of souls, tumbling headlong into eternal, conscious torment. The latest data from the World Christian Database and Joshua Project estimate that less than 10 per cent of missionaries work with the unreached, and only a paltry 0.5 per cent of the church's spending goes specifically to reaching the unreached. That leaves over 90 per cent of missionaries working among the reached and 99.5 per cent of the church's resources going to the reached.[5] Studies also reveal that Americans spend more annually on Halloween costumes for their pets than the church spends annually to reach the unreached.[6] While whole clans and language groups plunge into God's eternal wrath, affluent Christians spend billions of dollars, innumerable resources, and countless man-hours in gospel-gluttonized countries. To be sure, they are doing good for Christ's sheep, but frankly, the great horizontal injustice of our day is that billions of people remain unreached and so few Christians care enough to do something about it. The term 'unreached people group' should be intolerable to us; it should taste like vinegar every time it comes out of our mouths. Kevin DeYoung and Greg Gilbert make a strong case:

> Since hell is real, we must help each other die well even more than we strive to help our neighbors live comfortably. Since hell is real, we must never think alleviating earthly suffering is the most loving thing we can do. Since hell is real, evangelism and discipleship are not simply good options or commendable ministries, but are literally a matter of life and death.[7]

Considering the common condition of evangelicalism's priorities, this charge and warning of Proverbs 24:10-12 is particularly haunting:

---

5. See Denny Spitters and Matthew Ellison, *When Everything Is Missions* (Orlando, FL: BottomLine Media, 2017), pp. 102-3.

6. Leah MarieAnn Klett, 'Americans Spend More Money on Pet Halloween Costumes Than Reaching Lost: Missions Expert', *The Christian Post*, 28 October 2018, https://www.christianpost.com/news/americans-spend-more-money-pet-halloween-costumes-than-reaching-lost-missions-andrew-scott.html (accessed: 8 May 2019).

7. DeYoung and Gilbert, *What is the Mission of the Church?*, p. 245.

> If you faint in the day of adversity, your strength is small. Rescue those who are being taken away to death; hold back those who are stumbling to the slaughter. If you say, 'Behold, we did not know this,' does not he who weighs the heart perceive it? Does not he who keeps watch over your soul know it, and will he not repay man according to his work?

In today's information age, there is no excuse to disregard the plight of the unreached. No one can say, 'We did not know this.'[8]

An analogy of a shipwreck

When I teach my students about how to discern the fruitfulness of a ministry's theology, I tell them to look first at their methodology. They may have a decent doctrinal statement on their website, but their methodology is the true barometer of their theological distinctives. Their methodology always betrays their theology; and almost always, the first doctrinal distinctive to suffer compromise is the doctrine of sin. This effectively contaminates all other essential doctrines.

To drive home the point to my students, I give an analogy: If I were to put before you six unbelievers— a Southern Baptist girl, a Catholic priest, a prostitute, a drug dealer, a Qur'anic Muslim, and a Hasidic Jew—which one do you think would be most inclined to repent and trust in Jesus? Usually people say the Southern Baptist girl or the prostitute. Now to be fair, those are not bad guesses if we are considering the unbeliever's level of opportunity to hear the gospel or the unbeliever's level of desperation to turn for help. But if we answer like that, we demonstrate that we do not fully understand the depravity of each person's heart and their inherited sin nature.

Here is how I answer my own question to my students: There was a shipwreck, and on the ship there was a Southern Baptist girl, a Catholic priest, a prostitute, a drug dealer, a Muslim, and a Jew. They are all dead, face down in the water. Which one do you think would be most able to swim to the nearest shore or reach out and grab a life

---

8. The teaching of Jesus in Matthew 25:31-45—pointedly within the context of the final judgment—is a similar warning about neglecting the responsibility to reach out to the 'least of these'. For a helpful discussion of this passage and the identity of 'the least of these', see DeYoung and Gilbert, *What is the Mission of the Church?*, pp. 162-4.

preserver? Or another way to ask it: Of those six people face down in the water, which one is most likely to take on the non-human nature of a fish and start breathing water and thriving in an underwater habitat? Well, the obvious answer is that dead people cannot make themselves come alive and humans do not breathe water because by nature we only can breathe air. It would take a miracle for a dead person to live and a human being to take on the nature of anything non-human. We are all born dead in sins and trespasses. And the new birth of an unregenerate person is equally miraculous for someone who grows up in the church with much opportunity to believe the gospel or for someone hostile or ignorant to the gospel, and for all kinds of people in between. Regeneration is a miracle for all types of people without discrimination or partiality. Everyone is dead in sin, not partially dead, not almost dead. Dead. Deadness requires a miracle to bring forth life.

The problem with so many ministry methods that do not hold to the biblical doctrine of sin is that instead of using the defibrillator and CPR of the Spirit-empowered, Christ-centered Word to rescue a person drowned in sin, they simply try to attract, persuade, lure, and entice dead sinners to experience what is only promised to those who have the Holy Spirit indwelling them. They sit in their lifeboats and talk about how delightful their boats are; they try pouring warm water on the backs of the dead people in the water just to be nice and love on them; they sing songs about peace and love with popular-sounding melodies and emotive chord progressions; they quote movies; and they just keep trying new things, hoping dead people will like them and join them. But they are like clouds without water (cf. Jude 12) or rescue boats without trained rescuers and life preservers.

Unmoored mission drift

Mission drift essentially happens, not because the Bible is unacknowledged, but because the Bible becomes one authoritative voice among many others—opinions, success stories, demographics, experiences, statistics, emotion, etc. And oftentimes the reason given for why these authoritative voices should equally instruct alongside the Bible is, 'All truth is God's truth.' The Bible may be referred to as authoritative, especially on the doctrinal statement of a ministry's website, but it is, in fact, not heeded as though it were sufficient. And when it is used, favorite passages are extracted out of context or quoted at the expense of other theological truths, thus proof-texting the ministry's preconceived narrative of the human condition and what corresponding deliverance must then entail. The Bible is indeed used, but it is used because it is viewed as useful and truthful, not because it is the supremely authoritative Word of God. In other words, whether it is said or not, there is an underlying perception that the Bible's record of the way of Jesus works for peace-filled living and personal development. Therefore, it must be true. Pragmatism, pure and simple.

Typical kickback in mission circles to such above-mentioned remarks is that the world will know we are Christians by our love, and we are called to preach the gospel with our lives. Again, here are two common sentiments that betray a squishiness of theology and lack of precision with the biblical texts and a disregard for the whole counsel of God. Not to mention, there is an underlying repulsion for heady theology that kills passion and ignores the real-life suffering.

Yet, the holistic transformation that so many big-hearted Christians desire has historically developed after gospel-inculcation among a people. Missiologist, Craig Ott, helpfully observes:

> There is no greater transforming power than the translation of the gospel message and entrusting that message to the work of the Holy Spirit in the local people. Even the best-intended missionary efforts at social development can smack of colonialism and culturally taint or even emasculate the gospel. But as, so to speak, the lion of the gospel is set loose among a people, then personal, ecclesial, and community change occurs in dramatic and unexpected ways.[9]

Moreover, Ott astutely argues:

> Biblical theology of mission provides the North Star by which the ship of mission must navigate. Though storms may rage and currents may pull, the ship of mission can stay its intended course as long as it

---

9. Craig Ott, Stephen Strauss, with Timothy C. Tennent, *Encountering Theology of Mission: Biblical Foundations, Historical Developments, and Contemporary Issues*, Encountering Mission (Grand Rapids: Baker Academic, 2010), 146.

reorients itself on the fixed point. Trends and fads, political correctness, popular opinion (inside and outside the church), ethnocentrism and myopia, and a host of other forces would blow this ship off course. The scriptures as the revealed Word of God must remain the fixed point by which we navigate the ship of mission.[10]

The evangelical Anglican bishop J.C. Ryle (1816–1900) compared the aversion to doctrine among young ministers and missionaries in his day to a spineless, powerless 'jelly-fish Christianity'. He lamented:

> A jelly-fish ... is a pretty and graceful object when it floats in the sea, contracting and expanding like a little delicate, transparent umbrella. Yet the same jelly-fish, when cast on the shore, is a mere helpless lump, without capacity for movement, self-defence, or self-preservation. Alas! It is a vivid type of much of the religion of this day, of which the leading principle is, 'No dogma, no distinct tenets, no positive doctrine.' ... They have no definite opinions. ... They are so afraid of 'extreme views' that they have no views at all. We have thousands of 'jellyfish' sermons preached every year, sermons without an edge, or a point, or corner, smooth as billiard balls, awakening no sinner, and edifying no saint.[11]

About sending qualified missionaries, Ryle maintained:

> How are missions to the heathen to be carried on unless the managing Committees are agreed about the men they ought to send out, and the doctrines those men are to preach? ... Can we imagine such a Board getting over its difficulty by resolving to ask no questions of its missionaries, and to send out anybody and everybody who is an 'earnest' man? The very idea is monstrous. If there is any minister who must have distinct views of doctrine, it is the missionary.[12]

Ryle would also argue that doctrineless Christian missions are powerless and fruitless:

---

10. Ott, et al., *Encountering Theology of Mission*, pp. xxi-xxii.

11. J.C. Ryle, *Principles for Churchmen,* 2nd ed. (London: William Hunt, 1884), pp. 97-8.

12. Ryle, *Principles for Churchmen*, pp. 82-3.

'If you want to *do good* in these times, you must ... take up a distinct, sharply-cut, doctrinal religion. ... The victories of Christianity, wherever they have been won, have been won by distinct doctrinal theology; by telling men roundly of Christ's vicarious death and sacrifice; by showing them Christ's substitution on the cross, and His precious blood; by teaching them justification by faith, and bidding them believe on a crucified Saviour; by preaching ruin by sin, redemption by Christ, regeneration by the Spirit; by lifting up the brazen serpent; by telling men to look and live—to believe, repent, and be converted.... Christianity without distinct doctrine is a powerless thing. It may be beautiful to some minds, but it is childless and barren. ... But, depend on it, if we want to 'do good' and shake the world, we must fight with the old apostolic weapons, and stick to 'dogma.' No dogma, no fruits! No positive Evangelical doctrine, no evangelization![13]

Unfortunately, rigorous theological and biblical training is increasingly disparaged and treated as peripheral for real ministry to real people with real problems. Doctrine divides, Jesus unites; deeds, not creeds; practical application, not propositional truth ... so goes the post-modern, anti-authoritarian mantra. One of the most oft-cited examples is that Jesus chose uneducated simpletons to be His disciples, not the highfalutin scribes and Pharisees. The argument maintains that the more you study the Bible and are competent to rightly divide the Word of truth, the less spiritual you are and the less useful you can be in His kingdom. After all, the Holy Spirit teaches and leads us all into truth, and we are all equal in Christ. Are we not told to imitate Jesus' loving and humble example (they mean 'tolerance' and 'uncertainty') in the Gospels, not Paul's dogmatic argumentation in Romans? The words and acts of Jesus in the Gospels are more sacred than the rest of the sacred Scriptures.

It is not uncommon for missionaries to downplay theological education as if it were a crutch for those who are so left-brained that they do not know how to encounter God with their heart. The stigma is that brainy seminarians prefer theological training because they are theologically

---

13. J.C. Ryle, *Holiness: Its Nature, Hindrances, Difficulties, and Roots* (Moscow, ID: Charles Nolan Publishers, 2001), pp. 355–6. Emphasis in original.

nit-picky and care little for reaching the lost and shepherding weary sheep. Of course, many of us could think of immature and prideful seminarians or young ministers who use the finer points of doctrine to ridicule others and boost their egos; unquestionably, they should be duly confronted head-on. However, one has to wonder whether such a proud person is really called of God to minister or whether he fits the qualifications for a Christian leader in such an immature stage of spiritual development.

Their points and critiques are well taken and sometimes well deserved, and it is true that the seminary experience does not promise to produce men and women passionate for taking the gospel to the world. It is true that many doctrinaire young ministers have received an education at seminary and then have caused havoc in ministries. However, there is no direct correlation between theological education and immaturity and cold-heartedness. Correlation does not equal causation. Seminaries do not produce that; however, they may provide opportunities for the sin in one's heart to manifest itself, through cheating, lying, pride, arrogance, lust, false teaching, etc. But that is not the seminary's job to root out.

Now ponder the argument that claims Jesus chose uneducated simpletons to carry on His revolution of love, over and against the highly educated teachers of the law. This is often a compelling observation, especially when someone is unfamiliar with the historical and religious context in which the Gospels were written. Eckhard Schnabel offers insight into the first-century Jewish culture that produced Jesus' disciples:

> The calling of the twelve disciples in Galilee must not be burdened with the view that Jesus called uneducated Galileans to the task of preaching and teaching. It is rather probable that Jesus' disciples, including the fishermen Simon and Andrew, were educated. According to John 1:44, Peter, Andrew and Philip came from Bethsaida, an up-and-coming town that was granted the status of a polis in A.D. 30 and was located in the vicinity of the Greek city Caesarea Philippi. Rainer Riesner argues that people 'who grew up in such close proximity to a Hellenistic city must have spoken more than a few scraps of Greek. Thus John 12:21 presupposes that Philip could speak Greek.' Andrew,

> Philip and Simon had Greek names, which may not be coincidental. Riesner observes, 'The Galilean fishermen in Jesus' group of disciples belonged not to the rural lower class but to the vocational middle class.... A Jew who came from a pious background 'had a solid, albeit one-sided, education. He could read and write and he could retain large quantities of material in his memory by applying simple mnemonic devices.'... The view that Jesus had untutored disciples is a romantic and entirely unwarranted one. Note, for example, the calling of Matthew-Levi, a tax collector.... A tax collector belonged to the higher levels of society. His position presupposed not only that he was wealthy but also that he had ... education.[14]

Why would a patient with a brain tumor expect a surgeon to be a credentialed doctor who is a well-trained expert in neurosurgery? Why not just get a massage therapist to give the patient a relaxing scalp massage? Why do we send into missions new converts who are not competent to teach the full counsel of God from both the Old Testament and New Testament? Why are our expectations of physicians of the soul devastatingly lower than our expectations of physicians of the body? If a surgeon misdiagnoses or commits malpractice, you may suffer prolonged sickness. However, if your soul physician misdiagnoses or commits malpractice, you may suffer eternal hellfire. It seems obvious that someone who has volunteered with the Peace Corps is not going to be as qualified to help cancer patients as would be a physician from an elite medical school and a rigorous residency program. Why do we expect less of gospel ministers and missionaries?

Our Word-consecrated mission

John records one of the most sacred scenes of Christ pouring out His heart for His disciples. Jesus' high priestly prayer in John 17 is worthy of our attention. As John records it, Jesus starts His prayer by praying for Himself (17:1-5), then He prays for His disciples (17:6-19), and finally He ends His prayer by interceding for all who would believe the message of the Apostles (17:20-26). The middle of Jesus' prayer for His

---

14. Eckhard Schnabel, *Early Christian Mission* vol. 1 (Downers Grove, IL: IVP Academic, 2004), pp. 277-8.

disciples is significant for understanding how the missionary should view the Word and mission.

Jesus prays in verse 17: 'Sanctify them in the truth; your word is truth.' And then He gives the reason for His prayer request in verse 18: 'As you sent me into the world, so I have sent them into the world.' Jesus is praying that His disciples would be consecrated for the mission to which He is calling them, and that applies to us in every generation, especially to missionaries, because the apostolic task and commission is yet unfinished. To execute the mission of going into the world (v. 18), the sent-ones must be sanctified (v. 17). This begs a few questions: What is the goal of being sanctified? What tool does the Father use for this sanctification?

The telos

The term 'sanctification' is commonly used for the process of being made holy, or more precisely, the process of being set apart. Being set apart has two sides: it requires leaving and cleaving, as it were. We are set apart from the world, the devil, and our sin nature, but we are only halfway there in the setting apart process; we need to go the rest of the way and be set apart for and to God. We can only serve one master, which means having no master is not an option. There is no neutral ground in our allegiance and loyalties. God is the goal of our sanctification. He sets us apart from the world, self, and the devil as a possession for Himself. God's *telos*—goal—of our sanctification is for holy service to Himself.

When Jesus prays for His disciples, 'Sanctify them' (v. 17), He is praying that the disciples would be set apart for something. What is that something? He highlights His purpose in praying this in the next verse: to be sent into the world on a mission just as the Father sent Him on a mission (v. 18). In other words, Jesus is praying that His disciples would be set apart for the holy missional purposes of God— consecration to engage the world with the gospel. Commenting on verse 17, D.A. Carson makes the helpful argument: 'In John's Gospel, such "sanctification" is always for mission.'[15]

---

15. D.A. Carson, *The Gospel According to John*, p. 566.

This request of Jesus was not solely for those eleven disciples (Judas notwithstanding), because He goes on to say to the Father in verse 20 that He is not only interceding for the eleven in His midst, 'but also for those who will believe in me [that is Jesus] through their word.' Clearly, the application of Jesus' prayer is for all Christians, and especially for those whose God-ordained vocation and calling in life is to literally go into the world, crossing cultures, taking the gospel to the unevangelized and undiscipled.

How often does our talk of personal sanctification revolve around being a 'better' (i.e., well-behaved) Christian? We hate the consequences of sin and how it hurts us or others, and rightfully so. Thus our motivation for sanctification often revolves around experiencing more joy and freedom from sin. This is not a bad motivation, but is it the only motivation? The sum of the Law and the Prophets is to love the Lord our God with all that we are, and to love our neighbors as ourselves (cf. Matt. 22:37-40). Christ fulfilled this Law for us, and now by His indwelling Spirit He enables us to progressively live in the same manner.

Could it be, however, that our motivation for sanctification is often only half full, focused exclusively on the vertical? Maybe the reason we do not view the purpose of sanctification as mission is because we are not broken enough over the plight of our global neighbors. Maybe if we prayed that God would increase our love for our global neighbors, we would start viewing sanctification as a means to a missionary end. If we are so enamored by the gospel's sanctifying power for us, so much so that we spend hundreds and even thousands of dollars on tuition, books, resources, and conferences celebrating the gospel for us, does not our motivation for gospel-centered sanctification seem disproportionate?

The tool

What is this tool that God uses to train and consecrate His servants for going into the world? The truth. Not truth, generically. *The* truth, with a definite article. Jesus then emphatically identifies what embodies *the* truth in the very next clause: 'your word is truth' (v. 17). Here Jesus refers to *the* truth as the Father's word, yet earlier in the evening Jesus identified Himself as *the* truth: 'I am the way, and the truth, and the life. No one comes to the Father except through me' (John 14:6).

This parallel of truth language suggests different levels. The Word of God is *the* truth (17:17) just as sure as Jesus is *the* truth (14:6). Mutually interpreting, it seems, the Christ-centered Scriptures are the truth about Christ, who is the truth. God sanctifies his servants for their mission through saturating them in the Christ-centered Word.

This reality that the Word of Christ should be front and center in how disciples are sanctified is underscored by Christ's final instructions to His disciples in Luke 24. On the road to Emmaus, Jesus explained to them everything written in the Law of Moses, the Psalms, and the Prophets that pointed to Him:

> And beginning with Moses and all the Prophets, he interpreted to them in all the Scriptures the things concerning himself. ... Then he said to them, 'These are my words that I spoke to you while I was still with you, that everything written about me in the Law of Moses and the Prophets and the Psalms must be fulfilled.' Then he opened their minds to understand the Scriptures and said to them, 'Thus it is written, that the Christ should suffer and on the third day rise from the dead, and that repentance and forgiveness of sins should be proclaimed in His name to all nations' (Luke 24:27, 44-47).

Now, consider the historical and literary context: What famous event follows Christ's instructions to His disciples to look for Him in the Old Testament as He fills up the Torah, the Prophets, and the Wisdom books? The next major event that followed His teachings here and preceded His final ascension into heaven was the Great Commission. In Matthew 28:18-20 Jesus gives the Great Commission: 'All authority in heaven and on earth has been given to me. Go therefore and make disciples of all nations, baptizing them in the name of the Father and of the Son and of the Holy Spirit, teaching them to observe all that I have commanded you. And behold, I am with you always to the end of the age.'

So, when Jesus gives the command to make disciples of all nations by teaching them to observe all that He commanded, He is not only talking about His parables or the Sermon on the Mount; He is also talking about everything He taught them about Himself from the Old Testament. And surely the Messiah-centered hermeneutics lessons He had just imparted to the disciples (that made their hearts burn) on the road to Emmaus were ringing loudly in their ears when He gave them the Great Commission not too long afterward. In imitation of Christ, the Apostles demonstrably used a Christ-centered lens in looking at the Old Testament (Acts 3:18, 22-24; 10:43; 17:2-3; 26:22-23).

All of the inspired Old Testament Scriptures point to Christ. Paul reminds Timothy that these Scriptures should lead to faith in Christ: 'from childhood you have been acquainted with the sacred writings, which are able to make you wise for salvation through faith in Christ Jesus' (2 Tim. 3:15; cf. 1 Pet. 1:10-11). Jesus Himself claimed that the Scriptures testify about Him (John 5:39-46), and He even scolded His disciples for not knowing things they should have known.

Matthean scholar Patrick Schreiner helpfully states regarding the significance of the Great Commission in Matthew's narrative: 'The Great Commission is predicated on the narrative preceding it.'[16] Schreiner explains: 'Matthew functions as the scribe who learned from his teacher and sage how to make disciples by illuminating how Jesus fulfills the old.'[17] Schreiner also points out:

> Matthew prominently presents Jesus as a teacher (διδάσκαλος) and instructor (καθηγητής). The later term is unique to Matthew and portrays Jesus in the role of a tutor (23:10). Jesus therefore has a unique instructor-student relationship with his disciples in Matthew. Matthew refers to Jesus as a 'teacher' implicitly or explicitly twelve times.[18]

As Christ discipled Matthew (and the other disciples), He was training him how to write, instruct, and teach as a scribe so as to bring out the kingdom treasures of the good news that Christ fulfills and fills full the Old Testament laws, judgments, promises, types, and shadows. Schreiner compellingly argues about the identity of Matthew as a trained disciple:

> *Matthew is the discipled scribe who narrates Jesus's life through the alternation of the new and the old.* The image I employ has its source in Matt. 13:52: 'Therefore every scribe who has been trained for the

---

16. Patrick Schreiner, *Matthew, Disciple and Scribe* (Grand Rapids: Baker, 2019), p. 188.

17. Schreiner, *Matthew*, p. 8.

18. Schreiner, *Matthew*, pp. 15-16. See Matthew 8:19; 9:11; 10:24, 25; 12:38; 17:24; 19:16; 22:16, 24, 36; 23:8; 26:18.

> kingdom of heaven is like a master of a house, who brings out of his treasure what is new and what is old.' ... The word usually translated as trained (μαθητευθείς) is related to the Greek word for disciple (μαθητής). Matthew's verse could therefore be translated: 'Therefore every discipled scribe for the kingdom of heaven is like a master of a house, who brings out his treasures new and old.' Jesus tells them that a scribe (someone who works with texts) who becomes a disciple (following Jesus as a teacher of wisdom) can produce great things for the kingdom of heaven.'[19]

Scribes functioned in four main ways, which Matthew himself certainly employed. Schreiner states, 'Though it can be tempting to think of scribes merely as those who wrote, most scribes in both Matthew's time and before Matthew's time engaged in at least four activities that mirror and illuminate Matthew's composition: (1) learning, (2) writing/interpreting, (3) distributing, and (4) teaching.'[20]

Though the Great Commission is the mission of the church universal, yet for those who are specifically sent into the world as missionaries to the unreached peoples, to reveal the hidden treasures of Christ filling full the plan and promises of God is part of the disciple-making task. To be sure, truncating the Great Commission to merely instructing new converts how to better obey Christ's rules to be better Christians completely misses the point. We have the privilege to train the nations to keep, observe, guard, and obey the holy, awesome Word of Christ, that the better Adam, the better Abraham, the better Moses, the better Israel, and the better David has made a way for sinners to be adopted as sons of God. Jesus is the Desire of all nations. The task of making disciples in the Matthean Great Commission sense surely expects the 'sent one' to be trained in explicating the excellencies of Christ in all of Scripture, as a missionary-scribe, a missionary-theologian.

This Christ-centered interpretive paradigm in which Jesus educated his disciples is essential for the establishment and maturity of Great Commission churches in every generation. If our disciple-making,

---

19. Schreiner, *Matthew*, pp. 9-10. Emphasis in original.
20. Schreiner, *Matthew*, pp. 21-2.

church-planting strategies, and leadership development do not include doing what Jesus did with the Old Testament, then our Great Commission discipleship remains unfinished. Church leadership remains embryonic until the pastor is competent to teach. Teach what? All the Scriptures. Does it not seem reasonable that a competent disciple-maker should emulate how Christ instructed His disciples on the road to Emmaus to understand the Christocentric Word before giving them the Great Commission? Does it not seem sensible that a Christian leader should follow the Christocentric pattern of teaching that the Apostles model in the New Testament? Our theology drives our methodology, and if we believe the Bible alone is effective and sufficient to bring sinners to salvation in Christ and sanctify justified sinners into Christ's image, then why do so few missionaries value biblical/theological training in their disciple-making efforts? The power is in the seed, not the seed-thrower. A sower may be well-seasoned in many other skills, but those are ultimately inconsequential when it comes to liberally throwing seed onto the soil. Granted, the sower may well discern where the fertile soil might be, but in general, the wise sower knows that there can be no harvest without dissemination because only the seed can produce life. No other agricultural methods can substitute sowing.

Scripture's authority and sufficiency

Jesus told a story in Luke 16 about a man named Lazarus and a rich man, the former in paradise and the latter in torment. The rich man, despairing of his tortuous confinement, cries out to Abraham, who is standing with Lazarus far outside the place of torment. After pleading for mercy in vain, the rich man pleads with Abraham to send Lazarus back to his hometown to warn the rich man's family of the dreadfulness of Hades lest they also die and suffer such torment. Consider the rest of the dialogue between the rich man and Abraham:

> But Abraham said, 'They have Moses and the Prophets; let them hear them.' And he said, 'No, father Abraham, but if someone goes to them from the dead, they will repent.' He said to him, 'If they do not hear Moses and the Prophets, neither will they be convinced if someone should rise from the dead' (Luke 16:29-31).

Do you hear what Jesus is saying in this story? This is profound: even if a person were to rise from the dead and warn people about the torments of Hades, if those witnesses of such a miracle do not already listen to the Word of God in the Old Testament, they will not listen to such a testimony even from a deceased person back from the dead who laid at the gate of their relative and who now claims to have a message from their relative in Hades. It would be one thing if someone claimed to come back from the dead and go tell random people on the street that he had been in Hades and is back now to warn people. That would not be difficult to shrug off as crazy and bizarre. But for people who knew such a person (presumably they walked around him to get into the house of their rich relative now in Hades), Jesus is saying that they would still not be convinced of the man's testimony if they did not already have ears to hear the Word of God.[21] That is a profound commentary on the deadness of the human condition. And that is an explosive defense of the effectual power of the written Word to regenerate dead hearts. *Sola scriptura*, full stop.

The implications of this story are staggering. If people do not have eyes to see the glory of God and ears to hear the truth of God in the Bible, they will not be convinced of the gospel no matter how many amazing and awe-inspiring works they might witness, even the raising of a known villager from the dead. Feeding them, rescuing them, providing jobs for them, 'loving on' them, and any other methodology emphasized over and against the sufficiency of the Word of God, will not finally deliver them from the dominion of darkness into the kingdom of light. Now, some will object that this is callously calling for neglecting the legitimate holistic needs of suffering people. However, supplying the Word of God as the forefront emphasis of our ministries does not rule out other ministries of compassion and mercy; it just

---

21. In his book, *A Peculiar Glory*, John Piper provides a helpful analysis of the role of signs, wonders, and the Word of God in opening eyes to see the gospel. He asserts: 'Wherever there is a spiritual deafness to the voice of God in the Old Testament, mere external miracles will not cure that spiritual deafness.' See John Piper, *A Peculiar Glory: How the Christian Scriptures Reveal Their Complete Truthfulness* (Wheaton, IL: Crossway, 2016), pp. 107-9.

prioritizes and puts ministries of works and ministries of the Word in their proper place.

I am fully aware that many well-intentioned people who value integral mission claim to place equal emphasis on eternal and temporal needs and see no distinction. And they argue passionately for such. However, until they can demonstrate an overwhelming proportion of imperative verbs from the text demonstrating that equal attention must be given to both eternal and temporal needs, we should remain convinced that the Bible teaches us to care about every kind of temporal suffering, indeed, but especially for that everlasting suffering in hell.

More to be desired than gold

When we are making disciples, we must impress upon them the value of God's Word, not the value of our ministries. Someday missionaries will depart, whether by death or attrition, and to put it in common terms, what we have won people with, we have won them to. The medium is often the message, and if the disciples in our care follow us chiefly because they trust and respect us, then we have done them a disservice. A true missionary leaves the Bible in the heart, head, and hands of the disciple. The authority and accuracy of anything you say have nothing to do with your ability to tell memorable stories, share sentimental reflections, entertain them with humor, charisma, and personality, motivate them with big vision, or impress them with academic knowledge. No, the authority and sufficiency of anything you say is directly related to the written Word and how it points to the Living Word. Your job is not to motivate, captivate, fascinate, entertain, or amuse. Your job is to 'preach the Word; be ready in season and out of season; reprove, rebuke, and exhort, with complete patience and teaching. For the time is coming when people will not endure sound teaching, but having itching ears they will accumulate for themselves teachers to suit their own passions, and will turn away from listening to the truth and wander off into myths' (2 Tim. 4:2-5). Heresy and false teaching are not always in what is said, but what is left unsaid. The missionary needs to be courageous enough to say what the text says in all its hard and countercultural places, and humble enough to say no more.

We live in a global culture that is increasingly anti-authoritarian and self-oriented. It is anti-authoritarian and egalitarian in that it increasingly despises differences of roles, hierarchies, and rank. Truth becomes relative to each person's personality and preference. Certainty is dismissed as arrogance; and tolerance is embraced as humility. When our confidence in absolute truth and authority has eroded, inevitably God gets de-godded—we re-create Him in our own image. Jesus becomes a lump of clay that we can mold and shape into whatever we prefer.

The culture of instant gratification and of access to anything creates in us a sense of pragmatism (if it works it must be true), impatience (if it takes too long then by all means, upgrade), a sense of entitlement (because some have it, all deserve it), anxiety (there are so many opinions and options that I am afraid to make a decision), a sense of self-orientation (how much am I recognized and how am I being perceived?), and a sense of dissatisfaction and despair (my life is boring compared to ____; I will never be good enough). So, because we are increasingly unsubmitted to authority and truth, we do what is right in our own eyes. Feelings, emotions, desires, social pressure, and popular opinion become the standards of right and wrong. Because we have low certainty in exclusive truth and high anxiety in diverse perspectives, and because we are so self-oriented, we have created our own post-modern pastors, churches, ministries, and sacred scriptures based upon our perceived problems. Our sin problem?: That our inner child has been victimized and bullied by external realities and identities forced upon us without our consent, thus threatening our happiness in the unique person we have imagined ourselves to be. Our pastors?: Experts, doctors, sociologists, politicians, analysts, psychologists, and celebrities. Our churches?: Clinics, hospitals, sports arenas, TV/movies, malls, and restaurants. Our ministries?: Education, self-discovery tourism, therapy, entertainment, hobbies, work, and play. Our sacred Scriptures?: Internet, social media, Christian books, conferences, and self-gratifying experiences.

Amidst all the haze and confusion of our globalized culture's *laissez-faire* approach to truth, be sure of this: Scripture is God's self-revelation; where the Bible speaks, God speaks. True, God reveals Himself through His creation and providence, but in no way different or unique to how He specially reveals Himself in the Scripture. Where the Bible stops speaking, God stops speaking. Period. The Bible does not contain the Word of God; it does not become the Word of God; the Bible *is* the Word of God. We should not look to the Bible to support *our* thoughts and vision; we should look to the Bible to submit to *God's* thoughts and vision. Moreover, God upholds His Word equally as He upholds His holy name: 'I bow down toward your holy temple and give thanks to your name for your steadfast love and your faithfulness, for you have exalted above all things your name and your word' (Ps. 138:2). This is a Hebrew parallelism, where two things are put together as complementary and mutually interpreting. Show me a missionary who honors the Word of God, and I will show you a missionary who honors the name of God. As much as you know and enjoy the Word of God, likewise you know and enjoy Him. If you do not hunger and thirst for God's Word, then you do not hunger and thirst for God.

Consider one of the most explicit passages on the supreme authority and comprehensive sufficiency of the Scriptures—Psalm 19:7-11:

> The law of the LORD is perfect, reviving the soul; the testimony of the LORD is sure, making wise the simple; the precepts of the LORD are right, rejoicing the heart; the commandment of the LORD is pure, enlightening the eyes; the fear of the LORD is clean, enduring forever; the rules of the LORD are true, and righteous altogether. More to be desired are they than gold, even much fine gold; sweeter also than honey and drippings of the honeycomb. Moreover, by them is your servant warned; in keeping them there is great reward.

First, this second half of Psalm 19 is being compared with the revelation of God in creation, recorded in verses 1-6. Creation declares God's majesty, wisdom, and power. Verses 1-6 declare knowledge about the Creator-God.

Now look at the text to see the effects of the revelation of the Lord in the Scriptures. Verses 7-11 declare knowledge about the Redeemer-God. Here, David is using synonyms for the Word of the Lord: law, testimony, precepts, commandment, fear, and rules, because these are all the ways Scripture refers to itself in the Old Testament. This is supposed to communicate comprehensiveness, that all of the words of the Lord are supreme and sufficient.

This text (vv. 7-8) lists four explicit benefits that encourage us to treasure and love the Word of God. And then, the text (v. 10) tells us that the reward of keeping the Word of God is greater treasure than gold and sweeter to the taste than honey.

The four benefits set forth are illustrative of the life-giving power of the Word:

1. God's Word is perfect (blameless), so it revives the soul. It restores, refreshes, and awakens us.

2. God's Word is sure (dependable, trustworthy), so it makes wise even the simple, not just the educated or elite.

3. God's Word is right (just), so it gives joy to the heart. There is joy in absolute truth. In our day of lawlessness and tolerance, there is something life-giving to the heart to know that God's Word is right and just, about everything it says.

4. God's Word is pure (radiant), and it gives light to the eyes; enlightened eyes is a Hebrew expression for internal joy radiating through the eyes.

Just as Elohim made the sun for light in Creation, so Yahweh has given us His Word for light in redemption. When you see Christ stand forth from the text, it illumines your heart and makes you rejoice aloud. So now, back up, and notice the life-giving imagery used here. The Word of God is supremely sufficient to breathe life into our souls, to make our minds wise, to make our hearts joyful, and to open our eyes to see beauty. This is theological and poetic imagery of YHWH giving spiritual life to His people, similar to how He breathed physical life into Adam.

And then in verse 9 it describes the fear of the Lord as clean, enduring forever. This is a reference to keeping/treasuring/applying the Word of the Lord. Fearing God and keeping His Word work together; they go hand-in-hand: 'You shall keep the commandments of the LORD your God by walking in his ways and by fearing him' (Deut. 8:6). How much you seek to keep and obey the Word of God reveals how much you fear God.

Verse 10 of Psalm 19 says that the Word of God is to be desired more than gold, even much fine gold. In other words, the Scriptures are not just more valuable than money, they are more valuable than much money, even much of the best money. It also says that the Word of God is sweeter than honey, even drippings of the honeycomb. In other words, the Word of God is better than the most excellent tasting food, even an extravagant amount of food, more than you have capacity to eat. The Word of God is not just sweet as honey; it is a dripping honeycomb that you cannot get all in your mouth. Lavish fulfillment. Inexhaustible goodness. You can never master the Bible; you need to be mastered by the Bible. It is more than enough. If it is boring to you, the problem is not with the Bible.

Imagine if the richest man in the world were to tell you that for every verse of the Bible you memorized this year, you would be rewarded $1 million, and as you mastered the Scriptures, every day you would be served the healthiest and best-tasting food, and more food than you could even eat. How diligent would you be, then, to memorize, know, and keep the Word of God? How jealous and hungry would you be for the Word of God? In verse 11 it says, in keeping the Word there is great reward. Famished people walk across deserts just to find water and food; how many of us walk across the room to pick up our Bibles and feed on the Word even once a day?

If this is what the Bible promises of itself, why do missionaries and mission agencies settle for anything less in their preparation, methodology, and even theology? May God raise up a generation of godly missionaries who will stand on the Word of God alone.

Conclusion

Just as the chapter opened with mission statements that betrayed an absence of theological discernment and development, below are a few mission statements that are demonstrative of carefully crafted, theologically responsible missions philosophies. Granted, these mission statements are not the organizations' detailed doctrinal statements, but they indeed illustrate theological ambition behind the mission:

- Our mission exists to glorify Christ among the least-reached peoples, by taking the gospel to the unreached and training the undiscipled, with the Christ-centered Scriptures, in partnership with the global church.

- We seek to glorify the Triune God through preaching the gospel of Christ, establishing biblical churches, and developing theological resources that equip indigenous pastors.

- Our mission is to honor Christ among Bible-less people groups through translating the Scriptures, creating theological resources, evangelizing the unreached, and training native pastors to shepherd the flock with the Word.

- We believe the gospel of Christ in the Word of God is the only hope for sinners, so our aim is to establish training centers that develop literacy, teach evangelism and apologetics, provide biblical counseling, disciple women and children, and equip pastors for making disciples.

A missionary without a Bible in his hand, in his heart, and in his head is a Christianized philanthropist. Eternal torment or eternal bliss and the honor of the Ancient of Days are all at stake. No room exists for a casual, self-styled approach to missions. The Great Commission requires making disciples through going and teaching, which suggests a level of training and competence to interpret the biblical text, learn the target language, and teach the biblical gospel in a way that communicates clearly and accurately to the local worldview. The answer for discipleship in missions is not mainly to give away free resources or to provide services, but to go teach the nations to read, think, and observe the Word. We need biblical thinkers, translators, teachers, and theologians, all of which demand the missionary to be a servant of the Word. In missions there are many players but very few stayers, many pragmatists but very few preachers, many anthropologists but very few apologists, many doers of mercy but very few makers of disciples, and many cultural enthusiasts but very few courageous evangelists. In the words of the old hymn:

> 'Rise up, O men of God! Have done with lesser things;
> Give heart and soul and mind and strength to serve the King of kings.
>
> Rise up, O men of God! His kingdom tarries long;
> Bring in the day of brotherhood, and end the night of wrong.
>
> Rise up, O men of God! The Church for you doth wait,
> Her strength unequal to her task; rise up and make her great.
>
> Lift high the cross of Christ; tread where His feet have trod;
> As brothers of the Son of man, rise up, O men of God!'[22]

---

22. William P. Merrill, 'Rise Up O Men of God!' in *Hymns for a Pilgrim People* (Chicago: GIA Publications, 2000), p. 458.

CHAPTER 5

THE MISSIONARY AS 'SENT ONE' OF THE SENDING CHURCH

'I will venture to go, but remember that you must hold the ropes.'
—WILLIAM CAREY

INCREASINGLY pastors and church leaders are declaring that missions activity is the work of the local church, not mission agencies. Much confusion exists about the role of the local church in missions, and frankly, much confusion will probably remain till Jesus returns. This chapter does not claim to straighten out all the wrinkles and bring award-winning clarity to the issue. My main goal is to identify complex factors for overseeing distant missionaries and discuss it in a way that church leaders and missionaries can reconsider together their presuppositions and perceptions. Additionally, I will propose ways that missionaries can lead and serve alongside local indigenous Christians.

The local church and the missionary

If a missionary has ever been asked who is in charge of him, undoubtedly he has felt the same level of confusion as if he were asked where he is from. The mind of the missionary is bicultural and does not find security in where he was sent from, but where he is planted. For those who are senders and supporters of missionaries, it would help a missionary if they did not assume too much oversight and also trusted the missionary's support structure on the field for much accountability. Centralized missionary oversight is essentially a bureaucratic train wreck waiting to happen. This is why some of the fastest growing mission agencies are decentralized and field-led and field-driven, not directed from the home office in the home country. It is noble when a local church says, 'We don't need an agency. We can send missionaries ourselves.' Yet I cringe when I hear that because I have witnessed multiple, once-thriving supporting churches dwindle, fracture, and go through massive leadership turnover that shakes the whole culture and structure of those churches, leaving the missionaries on a distant field feeling very vulnerable because of the instability and massive changes happening at their home church. Moreover, the people in church leadership, apart from some short-term trips, usually have never served as long-term missionaries. And the needs of caring for and overseeing missionaries are much more complex than the needs of local Christians in the church's immediate setting.

Below are three real-life scenarios that highlight the inconsistencies of church leadership and their ongoing relationship to the missionary, demonstrating the good, the bad, and the ugly in church-missionary partnerships. The names and places of these case studies have been changed.

First scenario

In the first example, there is a young church-planter named Mike who is sent out to plant a church in Brooklyn from a growing church in Toronto. He has submitted himself to the process of training and pastoral qualifications for this assignment. Since they view him as an extension of their church leadership, the church in Toronto commissions Mike and financially supports him as he moves to Brooklyn. After several years of receiving full support and doing the hard work of sharing the gospel and gathering young believers for worship, the church-planter has trained another elder to co-lead with him, and they have enough money from tithes to rent a small little church building on Sunday mornings from a Seventh-Day Adventist church which meets on Saturdays. The supporting church in Toronto has stopped requesting Mike to come back for annual missions conferences and other meetings with the missions committee and elder board. They know he is busy and do not want to detract from his duties. Now in the eyes of the once-sending church in Toronto, Mike has successfully planted a church, and they no longer view themselves as the church-planter's oversight. They merely serve him by praying for him and sending him funds because the fledgling church in Brooklyn might never be able to afford the living expenses of the church-planter and his family. The Toronto church surely has the financial capacity to subsidize Mike's cost of living, but they have ceased overseeing him and his ministry.

As time goes on, Mike continues to serve the little church in Brooklyn, though he still needs financial help from the church in Toronto. With the influx of immigration, the Brooklyn church has become a Spanish-speaking church. They are able to train up other men to do the work of the ministry in their context and around the borough. And, with relational networks to other Hispanic churches in the area and around the country, they are able to establish a nonformal modular pastor-training center. Increasingly, the elders at the church in Brooklyn hear of the emerging need for a Bible-preaching, Spanish-speaking church to be planted in the greater Toronto area. They commission Mike to return to Toronto to help plant a Hispanic church. Mike is still on support from the church in Toronto, and his church in Brooklyn is able to help him a little, but they are also sending another young man with him to serve part-time in the Toronto church-plant, who needs some compensation as well, though he intends to find part-time work to offset what he does not receive in financial support from their church in Brooklyn. By this time, the original sending church in Toronto has long stepped down from that role of sending/home church and has become a supporting church. But truly, they are no longer only a supporting church; they have become a partnering church, even a sister church.

Second scenario

In the second example, a missionary named Grant is sent out by a church in Cape Town to plant a church in Chengdu, China. Grant spends the first four years of his work there studying the language and trying to share the gospel in a culturally and linguistically communicative way. He is able to locate a small fellowship of believers, mixed between Chinese and expatriates. They are not part of the state church for doctrinal and practical reasons, so they meet on different nights of the week in someone's apartment unit. Every year the Cape Town church wants 'their missionary' to come back for a month to share at their missions conference, meet with the missions team, and update the elders. Not to mention, the Cape Town church wants Grant to conference call bi-weekly for elder meetings, and monthly for missions committee meetings. Even though they are a significantly established church, they do depend on other supporting churches to help him pay for his cost of living and travel. Because they are aware that Grant has these other supporting churches, they assume the responsibility to communicate and update the elders of those churches of their perception of their missionary's progress.

After approximately ten years, the leadership in the Cape Town church has turned over and the elder board and missions committee are almost an entirely different group of men. In the meantime, Grant is able to learn Mandarin and train up another young man who can help him shepherd the small persecuted house church that still meets on random evenings of the week in various apartments around the city. (They need to keep changing days and locations to prevent being tracked and followed by the authorities or suspicious neighbors). But, other than the unconventional meeting times and places, this missionary has successfully planted a little church and is co-leading it with a young apprentice.

Grant's mind has crossed the common seven-year threshold that usually marks the psychological transition to a bicultural identity and to a sense of belonging. He has made the mental jump. He is Chinese, and his home is there with those precious few saints in his house church. He dreams in Chinese, laughs at Chinese jokes, cheers for Chinese sports teams, views his little flock as his true family, and has forgotten what it means to be anything else. He cannot even recall some English vocabulary very easily. The church in Cape Town, on the other hand, sees their missionary still as an extension of their staff.

In the meantime, Grant's young child develops a health challenge due to China's hazardous pollution that only doctors in South Africa can evaluate. Moreover, he is slandered by some supporters in South

Africa who claim he has neglected his family and sacrificed them on the altar of ministry. He must go back to Cape Town to see a medical specialist, clear up any slander-causing misperceptions, and raise more support because he lost approximately half of his monthly donor-based income due to turnover from people leaving the church and others who have heard gossip about his questionable and irresponsible decision-making.

During this time, the Cape Town church's new leadership asks him questions about who is overseeing his work in China and to whom he is accountable, since according to their records, he has not communicated as often as he used to in the beginning. Part of that is true, since Grant has been functionally adopted as a member of his church in China and does not feel the need to communicate as frequently to the church in Cape Town. And part of that is due to the fact that the previous pastors and missions committee leaders did not keep written records of conversations and updates. Also, part of their concern is that they have heard the slander, and they are unaware that Grant's family knowingly accepted the risks of living in a severely polluted city in order to see a Bible-preaching church established there.

In response to the direct question about why he has not communicated with the desired frequency and detail, Grant stammers. He manages to explain that he is thankful for their much-needed generous support, but he sees his church in China as his accountability and oversight. He even informs them that he is a member of his house church. He means no disrespect by it; he only speaks plainly and honestly because he is used to speaking openly to church leaders in his context and he assumes these elders view him as an equal since he is, after all, a pastor in his own context in China.

This statement riles a few leaders and leaves others insulted and fuming. What they hear in his statement is that he is rebellious, does not want to submit to their authority, and that he has unilaterally treated his membership to their church as cheap and trivial. He is, after all, not a paid pastor on staff at an established institutional church with a large elder board. He is just a cocky missionary who understands very little about real leadership in a real church. The lead pastor retorts that rebellion is as the sin of divination, and that Grant cannot expect God's blessing and protection if he steps out of the spiritual authority and umbrella of protection of his elders. Another man on the elder board argues that they will not give their missionary permission to return to China until they are certain he is submitted to their authority and will happily receive without reservation their decisions for him, even if those decisions are bad and prove to be unhelpful.

He replies that his previous relationship with the former pastors who have since moved on was strong and vibrant, that they put him through the extensive ordination process, and that he even carries a copy of his ordination certificate folded up in his Bible to remind him who he has been set apart to be. The current elders and pastoral staff dismiss the reputations of those former pastors because of their significant disagreements with them previously, which essentially undercuts any credibility their missionary once thought he had.

The elder board ends the meeting by outlining their requirement for Grant to maintain support and return to China: get regularly involved in the Cape Town church and serve for at least a year or maybe two, until the elders can determine whether God wants the missionary to go overseas again. And the litmus test for whether he is ready to return to China is whether he and his family are happily submitting to their requirements for him. Then one elder adds the caveat, 'We own you because we pay for most of your support; and you need to do what we say because we are like your parents. Even if we are wrong, you must obey us because we are your chain of command.'

Needless to say, the missionary is flabbergasted and leaves that meeting feeling a mix of shame, failure, confusion, anger, guilt, doubt, and worry:

> What should I do? If I stay, my little church in Chengdu will struggle; they have already lost so many to prison and persecution. It is hard enough being away for a month, let alone a year or more. What about my family? They cannot just leave their home in China and move to South Africa. My children only know life in China, and now we know that we can get in China the medical treatment necessary for our child. What about my visa platform? If I leave for such a long time, it may be impossible to ever regain that visa again, and it will

adversely affect so many co-workers. And it took me the last seven years to develop that visa platform. But, if I refuse to comply or even try to make a compromise, I will be labeled as insubordinate, and I will surely lose all our financial support, plus this church will call all our other supporting churches and tell them they are not confident that I am fit to be a missionary anymore. Am I really rebellious like they say? What if they are right? Am I under God's judgment? What have I done?

Third scenario

This third example involves a young man named Scott who senses a missions impulse to go to Mozambique. He communicates his burning desire to the Sydney megachurch of which he is part. The missions team only knows Scott superficially, but they know his parents, who are founding members of the church. They admire this young man for wanting to spend a few years of his early twenties to work in Mozambique. They ask him what he wants to do, and he says that he wants 'to go "love on" children and orphans and just give them Jesus, since pure and undefiled religion cares for orphans [cf. James 1:2].' They respond enthusiastically, commenting that they are so thankful that Scott walks in 'the reckless love of the Father' and wants to spread it to the 'least of these'.

Scott is able to quickly raise support since a few of his wealthy relatives, who also attend the 4,000-person church, donated generous sums of money in addition to the large pledge from the church missions team. At the sending-out service, someone asks Scott in passing if he had been to Bible college or seminary, and he cracks a joke about seminary being 'a cemetery where passion for Jesus goes to die'. They sort of roll their eyes and say, 'Yeah, it's great that you are not going to shove theology down their throats. They just need to experience God's love for them.'

Fast forward two years. Scott has been in Mozambique and has traveled back to Sydney every Christmas and for holidays and family gatherings. The missions team and church leadership never hear directly from Scott, but they assume he is too busy because they follow him on social media and observe that he is always out on exciting adventures with kids and taking pictures of exotic experiences. They are able to connect with Scott during one Christmas break, and he tells them about the orphanage where he works. They ask him about his ministry to the orphans, and he kind of shrugs it off and says he wants the kids to experience God as they play. They ask him about how the kids experience God, and he tells them that they practice imaginative prayer and employ dream interpretation, since after all, people in the Majority World rely on dreams much more than rational, anti-supernatural Westerners. This piques the interest of a few people on the committee, and they celebrate it as cutting-edge power evangelism.

Not many months later, Scott's cousin from Sydney is killed in an accident, and Scott has a crisis of faith. He has traumatic dreams night after night, and he no longer feels God's intimate presence. His foundations are crumbling, and over time, he abandons his 'faith', temporarily hooks up with a young woman to fill the intimacy void in his heart, returns to Sydney, moves in with some childhood friends, lands a bartending job at a local nightclub, and abandons the church and Christianity altogether. As for his church in Sydney, they are sad that Scott has been through so much brokenness. They believe he will come around after his wounded memories are healed and he hears the still soft whisper of Jesus calling the prodigal to return. Needless to say, he never returns.

The three scenarios

These are altered versions of true scenarios I have known. I do not describe these in order to gawk at the good, the bad, and the ugly details, as much as I include them to demonstrate how vast and varied are practiced models of church-missionary partnerships. Some are humble, where the church trusts the missionary and grants him much freedom, humbly admitting they know nothing about serving in his cross-cultural context in another language. Some are spiritually abusive, demanding blind obedience of the missionary to the church leadership irrespective of the missionary's integral connection to the indigenous Christians with whom he serves. And some are negligent, requiring no objective confirmation of a call to ministry, no preparation, and no accountability. And then many are some combination of all three. What all these scenarios show us is that church-missionary relationships are more complex than we think, and each situation is as diverse as the personalities involved.

A theology of presence and the local church

In recent years, much published literature has detailed the nature of the church and even the identity and requirements of church membership. Much good fruit has come from such renewed attention to the church, leadership, and membership. And, as with most things that evangelicalism touches (especially the celebrity-driven sort), it is probably a fad that will prove to be the latest reactionary movement to the seeker-sensitive church model. The Emergent church movement reacted to the same model and crashed into oblivion. This church-centric movement has a much more established power base, mainly supplied by popular publishing companies, professionally advertised speaking circuits, massive web platforms, and niche branding that could compete with many secular companies.

If you survey the history of the church, very rarely do you find tomes written to unpack the nature and function of the church, polity, and membership. Often historical church leaders have spilt ink in areas such as, but not limited to, bibliology, soteriology, theology proper, Christology, sacraments, and eschatology. Indeed, there are some historical works focused on ecclesiology, but they are typically not what evangelicals remember to be the highlights of church history.

Why has there been such a recent uptick in writings on church polity and membership? Remember that the era we live in is incomparable to the rest of humankind. For most of human history, people commuted most places by foot, and most places they would need to go were within a short walk. The 'mega cities' of ancient times were the population size of moderate-to-small American cities with a fraction of the land space. Rarely did cities crest the million-population threshold, and most cities were in the thousands and so concentrated that families and clans rarely moved and worked outside of their little neighborhood. Accountability, in many ways, came easy because everyone knew each other in their respective zones of commerce, community life, and culture. Accountability was possible even more so in the church. Church gatherings were typically quite small, and it was not difficult to keep track of who was in and who was out. Of course there were exceptions, like Spurgeon's Metropolitan Tabernacle, but they were very few.

It was not until the invention of the automobile that average persons could commute across the city, do whatever they wanted anonymously, and never be held accountable to the honor and shame functions of their once tightly knit community. With the automobile people can now travel across town to sin secretly, work a job of their choosing, and attend a church that fits their liking. Vocation, recreation, and home/family location are generally in separate places apart from where the church gathers. Moreover, with the advent of radio preachers, televangelists, instant social media communication, and digital ministries, Christians are gradually losing incentive to get up on Sunday mornings, drive across town to a church service, yawn through a 1-2 hour service of unprofessional 'performances', chit chat with people with whom they have no affinity, and stay physically present and involved throughout the week. With the incredible influx of busyness, change, and rapid transience, it is no wonder that church-centered ministries promoting church membership, polity, and healthy church life have emerged onto the scene.

What this immense emphasis on church membership and pastoral oversight has done for missions has not been as helpful. Most literature written about how to do church leadership, church membership, and church-planting is written by Western pastors in wealthy cities with well-educated, seminary-trained staff and a very affluent congregation that values professionalism and efficiency. But often their proposed principles are based upon their theologically unchallenged opinions that brothers in their circles all value as good and true. What they rarely acknowledge is that the biblical text is actually quite silent when it comes to church polity. And so, trying to retrofit their healthy-church-models into rural America, unchurched Canada, post-Christian Amsterdam, inner-city Bangkok, non-evangelical Coptic churches, underground churches in Tehran, and mountain villages in Peru is a fool's errand. Just because some form of church government 'works' (however you qualify what is successful) in Washington D.C., Manhattan, and Dubai does not mean that is a silver-bullet model that everyone should adopt.

And I realize that the authors of most of those popular resources would agree and not claim they have a surefire method; but, the problem is that when someone goes into print and has his conference message converted into a viral video soundbite, whether they like it or not, people around the world uncritically assume they are the authority on that issue. And in most countries, you never question authority. Nonconformity is shameful.

We have lost a theology of presence in our churches by and large, which is probably why, subconsciously, the focus on church membership and the healthy church movement has been so welcomed by many pastors. We are realizing that it is insufficient to stream in a pastor from one site to the screen of another gathering across town or in another city altogether. Something is lost in the absence of presence. There is an aching emptiness to the digital age that efficiency, speed, and remote connectivity have not only left unsatisfied but made more apparent. People crave the presence of people, which is why in all our hyper-connectivity, depression and loneliness-related suicide is skyrocketing. This is why people enjoy going to the game as a family more than watching it on TV, driving to a concert with some friends than purchasing the album, attending a pastors conference with some colleagues than listening to a later recording alone in the office, going to a family wedding than just looking at a photo album, making a road trip with a roommate to the Grand Canyon than just watching a documentary. We all know this need for presence is true, which is why we celebrate the Incarnation at Christmas—God with us: 'Veiled in flesh the Godhead see, hail incarnate Deity; pleased as man with man to dwell, Jesus our Emmanuel.'

The problem? In the well-intended attempt to circle the wagons and focus on church health, authentic community, and presence, church leaders have often placed unbearable burdens upon missionaries to stay unduly connected to their sending church. Consequently, as hard as he tries to enculturate and become part of the target culture and local people, the missionary always feels the nagging expectation to return to the sending church for support-raising, to ask the elders for counsel and permission before making a big decision, to call in for elder meetings and missions committee meetings, and to receive annual teams of volunteers from the sending church to 'partner' with the missionary's local efforts.

Supporting v. sending churches

It seems that a healthy sending church should be able to recognize that even though a missionary who is sent out from the body, though he may start out like an extension of the staff, should ideally be able to plant, establish, and/or become part of a local church assembly, in whatever context, whether it be as established as a high church of 1,000 people or as unpredictable as an underground house church of ten people. Just as parents might initially groom their child to choose a college wisely, they are not going to live there in college with the child to counsel him or her at the same level. In a similar way, the sending church should groom a would-be missionary and help him find the right biblical/practical training, but once that missionary departs, it would be wise for the sending church to mainly offer prayer, support, and occasional proverbial wisdom but not presume the privileges and responsibilities of presence in the missionary's cross-cultural setting. Just as parents should step back relationally and authoritatively after the marriage of their child, so should a sending church do similarly with their missionaries. It might sound pedantic, but it is important to note that missionaries are 'sent ones', not 'being sent ones' or 'sending ones'. Once a missionary is commissioned and sent, that is a point-in-time event, just as an ordination ceremony for a pastor or a graduation ceremony for a seminarian. The relationship of the ordination committee to the newly minted pastor and of the seminary faculty to the freshly graduated doctor changes. There is a shift in authority, accountability, and oversight that must take place if the missionary is truly to flourish in another culture and fly on his own in another country.

The sending church should have a goal in mind to hand over the missionary to the local indigenous church as though a father were to hand over his daughter to the bridegroom. There must be a spoken acknowledgement of the need for leaving and cleaving. To be sure, this wedding/marriage analogy is imperfect, but a theology of presence should urge sending churches to relinquish degrees of oversight and involvement as the missionary progressively invests into the local ministry. The sending church should plan to gradually step back, with open and honest communication with the missionary, and serve more as a supporting church than an overseeing church. Such an approach necessarily requires maturity, humility, and patient *finesse* for all parties involved. All missionary contexts and sending church situations are different and require careful discernment.

Another challenge to consider is that the missionary might be tempted to hold on tightly and not to leave the rich relationships of the sending church. Instead of hanging out with locals, he is in his room updating social media pages and calling friends and family. Culture shock has a way of crippling the early enthusiasm of getting to know locals. The sending church needs to understand this so that they can gently encourage the missionary to not lean upon them remotely but to seek ways to establish local indigenous relationships. These indigenous relationships, as hard as they are to develop, are a proven key for longevity and long-term commitment. The sending church should encourage and pray for the missionary to receive grace to leave and cleave.

The missionary must realize that part of being a missionary-theologian is thinking through these issues himself. Though many churches might have strong elder boards and established membership structures, the writers and speakers who supply those churches with such useful resources typically have not been long-term foreign missionaries themselves, and their understanding of a church-missionary relationship is often myopic and/or based upon one or two 'successful' experiences in their contexts. But just as church leaders know that a Facebook group, a live-stream video feed, and listening to Christian radio is no substitute for assembling together as a covenant community of faith under the proclamation of the Word, so a consistent theology of presence should not allow for a sending church to assume long-term oversight of a missionary via emails, conference calls, social media, regular home assignments, and short-term teams. The missionary, then, must sensitively communicate to the sending church how he views his role as a 'sent one'.

Just because we can send emails, instant messages, and communicate face-to-face via our innumerable devices of choice, does it mean we should? When the church in Antioch initially sent out Paul and

Silas, they did not have the same functional relationship to the leadership of that church thereafter. In fact, if you look at the biblical records carefully, Paul seems to have multiple sending churches along the way. This does not mean he disregards those with whom he once was closely connected, but he does seem to leave and cleave, as it were. He goes to one area, plants a small church, trains the elders, and they send him out on his way to wherever the Holy Spirit makes clear. Paul stays connected to them at one level, writing letters and praying, but to say that their partnership exceeded financial support, mutual prayers, and evangelical encouragement would be an over-reading of the text. It seems that wherever Paul served, he became deeply part of that gathered assembly as though he were a member himself.

Home churches, sending churches, and supporting churches

Furthermore, the missionary must determine the role of his churches. Often times those churches have not thought through their missions policies, and a missionary-theologian who can articulate the models and what might work well for his situation can actually be very helpful for overworked pastors and busy missions committee members. Sometimes such advice from the missionary, especially a missionary who has no experience and field-tested wisdom, might not be as welcomed as other times. So, use mature discernment and interpersonal sensitivity.

Very few missionaries have one singular church that financially supports all their needs. Most sending churches must rely upon other churches to support the missionary as well. There are many models for what it means to be a sending church versus a supporting church. Also, there are some models that incorporate a triad model of a home church, sending church, and a supporting church.

Though some church leaders cannot fathom such a model, many missionaries view one church as their home church, one church as their sending church, and other churches as their supporting churches. Or sometimes, two churches might serve as co-sending churches and others as necessary supporting churches. And of course, there are those who have a strong home church that is also their sending church, and they also have a few supporting churches alongside as well. There are other variations I have heard from co-workers, students, and mentors, but these above-mentioned are most common. These are not uncommon paradigms of missionary-church partnerships. So, how do missionaries typically explain these models? Consider how these practically function.

Model 1

Ben was raised in a small rural church, was baptized there, first sensed a call to missions and was objectively confirmed there as competent to teach and elder-worthy. Ben goes to seminary in another town. Along the way he realizes that his home church can barely keep their doors open, and there is no possible way they can give more than $50 per month. And, while he is at seminary, Ben gets deeply involved with a larger suburban church that notices his missions calling and wants to get behind him and send him. That church has a few connections to some other churches in the area that also want to contribute financially a little sum as supporting churches. Ben keeps in close connection with his rural home church, and his larger sending church realizes his loyalty to that small flock back home; they honor and encourage his organic connection to that home church and agree to send him through an agency and oversee much of the logistical necessities that a sending church must adopt. The other like-minded supporting churches pitch in and help when necessary.

Model 2

Nick's home church is his sending church, where he has been objectively confirmed as called to ministry and has been commissioned for the task of foreign service. They have the leadership and financial capital to oversee and help him transition to the field and cross-cultural living. Even though they have significant capacity, they desire Nick to find a few other supporting churches who can come alongside prayerfully and financially.

Model 3

Pete is raised in one church, and that church plants a sister church on the other side of town. They initially operate like one church in two locations. There are many organic relationships between the two churches. Over time, after being confirmed for missions service and after undergoing biblical/ministry preparation, Pete starts getting involved at those two churches equally. He alternates Sunday church attendance between the two, and he is involved in small groups at both. He visits both churches' elder meetings and helps out with the missions committee meetings of both. When it comes time to move overseas, Pete's mission agency asks what the name of his sending church is for their records. Since both of his sending churches share a similar name but qualify their name by the location of where they are in the city (i.e., Faith Bible Church-North and Faith Bible Church-South), he writes down 'Faith Bible Church'. Eight years go by and those two sister churches grow apart and become two independent and unique gatherings; they also see a turnover in many of the original leaders. They even change their names (The Gathering, and True North Church) and update their doctrine and vision statements. But in Pete's mind, having only memories of what it once was, he still has two sending churches.

Challenges are opportunities

There are so many complicating factors that the average Christian does not see in the life of the missionary. It is not uncommon for the missionary to feel like he has innumerable bosses to please:

- the multiple supporting churches whose elder boards want to keep up with him in depth even while on the field and want him to visit them for a season while back on home assignment;

- the few generous supporters who seem to always have an opinion to share about what the missionary should do differently, the team leader on the field who keeps track of the missionary's progress or lack thereof;

- the extended family who often drops a discouraging word about how the missionary's distance is causing so much heartache back home;

- the platform where the missionary obtains his visa that demands 20-40 hours per week of his time;

- the unique needs and wishes of his nuclear family unit who so heavily depend on him to hold it all together;
- his own interior ambition to do the work of the ministry to which God has called him with zeal and faithfulness.

Not wishing to address all the types of leadership and authority issues, suffice it to say, the missionary-theologian needs to know his sending church's polity, respect the inquiries and suggestions of the elders, and work with the mission agency's established leadership structure in order to find common ground that lets all parties be heard and still allows for the missionary and his family to feel a sense of independence, support for their needs, and respect for their capacity. There is a good reason for mission agencies to depend on churches for relational, spiritual, and financial support, and at the same time, both parties need to realize that many factors change during a missionary's lifespan. Pastors move on who once knew the missionaries really well, and their replacements do not have the same opportunities to get to know the missionaries like the previous pastor did before the missionaries were sent out. Elder boards shift. Missions-minded families leave the church. Churches split. Mission committees change their policies. The missions pastor that groomed the missionary has left the sending church on bad terms, which leaves the missionary on the field in a tense situation since some people in the sending church now view him as guilty by association. Congregants get excited about a new venture to support and grow bored with the little return on investment from the long-term missionary. Often when a missionary family returns to the church to visit, they and a handful of old-timers are a faint resemblance of the church family that the missionary remembers from years ago. So much in the home church has changed, and so much in the missionary family has changed. It is truly harder to come back than it is to leave.

Churches and pastors alone cannot successfully manage or foresee all the challenges of the missionary life. But agencies cannot do it alone either; they need the local church's leadership and oversight to help prepare, encourage, and support the missionary unit before, during, and after their field work. To be sure, agencies should never replace the local church but seek mainly to serve and enhance the ministry of the local church. This three-party dance between the missionary family, the agency, and the sending churches is very complex and delicate. Below are some huge differences that complicate the three-party relationship and thus necessitate grace, flexibility, and humble deference:

- Generational issues—the way Baby Boomers, Generation X, Millennials, and Generation Z understand decision-making, guidance, leadership, accountability, task orientation, long-term commitment, responsibilities, and support.

- Denominational and theological issues—the reason the missionary should be a trained theologian at some level is so he can competently talk theology with both elder boards and mission agency leadership personnel.

- Cultural issues—differing applications of leadership and oversight, such as the way a sending church and agency in Australia functions (egalitarian with a low-power distance) vastly differs from a sending church and agency in South Korea (authoritarian with a high-power distance).

- Medical issues—health factors that the missionaries are not obligated to divulge to anyone for legal and confidentiality reasons, but the sending churches and agencies still need to be aware and accommodate at some level.

- Financial issues—perspectives for how the missionary family wishes to accrue support and wealth (do they solely raise financial support, or get a part-time telecommuting job, or rent their house for income, or work bivocationally in a local business, etc.?). If they have part-time work for income or even for obtaining a visa, their work responsibilities to their employer need to be highly respected, especially in countries that are deeply relational and less contractual.

- Children and family issues—challenges the missionary family faces in pursuing education for their children; for instance, in many countries home-schooling is illegal, so the only option then is for the children to attend a local government school in the local language. Some international schools are either not affordable or not in proximity. Or, the family might make the decision to move away from the target people group in order to relocate to the capital city so their children can attend the international school. The family will also need to make tough choices about whether to return to their passport country to help their children transition to college or even whether to return to care for their aging parents. Missionaries will need to make hard choices that few can understand. This is not merely a decision of where to live; rather, this is a painful breaking away of a ministry, places, memories, names, and faces whom the missionary family has served so diligently for decades. There is no dry eye for months afterward.

These illustrations have multi-faceted complications; yes, they are challenges, but I would propose that they are actually opportunities for the church leadership, agency structures, and missionary families to grow in grace, mutual respect, and long-term endurance for the mission. With all the uncontrolled variables to consider, it is presumptuous to propose a one-size-fits-all solution. Truly these are case-by-case scenarios that require flexibility, wisdom, biblical depth, and lifelong devotion.

Making sense of it all

So, what comprises a home church, a sending church, and a supporting church? And when should the missionary consider his local indigenous church his home church to whom he is accountable? I am not going to offer impenetrable solutions to these questions because the biblical text does not exhaustively clarify how these should work out. I will, however, offer some suggestions for consideration based on what I have learned from veteran missionaries.

In terms of financial support as it corresponds to the missionary-church relationship, a model that I have seen work well is for a church to commit to giving no less than 10 per cent and no more than 20 per cent of the missionary's monthly budget. That way a missionary can afford to visit a supporting church but not be too concerned if a church needs to withdraw its funds. And this donation amount does not need to be the initial start-up amount; it could just be the goal that the church body incrementally works toward.

Every missionary should be a theologian and should think through these issues because rarely do church leaders have the discernment to foresee the need to delineate how these partnerships should work. It is often up to the missionary to think through these and help his church leaders to find a common way forward.

Here is an option of how we could describe a home church: They are churches who hold the missionary accountable morally, theologically, and ministerially. The missionary adheres devoutly to their doctrine and views the elders as his shepherds. In other words, there is a sense of responsibility among the elders to strengthen, pray for, and listen to the missionary, and if need be, correct and restore the missionary. The missionary, likewise, views them as his church family to whom he gladly belongs. This body of believers can be the initial sending church, another supporting church that later steps into that role for unforeseen reasons, or it can become the local believers in the target culture to whom the missionary has eventually transitioned his devotion. In order for these transitions to take place well, the missionary must communicate well and clearly with all parties involved so as to not confuse expectations, roles, and needs. These transitions should be both expected and welcomed.

Here is an option of how we might describe a sending church: They could be either the same as the home church and/or they could be also the church that has staffing and financial stability to oversee and send the missionary. We might also describe them as the church that has taken the *initial* responsibility in sending out the missionary. But, the level of that initial responsibility could diminish over time, and they might functionally slip into a more supporting church role due to lack of personnel or change of leadership while another previously supporting church steps up and transitions functionally into a sending church role.

Here are some options of how we might describe a supporting church: They are churches whose doctrine and missions vision aligns

THE MISSIONARY AS 'SENT ONE' OF THE SENDING CHURCH

with the missionary's and his home/sending church's doctrine and missions philosophy. They are unable to be the sending church of this missionary since they are already that for a few others. But they do have interest and desire to support this missionary in whatever way they can. This supporting church relationship might grow over time, and it is possible that they might be in a place to assume a home/sending church role in the future if the missionary needs that.

As you can see, there are no clear-cut easy answers here. There are a few things to keep in mind: We must be careful not to speak too authoritatively about what the Bible does not specifically prescribe and might only imply through analogy. Also, we must make sure that the missionary is freed up and encouraged to view his local indigenous church (even if it is an unremarkable and small group of believers) as his home church when that time comes. Moreover, the missionary must be a theological leader and servant in all these decisions and discussions, but that does not mean the missionary can ridicule or lecture the elders and pastors of his churches. They are godly, kind-hearted men who want to help, not hurt. They just might not understand all the complexities at first, and they never will completely. It takes much conversation, listening, prayer, and patience to establish a supportive team of churches.

Also, missionaries need to remember that they usually have a very stubborn, ambitious, driven personality that God uses in the struggles of international service. And because the missionary life is not just a job but a whole way of life, the missionary needs to be aware of his propensity to hasty defensiveness and resentment to church leaders and supporters for questioning, commenting, and not affirming what the missionary values so deeply.

Furthermore, a servant-heart in the missionary does not mean he should be a pushover or a quiet yes-man. A missionary who is a theologian should be able to winsomely articulate his conviction and persuasively argue from Scripture where it is clear. Most church leaders have no clue what it is like to travel around, talk about your needs, and pray that some people might want to support you. If all pastors were forced to travel around to other churches and tell people why they need to be supported so they can preach on Sundays, counsel broken marriages, oversee committees, and make disciples in their local church, very few pastors would actually get much ministry done. And very few would even step into that position in the first place. Moreover, very few pastors would find it helpful if some elders from another church in another city or country were to exercise oversight over them and their ministry as though they were right there with them. This is why a theology of presence in church-missionary relationships is so helpful.

Conclusion

A brief survey of missions history will demonstrate that God always accomplishes His sovereign purposes through weak, well-intended servants who do their best with what they know. There are hundreds of moving parts that God's people never see—the elderly woman in a small rural church who prays faithfully every day, the pastor who tirelessly promotes the missionary family to others so that they too will support the cause, the indigenous unbelievers who kindly assist the missionaries to get established and enculturated, the local police chief who is secretly in favor of the missionaries' work and disallows his officers to harass them, and the mission team leaders who guide and mentor the missionaries through the ups and downs of cross-cultural living.

Moreover, numerous unpremeditated words and actions can lead to painfully drastic changes in a mission—that hasty email sent late at night that ignites a conflagration that should have never happened, that anxious decision to send a child to a boarding school that later uncovers years of secret abuse, that difficult move to a remote city that plunges into war and chaos after years of tirelessly working to establish a legitimate visa platform there, and that tense relationship with a parent who despises everything you stand for and thinks that you have robbed them of their grandchildren. But God in His kindness and wisdom works through those sad situations to advance His cause in surprising, but rarely immediate, ways.

Missions philosophies, vision statements, and strategies are certainly helpful for planning and goal-setting, but too often our announced initiatives are uncomfortably close to sinfully boasting about tomorrow, claiming we will go to such and such a town and do ministry. In principle, James 4:13-16 warns about this:

> Come now, you who say, 'Today or tomorrow we will go into such and such a town and spend a year there and trade and make a profit'—yet you do not know what tomorrow will bring. What is your life? For you are a mist that appears for a little time and then vanishes. Instead you ought to say, 'If the Lord wills, we will live and do this or that.' As it is, you boast in your arrogance. All such boasting is evil.

In light of all the uncontrolled variables and unforeseeable challenges, missions senders and missionaries should consciously make a habit of qualifying most plans and ideas with, 'If the Lord wills.' And in the same unassuming posture, maybe our best vision statement would be to emulate Jehoshaphat's humble prayer as Judah was surrounded by Ammonites and Moabites: 'We are powerless against this great horde that is coming against us. We do not know what to do, but our eyes are on you' (2 Chron. 20:12). All pastors, field directors, and missionaries should contemplate the daunting task that remains, kneel in quietness and yet confidence before the King of the Commission, and confess, 'We do not know what to do, but our eyes are on you.' Visionaries and activists are not quick to speak in such self-effacing and God-exalting terms. Nevertheless, God uses our naïve enthusiasm for His purposes—always in spite of us, never because of us. After a hard life of unremitting losses and sorrows, Adoniram Judson reflected on humility in ministry: 'O, when will Christians learn ... that their puny, polluted offerings of works are not necessary to God? He permits them to work, as a favor, in order to do them good, personally, because he loves them, and desires to honor them, not because he needs them.'[1]

The history of missions is the history of good intentions, failed attempts, unnoticed triumphs, haunting silence, ordinary obedience, quiet contentment, and late-night sobs all through which God powerfully works for His glory and our eternal gladness in Him. There are so

---

1. Wayland, *A Memoir*, p. 2:368. For a developed synthesis of Judson's self-denying trust in God's providence in the joys and sorrows of missionary life, see E.D. Burns, *A Supreme Desire to Please Him: The Spirituality of Adoniram Judson* (Eugene, OR: Pickwick, 2016), pp. 94-110.

many joys a church body experiences in reaching the nations. The return on investment in missions is never a loss. It is the highest privilege God could give his people, and he provides magnanimously for it; because of Christ's final sacrifice, obeying the Great Commission is never finally a sacrifice for us. In the end, on that great Day, the senders, the sent ones, and the reached people groups will sing for joy and celebrate together in the awesome presence of the smiling providence of God.

CHAPTER 6

THE MISSIONARY IN THE GLOBAL CONTEXT

> 'The church was first established and organized with a
> worldwide mission for a worldwide work.'
> —Roland Allen

A MISSIONARY-THEOLOGIAN is not only an exegete of Scripture, but he is also an exegete of the target culture, which requires studying the local language, learning cultural cues and values, and listening to diversity of perspectives. There are many ways a missionary-theologian can serve local, indigenous Christians. One of the most obvious ways is through leadership, while another less-common way is through theological partnership.

Leadership principles for cross-cultural ministry

In recent decades, it seems that there has been an over-emphasis on leadership techniques and strategies in the Western church. When I read the Bible, there is little explicit teaching on leadership theory and practice but much explicit teaching on the necessary character and strengths of a godly leader. Most of what I learned about leadership techniques and strategies in the West was not directly applicable once I first started serving in Asia. Christian leadership in any culture is much more than pragmatic techniques; it is character-oriented and spiritual in nature. I work in Asia among unreached peoples and with underground church leaders whose culture and struggles are unique and whose ministry context is very different from the archetypal Western church. The following spiritual leadership principles, I believe, should transcend culture. This list is obviously not exhaustive by any means; I teach whole seminary courses on this topic alone, so this list is merely a conversation-starter, generally illustrative of spiritual leadership that I typically emphasize in my disciple-making and leadership-training in Asia, Africa, and the Americas:[1]

Resting in the work of Christ alone

Many missionary leaders have ambitious personalities. Those who are theologically trained usually know better than to publicly admit that they are trying to earn God's approval or pay back their debts to God. This is works-righteousness, plain and simple. Most missionaries will verbally claim the gospel is their motivation, but the way they speak, think, and teach often emphasizes the need for doing more and doing better. They operate from a guilt-driven, not grace-driven perspective. The challenge of spiritual leadership as a missionary is to learn to rest in Christ, trusting in what He has accomplished in salvation and resting in His promise that He will build His church, in His time, in His way. To be sure, we should work hard and obey the Scriptures, but at the end of the day, we have the sweet privilege of laying our head down and thanking God that He is sovereign over the seed and the soils. He brings the growth. And yet, in our lust to earn God's approval, many times the guilt-driven leader treats his disciples and family as he views his relationship with God. He seeks to use God for his own purposes. And he uses God's Word just enough to come across as spiritual, though his obedience is only partial and half-hearted. This is the difference between a heart that prays 'Lord, I want to be used greatly', which actually means, 'I want to be famous for Jesus' versus the heart that prays, 'Glorify Your name in my life no matter what,' which means, 'I want Jesus to be famous; do what You will.' And if the driven missionary-leader is using God, then people certainly become stepping-stones for his self-fulfillment as well.

---

1. Most of these points were originally published by the author in the magazine of Toronto Baptist Seminary, *The Seminarian*, in March 2015.

True grace-amazed leaders use the Bible to point our eyes to the better Leader—Jesus Christ. Like King Saul, the influential leaders we aspire to imitate are often handsome and attractive, but God's Leader 'had no form or majesty that we should look at him, and no beauty that we should desire him' (Isa. 53:2). Like King Saul, the influential leaders we emulate are cool and entertaining, but God's leader 'was despised and rejected by men; a man of sorrows, and acquainted with grief; and as one from whom men hide their faces he was despised, and we esteemed him not' (Isa. 53:3). Like King Saul, the influential leaders we often choose for ourselves are dynamic, ambitious, successful, motivational, self-confident, and assertive; but God's Leader 'was oppressed, and he was afflicted, yet he opened not his mouth; like a lamb that is led to the slaughter, and like a sheep that before its shearers is silent, so he opened not his mouth' (Isa. 53:7). Here is our true King, our true Leader, whom God has given to all who trust in Him:

> Christ Jesus, who, though he was in the form of God, did not count equality with God a thing to be grasped, but emptied himself by taking the form of a servant, being born in the likeness of men. And being found in human form, he humbled himself by becoming obedient to the point of death, even death on a cross. Therefore God has highly exalted him and bestowed on him the name that is above every name, so that at the name of Jesus every knee should bow, in heaven and on earth and under the earth, and every tongue confess that Jesus Christ is Lord, to the glory of God the Father (Phil. 2:5-11).

The following list of missions leadership wisdom principles grows out of the reminder to rest in our union to Christ and in His work on our behalf. There are so many discouraging, frustrating, and downright miserable experiences unique to the missionary life, but the good news is that you can never improve upon God's love for you, nor can you do anything to detract from His love for you. The Father delights in you as He does His own Son, who fulfilled all righteousness for you, fully, freely, and forever. Never will there be a day where the Father says to you, 'I love you now more than ever.' His love is immeasurable, eternal, and immutable. So, lead with all your might, steadfast in the Word, but rest with all your heart in the amazing grace of Jesus Christ. It is His work, from start to finish. He is the Leader and the Lord of the Great Commission. He is the true Missionary sent by God into the world.

Fear of God

Proverbs is a book written for princes who would someday assume the role of king and ultimate leader. If there is any book in the Bible written with leaders in mind, it is Proverbs. Proverbs makes clear that above all else, wisdom and knowledge are of utmost importance for the leader (Prov. 4:5-7). And, the fear of the Lord is the beginning of wisdom and knowledge (Prov. 1:7). The Christian leader must be so tethered to God's heart and holiness that there is never a question about where his allegiance lay. Because he has been undone by the holiness of God, the leader is an obedient God-fearer (Isa. 6:1-8). He does not fear man, nor does he serve himself. He conducts himself with fear knowing that God will impartially judge him (1 Pet. 1:17). It is the fear of God that makes the leader enjoy the friendship of God (Ps. 25:14).

Humility

The leader who truly fears God is deeply humble. God opposes the proud leader but gives grace to the humble (James 4:6). Because the humble leader is quick to repent and confess sin, the presence and favor of God marks his leadership (Isa. 57:15). The leader must surrender his will and sense of significance under the sovereign hand of God, knowing that he cannot serve God as though God needed anything (Acts 17:24; Job 41:11). A leader that trembles before the holiness of God is willing to follow Him wherever He wills (Isa. 6:1-8). The humble leader will also surround himself with those who are strong in areas where he is weak. He is not afraid to work himself out of a job. The humble leader does not view himself as indispensable and without replacement. He knows God alone promotes and demotes leaders.

Courage

Courage requires a steady endurance in the face of great adversity. God's most repeated command to Joshua was 'be of good courage' (Josh. 1:7-9, 18). Courage is not an inner strength that trusts in self and fears nothing. Rather, courage is a strong confidence in the abiding presence and sovereign purposes of God in all things that is willing to take risks in obedience to God's commands. People follow leaders because of their God-fearing courage, not because of their ascribed or achieved titles.

Bible-filled

God commanded Joshua to meditate on the Law in order to obey it and speak it. His leadership success corresponded to the quantity and quality of his meditation on the Word of God (Josh. 1:8). The sense that this is the way prescribed in the Bible is what gives leaders the strength to pursue the straight and narrow path. In the face of temptation to give in and try an easier way or a way that will bring quicker results, if a leader follows the principles of God's Word, he can be certain that God will honor him in eternity. A tight-fisted grasp on the Bible keeps the leader focused on objective, unchanging truths and not on passing trends or cultural fads. This security grounded in the Word keeps the leader fresh and encouraged.

Prayerfulness

The Son of God Himself is the greatest example of prayer in the Bible. Apparently, His prayer life was so influential and inspiring that His followers asked Him to teach them how to pray (Luke 11:1). This is the only instance where Jesus' followers asked Him to teach them to do something. Of all the things they could have asked Him to teach them to do, they asked about prayer. This speaks volumes to the role of prayer in the life of the leader and in his ability to influence people. Prayer is the most powerful weapon in the leader's arsenal. Through it he draws near to God in humility, gains fresh perspective, is made courageous, and lays hold of the promises of the Bible by faith. When a leader is prayerful, he demonstrates to his followers that his vision is bigger than he is, that he is on a holy mission, and that he is seeking to lead in a way that is supernatural. One of the greatest steps a leader can make is to inspire his people to pray.

Ability to teach

There is a big difference between desiring to teach and being able to teach (1 Tim. 1:7; 3:2). A leader cannot merely desire to teach that about which he is unskilled. He must demonstrate competence to teach (2 Tim. 2:15). The Bible assumes that leaders teach the Word (Heb. 13:7). Those unable to teach the Scriptures are not qualified to be church leaders, specifically elders. This is the one skill demanded of the Christian leader that is not character-related (1 Tim. 3:1-13). It does not mean gifted to teach, but mighty to teach the Word. Moreover, all Christians should develop in some degree the ability to teach the Word (Heb. 5:12), yet the Christian leader must be not only mighty in the Scriptures but proven in his ability to rightly handle the Word.

Lifelong learner

The Christian leader must see his work as theologically-oriented, since his leadership in the Kingdom of God is much like that of a prophet, priest, king, and sage. Due to the nature of spiritual leadership, the leader must posture himself as a lifelong learner—one who studies and holds firm to the doctrines of the faith in order to be alert and guard the deposit entrusted to him (1 Tim. 4:6-16; Acts 6:4). The Christian leader must have a theological orientation that connects all aspects of life back to God's glory (1 Cor. 10:31). This prevents him from being jarred by unexpected situations and new doctrinal trends. In order to make wise decisions, a teachable leader esteems lifelong learning.

Passion

There needs to be a spiritual energy and urgency in the heart of a leader. The Bible says leaders should lead with zeal (Rom. 12:8); 'Never flag in zeal, boil in the Spirit!' (Rom. 12:11). In order to implement change, urgency is required. A leader on fire will inspire.

Strategy/Objectives

The spiritual leader must not only be a visionary; he must also be a planner. The leader that fails to plan, essentially plans to fail. Jesus was called to preach the kingdom of God, and He strategically implemented that mission by targeting certain towns, choosing certain disciples, training them to imitate his leadership, and then giving them assignments to go to certain areas and declare certain truths within a certain time frame (Matt. 10:5-16). Strategic planning comes from God, not from the corporate world alone. The leader, in collaboration with his team, must create strategies that implement the vision and then delegate responsibilities to execute those strategies. Such objectives should be measurable, attainable, and challenging.

Endure Disapproval

The Christian leader will not only face demonic opposition, but he will also suffer criticism from the people he is seeking to lead. The reality of constant criticism requires the leader to not seek man's approval (Gal. 1:10). In fact, if a leader never knows criticism and only praise, likely he is not following the Lord as he ought (Luke 6:26).

Servanthood

Jesus came not to be served, but to serve (Matt. 20:28). His model of leadership was one of compassion and ministry to the sick (Matt. 9:36) and serving His followers (John 13). Instead of only seeking out affinity for those with whom leaders easily get along, biblical principles call leaders to pay the price in identifying and enduring with a group to which he is committed even when it is frustrating to do so. Learning to pay the price of servanthood is a key to developing deep fruit in ministry anywhere in the world. Identifying with people and being patient with them through frustrating situations will help leaders minister more effectively.

Growing and empowering young leaders

The leader has a responsibility to grow young disciples by intentionally teaching them. The leader should set aside times to directly speak truth at length with young disciples and not only limit teaching truth to mutual conversations. Nevertheless, part of his responsibility is to reveal God by his life as he trains young leaders. Leadership does not have to do with status; it has to do with responsibility. There is a longsuffering that leaders must endure during the slow growth of their followers, much like a parent who endures the gradual development of a child. As a disciple grows, so does his level of freedom to explore his ministry passions and gifting. A young disciple who is well led will step out and take risks not merely because of confidence in acquired skills but because of confidence in the culture of love, nurture, and trust demonstrated by his leader. Christian organizational culture is primarily relational and not project driven. A wise leader will look for very trainable people to grow up into leaders who eventually take the reins of leadership.

Much more could be said about the anatomy of a godly leader. There are numerous more character qualities that are required of Christian leaders, such as those listed in 1 Timothy 3.

The above leadership principles are a blend of examples of character and practice of godly leadership. There is always need to refocus our vision for leadership development and reapplying its principles. Though not exhaustive, these leadership principles are especially relevant to the variety of cross-cultural contexts in which I have served. I believe that these leadership principles are helpful for any man of God who wishes to lead God's people into mission.

Learning to interpret and apply Scripture through global lenses

One of the greatest challenges a missionary-theologian might have is stepping out of his theological comfort zone to discuss issues of biblical and theological interpretation with indigenous Christians that do not hold the same original worldview. These are tough conversations of humble listening and deferential learning. One way this discipline of articulating theology in the global community can be learned is through the study of church history.

Church history as a cross-cultural lens

To their credit, many evangelical institutions in the last century have created departments of missions to help prepare missionaries-in-training to adapt to foreign cultures well. Much ink has been spilt in the field of missiology. Degrees of contextualization have been at the forefront of mission philosophy and resulting methodology.

The motivation has generally been to see the Bible first translated into a dynamically equivalent translation of the Greek and Hebrew texts. In order to do that, linguists have studied linguistic theory, phonetics, and the theory of communication. Moreover, anthropologists have dissected the meaning of culture, its norms, and how it intersects with language and the meaning of words. Missiologists have labored at contextualization theory, proposing that the missionary who thinks according to his target culture's language and worldview will be able to translate and teach the Bible in a culturally relevant way and in a way that is less like the missionary's home culture. The goal here is twofold: communicate the gospel and the biblical culture in a way that is understandable in the target culture and communicate the gospel in a way that does not echo the unbiblical presuppositions and preferences of the missionary's home culture.

What is amazing is that missionary preparation programs generally do not require any sort of church history education. To their credit, churches, mission agencies, and some missions schools may require some Bible and theology courses, courses on cultural adaptation, and maybe one history of missions course, but very rarely is much attention given to the history of the church in general. Missions history courses cover the famous missionaries who have influenced the mission philosophy and practice throughout the ages. But those courses are commonly devoid of any sort of attention given to the development of theological categories, the diverse cultural perspectives behind those categories, and how foreign our contemporary globalized culture is to every other culture before it, including those English-speaking church leaders of generations past who contributed to what we call 'Western theology'.

Studying the Latin and Greek Fathers, the Medieval apologists, the Reformers, the Puritans, the Particular Baptists, and the leaders of eighteenth-century evangelicalism is an exercise in cross-cultural hermeneutics. They looked at Scripture in ways that seem so foreign to us today. To be fair, they did not have a fraction of the resources that we have at our fingertips today, but in spite of that, their influence was prodigious and powerful. Much can be learned from how Christian leaders of generations past have handled Scripture, articulated theology, contended for the gospel, and counseled disciples. Many of these historical church leaders wrote in Latin, Greek, German, French, and Spanish, and some were from the African continent. Immersing oneself in the minds and worldviews of such diverse writers can be instructive for a missionary who is seeking to understand how the people of God have contextually practiced Christianity throughout the ages in numerous cultural/worldview backgrounds. This helps the missionary realize what is essential, and how those essentials have been disseminated and received expression in various languages and cultures throughout the ages.

For instance, as a fifth-century missionary in Ireland, Patrick's methods of community evangelism were much different compared with an eighth-century missionary, Boniface, and his confrontational evangelism among the Saxons in Germania; and Protestant Reformer John Calvin's (1509–1564) methods of training pastors and church planters in France were much different to Adoniram Judson's methods in Burma. But all these methods of the above-mentioned church leaders were not devoid of some theological basis. Instead of only studying their methods, the missionary-in-training should go deeper and study their theology so as to understand how their worldview connected what they were reading from the Bible to how they were applying it in missions. Missionary methods are always downstream of missions philosophy, which is directly connected to the missionary's theology: bibliology, anthropology, hamartiology, theology proper, Christology, soteriology, ecclesiology, and eschatology.

Global partnership as a cross-cultural lens

The same discipline of learning from historical leaders who have communicated the gospel and made disciples in different eras, languages, and cultures can be applied similarly today to various Christian leaders who are not of our own home culture. That many educational institutions increasingly promote inter-cultural dialogue and learning opportunities with global church leaders is a healthy practice. The global church has much to learn from the diverse perspectives of various cultures.

For example, if a German missionary were to teach on the sin of idleness in Nigeria, he may indeed scold people for napping during the middle of the workday. Those are precious hours that are slipping away. But for the Nigerian, those are the hottest hours of the day, and they do not have the luxury of sitting at a desk indoors where the air conditioning is always on. On the flipside, if a Nigerian missionary were to be in Germany, he may be repulsed at the perceived coldness of German Christians. He may consider pointing out that they seem more concerned about being on time, not a minute early and not a minute late, as socially rigid and caring too much about what others think. But the Nigerian missionary might not consider the fact that the German society values professionalism, efficiency, optimization, and industriousness in a way that very few societies can rival. The cost of living in Germany is so high that to relax, take hours out of the workday to chat, and often show up noticeably late would possibly result in job termination, loss of income, and eventually an inability to provide for basic needs. Not to mention, Germany has four strong seasons, and if a person does not keep a job, there will be no way to buy food and survive a harsh winter. Tropical countries have their own challenges, but they do not have to worry about storing up food and staying warm to avoid death and starvation during months of freezing cold.

Christians from both cultures (German and Nigerian) can significantly contribute to one another's discipleship, spiritual maturity, and application of the Bible. Neither perfectly applies the full counsel of God to every issue, for we all have blind spots and do not see our own culturally acceptable preferences. What is an excusable blind spot for one is a glaring vice to another. We need to listen to one another in the global church as much as we need to listen to the diversity of Christian voices throughout the ages—the great cloud of witnesses who have gone before us.

Theological imprecision in the global church

Missionaries sometimes offer a grave disservice to emerging leaders in the global church. In a desire to be friendly and affirming in spite of theological imprecision and biblical errors made by the local leaders, missionaries sometimes permit and promote whatever theological notion the local indigenous leaders propose. The gesture is noble, and usually the process of trust-building requires listening more than talking. Yet frankly, the tendency to never offer insight and sharpen one another will help and empower no one. Many missionaries come from historically dominant cultures that have suffered chastisement over the years for being colonialist and domineering, and in many cases, rightly so. Though there are plenty of abuses in history that we should regret, renounce, and resolve never to repeat, unless it is our sin directly, we have no biblical mandate to repent and repair damage done from bygone generations (cf. Ezek. 18:19-20).

This anxiety of offending and fear of appearing culturally overbearing can sometimes hurt our discipleship more than help it. We need not feel like we are walking on proverbial eggshells if we have a different perspective. Duane Elmer, the eminent missiologist, helpfully reflects, 'I needed to learn and adapt to the cultural lenses of the local people. That would require not setting my lenses aside, but adding theirs to mine. I did not need to give up my own cultural frame of reference to accept and appreciate one different from mine.'[2]

Ideally, we would develop an open, honest, and warm friendship with our global brothers and sisters that unites around the text of Scripture, the message of the gospel, the person of Christ, and not around a common emotion of unified humanity that celebrates togetherness for the sake of the sentimental feeling it produces. Cross-cultural and multi-cultural Christian unity that esteems relationships higher than the biblical gospel of Jesus Christ can devolve into a functional microcosm of the humanist quest for the brotherhood of man. Because so much emphasis is put on unity and not on truth, what happens is that untrained indigenous Christian leaders, often at the encouragement of untrained or theologically indifferent missionaries, sometimes propose theological applications that sound like a syncretistic blend of local ungodly practices and Christianized culture: when African leaders want to practice healing services that employ nearly verbatim mind-numbing spiritualistic mantras common to indigenous shamanistic rituals; when Buddhist-background believers want to mine the Bible for rules to merit and maintain God's favor and blessing; when Muslim-background believers want to worship in the mosque and not gather with Christians lest they be found out; and when American believers conflate left-wing or right-wing political trends with the gospel, labeling the latest cultural outrage a 'gospel issue'.

---

2. Duane Elmer, *Cross-Cultural Conflict: Building Relationships for Effective Ministry* (Downers Grove, IL: InterVarsity Press, 1993), p. 12.

There are many things that Majority World Christians have to say to Christians from traditional missionary-sending countries. For instance, the Chinese church will often discipline and sometimes excommunicate a believer who is not habitually sharing his or her faith. Their reason? Since this gospel is good news and we are good-news-people, then we must *de facto* be publishers of that news. If we do not seek ways to proclaim it regularly, we demonstrate that we do not believe it to be good news at all; our reticence to share the gospel may prove that we merely accept it as good advice or a good idea, but not good news. And the reasoning goes, trusting good news alone saves, not adhering to good ideas and practicing good advice. Many persecuted Chinese Christians have no categories for a non-good-news-sharing evangelical that tries to accommodate the culture and just be nice. A silent evangelical is a contradiction in terms. It is a logical and theological impossibility.

Moreover, many persecuted Christians refuse to mix temporal politics (whether conservative or liberal) with their faith. They view Christ as the reigning King, as they should, and their allegiance to Him is political defiance of the tyranny of the State and cultural gate-keepers. Over their dead bodies, literally, would they put their country's flag in their corporate place of worship. They pledge allegiance to Jesus, and Jesus only. Is that not a gut-punch to the average culture-affirming, politics-addicted Western Christian? We should be concerned at how deep we are in our own syncretism and how prevalent and intoxicating are our sacred cows.

A Christian form of patronizing

Missionaries from traditional sending countries can err on the side of theological spinelessness: propping up indigenous leaders, overlooking damaging theological errors, syncretistic practices, and unknown heresy all in the name of encouraging them to 'develop indigenous theology' and not wanting to 'colonize their minds'. There is a growing notion that Western Christians have little to offer other than uncritical affirmation, confessions for the errors of generations past, and sometimes even reparations to the Majority World church. Some reasons I have heard for this negligent permissiveness is that these Majority World leaders are often overlooked, that they should be respected for their advanced age, and that they have had mystical experiences that most rationalistic Westerners would not understand. Plus, some missionaries suggest, they do not have the privilege of excessive education like Western Christians, so God speaks to them in different ways. And all they really need is a Bible and the Holy Spirit, not historic creeds and doctrinal confessions from pre-modern Western theologians—a sentiment which is, ironically, indicative of a Western-oriented, post-modern, reader-centered hermeneutic.

I have seen heresies, such as Modalism—believing God manifests Himself in various modes—proposed by Majority World Christian leaders in major publications. Some Western-educated editors will green-light false doctrines, like heretical descriptions of the Trinity, claiming we must celebrate indigenous theological interpretations that are not influenced by oppressive colonialist theology, that their oppressed perspective deserves its own undiluted interpretive grid. Similarly, some Western-educated leaders opine that contextual theology is situated and messy, and like a piece of post-modern art, it can be bizarre or crude, and it should be uncritically affirmed and celebrated because it represents their culturally unique identity and interpretation. But the reality is that the Majority World leaders might not even be aware of any historical/theological errors they are making. They truly mean well, and they are in fact quite intelligent and teachable. And to be fair, typically the theological error is directly traceable to a false teaching from the West or an untrained missionary. Furthermore, sometimes the Western-educated leaders themselves are oblivious to such egregious errors.

Conversely, the patronizing spirit of some Western-educated theologians and missionaries can be just as dangerous when the Majority World Christians are in the right, standing against the errors of Western-based liberal theology. Increasingly, there are occasions where church leaders from the Majority World are standing up against the immoral, degenerate, and apostate notions advocated by self-proclaimed Christians in the West. For instance, when Anglicans of Africa stand up against what they see as the perverse hypersexual activism of the American Episcopalians, declaring them to be apostate, the response of liberal Americans is to lament that those disadvantaged Africans have not benefited from a multi-perspectival religious education and that their minds have suffered colonization from puritanical sexual mores and desperately need erotic liberation. More of these scenarios will likely increase as the West nosedives into decadence. In most of these occasions, the main problem (not the only problem) lies in the condescending, unteachable, and unrepentant attitude of the Westerner.

Frankly, this sort of theological accommodation is actually offensive and demeaning to the indigenous leader. To put it bluntly, the way local Christians can interpret and perceive this accommodation is that educated Westerners are speaking down to them: 'We realize you have had less privileges and opportunities, and we don't expect you to know what the Bible and church history have taught about this issue. So, we'll quietly let it pass.' To be sure, there are situations where the missionary needs to wait for an opportune time to discuss the issue, but *consistently* and *consciously* dismissing and excusing a systemic theological error is kind to no one. Ostensibly, this might seem unfair to the gracious intentions of the Westerner. But I hear even more colorful language and great disgust from my Majority World friends when they discover that Western church leaders have been accommodating and excusing them with lower standards for fear of causing offense. I can understand the hesitancy because I myself fear offending, appearing overbearing, insulting, and disrespecting people, which is a risk I face because of my teaching role and my status as professor and PhD. Unquestionably, we should employ any correction or teaching with a sincere smile, genuine respect, sensitivity, affirmation, at the proper time, a suspicion of our own cultural biases, a teachable heart, and always letting the biblical text authoritatively win the day.

When they are not privy to some great time-tested historical and theological resources, they most certainly want to know the truth. They are ready to die for the truth, while casual Western Christians are too often embarrassed by the truth. Our togetherness should be grounded in biblical truthfulness lest our multi-cultural Christian relationship become just another anthropocentric and altruistic alliance upholding diversity as our chief end.

And this ability to speak truth to one another has equally benefited my life in so many ways. I am grateful for those brothers and sisters who have challenged my parochial, prideful, and ethnocentric thinking. I respect their candor and courage, especially since often I am their professor, and they are my students. I remember one example where I was carefully critiquing the so-called 'Insider Movement', in which some Western missionaries encourage Muslim-background believers to still attend the mosque, read the Qur'an, and pray to Allah, lest they identify with an underground church and suffer persecution.[3] One colleague from the Majority World, through clenched teeth, condemned this soft approach to discipleship, calling it 'diabolical' and 'demonic'. He said they view persecution and martyrdom for Christ to be the highest honor; why rob them of such a reward? I was stunned. Such bald gutsiness should confront the anxious, security-obsessed Western missionary who wants to avoid persecution at all costs.

As a professor who teaches doctoral students of intercultural studies, chairs dissertation committees, and interacts with some of missiology's brightest minds, the level of academic acumen, methodological scrutiny, and theological discernment I see in my Majority World students' research is astounding. God is raising up strong-hearted and sharp-minded men and women of the Majority World who are leading the charge of mission in their regions and beyond. My prayer is that their research, faithful service, and unique perspectives would be increasingly respected in global Christian leadership. They improve and challenge my thinking and praxis in numerous ways, for which I am deeply humbled and grateful. The future is bright for the global church.

Truth-based friendship

Speaking of a wholly different situation yet principally applicable to this topic, the Greek philosopher Aristotle (384–322 B.C.) once said: 'For though we love both the truth and our friends, piety requires us to honor the truth first.' Truth-telling should never be a battle-axe in the hands of doctrinaire missionaries. Of all people, those who have had the privilege to formally study the deep truths of Scripture should be most humble. Truth-telling malfunctions if not done in love and humility; and equally, love and humility are mere empty sentimentality if not bolstered with truth-telling. Truth-speaking should be winsome

---

3. For a developed treatment of the philosophy of insider movements, see Harley Talman and John Jay Travis, eds, *Understanding Insider Movements: Disciples of Jesus within Diverse Religious Communities* (Pasadena: William Carey Library, 2015).

and courageous, with a sincere smile, a deferential demeanor, a kind voice, and gravity of spirit.

Truly, our fellowship with believers of any nationality, age range, socio-economic status, and biological sex must be grounded in a fidelity to and celebration of the true doctrine of Christ as revealed in the Word, the historical confessions, and ancient creeds, which the Reformers called *sola scriptura*. If merely the title 'Christian' is our entry point into multi-cultural and multi-generational relationships and if those relationships are then developed and retained upon the premise of celebrating cultural diversity and upholding political correctness, then we have abandoned the truth and prove that we are not a community united around the doctrine of Christ. We are then a mere affinity group that upholds amiability, diversity, and tolerance as its highest values, labeling them as Christian love, theological open-mindedness, and mutual respect. Just because any of us claims to be a Christian, that does not mean we are immune to heresy, false teaching, and unrepentant sin. Just because we claim to serve Jesus, that does not mean we are talking about the Jesus as revealed in Scripture. Just because we celebrate the fact that we can get along and enjoy each other's presence and cultural uniqueness, it does not mean we are one in Christ. The world celebrates diversity for diversity's sake; Christians celebrate Christ, and a diversity of people groups simply enhances that enjoyment of Christ together.

The record of mission drift and theological downgrade in previous generations often demonstrates that key leaders historically relished relationships over revealed truth. Congeniality over controversy. Paul scolds the Galatians for being bewitched (cf. Gal. 3:1) by a false gospel. Paul confronts Peter publicly for willfully practicing a works-oriented gospel (cf. Gal. 2:11-14). Peter was likely doing what he thought was most expedient and effective. Surely, he was not masterminding a false gospel incursion. If the devil could influence Peter to act and talk in ways contrary to the gospel because Peter was afraid of upsetting the Jews, let us remember that none of us are invulnerable to acquiescing to demonic doctrines and walking contrary to the gospel. I am concerned that this is what happens too often when Christian leaders should know better but do not speak up for biblical truth for fear of offending someone with whom they have an enjoyable relationship. Christian leaders of all cultures should rightly aspire to be Barnabas-like: supportive, courteous, irenic, peacemaking, and bridge-building. In today's cut-throat social media wars, such a gentlemanly spirit is a rare commodity. Nevertheless, soberly remind yourself of this: deference without discernment can be destructive; 'even Barnabas was led astray' (Gal. 2:13).

The great Welsh preacher of the twentieth-century, D. Martyn Lloyd-Jones (1899–1981), called this friendship-at-all-costs a 'false ecumenical tendency'. He was concerned that Bible-believing evangelicals were indiscriminately welcoming fellowship and partnership with Christians of the broadest description, based upon mere 'niceness', whose unorthodox doctrine should have been the basis for separation:

> It is the danger of being so broad, so wide, and so loose that in the end we have no definitions at all. As I see things today, this is perhaps the greater danger because we are living in what is called an ecumenical age. People have reacted, and rightly, against the divisions in the past, these wrong and sinful divisions. But the danger is that you react so violently that you swing right to the other extreme and say that nothing matters except that we have a Christian spirit. ... Certainly we must all believe in unity. Our Lord has established that once and for ever in His great high priestly prayer (John 17). It is everywhere in the New Testament. Our great endeavor should be to be one, yet this must not lead to a looseness in our thinking. We must not become subject to a false, vague, nebulous, ecumenical type of thinking. ... I've met people who said ... the Church of Scotland people and others whom we did not know and with whom we had nothing to do in the past, we've discovered they're very nice people, and we've had a very happy time working with them. This was very subtle, because they found that they were nice people—whether they had thought before that these people had horns and long tails I do not know—but the point was that they had been impressed by their niceness, by their friendliness, and by their brotherliness. This had the effect of making these people take the next step and say, Well, I wonder whether these doctrines we've been emphasizing are so important after all. Isn't the great thing about us that we are

Christians, that we've got this loving spirit, and that we're prepared to work together?[4]

I have found that as I build truth-based, open, and honest relationships with global church leaders, they are more than thankful when I ask permission to sensitively point out theological and/or methodological errors in their ministries. And they are even more encouraged when I ask them to point out my own faults and blind spots. We grow to trust each other and love each other, united around a common zeal for gospel truth. They bemoan the fact that they have never had the privilege of studying theology formally, and they often wish they were stronger readers and had more resources. The privilege is mine to share with them what God has entrusted to me.

Today's over-application of the priesthood of all believers has not only leveled the playing field, as it were, but that field has become a latitudinarian wasteland where everyone does what is right in his own eyes according to how he interprets the Bible for himself and according to what secret words God directly says to him. Indeed, there is a crucial role for the priesthood of all believers just as there is a crucial role for family members to nurse a loved one after an operation in the comfort of their home, which presupposes the heavy lifting of the surgery was already done by a trained surgeon. Likewise, we need trained, proven surgeons of the soul who do their best to present themselves to God as approved, workers who have no need to be ashamed, rightly handling the word of truth (cf. 2 Timothy 2:15). This text suggests that there is a right way and a wrong way to handle the Word of truth, just as there is a right way and wrong way to handle a surgeon's scalpel. Those who do not cut the Word of truth rightly, the text suggests, have need to be ashamed. That is exactly my point. In our attempts to affirm and encourage untrained Christian leaders, instead of actually helping them grow by teaching them what we have had the privilege of studying, we are enabling their future shame and consequently, our own shame, though much more severe. In the text, the key to rightly handling the Word of truth and avoiding the shame

---

4. D.M. Lloyd-Jones, *What Is an Evangelical?* (Carlisle, PA: The Banner of Truth Trust, 2002), pp. 18-19.

of spiritual malpractice is to study and work hard to present oneself to God as one approved after being tested.

Local leaders might actually respect missionaries more if we would just be honest and helpful with theological precision. It can be an exciting discovery process where the Word of God unfolds with wonder and richness; it need not be drab and bookish. They want to hear the truth, and they do not want to be excused or ignored. Moreover, they would grow to respect us if we also would posture ourselves as learners and seek to learn from them as well.

Internationally accepted time-tested standards of excellence

There is an internationally acceptable and proven science for treating cancer that demands a trained and credentialed oncologist. Any well-meaning person would be immediately dismissed who claims to be an oncologist and guarantees effective treatment of cancer through generations of culturally inherited techniques that are akin to massage therapy or shamanism. Similarly, no internationally trained surgeon goes to a remote medical clinic full of cancer patients and gives his surgical instruments to local witch doctors without sufficiently training them how to prepare, rightly cut, and divide the anatomy so as to remove a tumor. Anyone from any culture who wants to be proven as rightly handling medicine and competent to treat cancer must put in the time and effort to study medicine and become the best doctor possible. Why do we tolerate less for physicians of the soul when eternity is at stake? It is the great demonic deception of the age: the death of theological expertise.

We all know this is a principle that carries over into most other fields of study and vocations. Lest we understand analogies that are only medical and science-related, there are other vocations that include more aesthetics and art that still employ international, time-tested standards for excellence. For instance, there is a science to the art of beautiful music. All around the world, people intuitively recognize beautiful music when they hear sound waves combine dynamic style and volume changes, the blending and balancing of harmony, warm intonation, notes in tune, and rhythmic and percussive movements on beat together. Any culture can take the proven science of sound waves and express it in a unique, culturally-nuanced form, but philosophically and even scientifically, the substance is the same. Another area of aesthetics that emerges out of science and physics is architecture. Think of all the beautiful buildings around the world. The visual form and aesthetic appeal changes from culture-to-culture. However, the hidden interior physics that support and uphold a massive structure through years of wear and tear, earthquakes, hurricanes, sub-zero freezing temperatures, and blistering heat are philosophically and scientifically the same. External cultural forms and aesthetic expressions may vary, but the laws of physics and sound waves remain the same. This principle is very similar for doing theology across cultures. For example, global Christians rightly commune at the Lord's Table, remembering and receiving from Christ His amazing grace; yet where a Scandinavian culture might reflect quietly with seriousness and awe, an African culture might celebrate with dancing, tambourines, and glad-hearted praises. The substance of both is true and biblical; the external forms of each are culturally unique and beautiful in their own way.

All this to say, in any other vocation, there are tried-and-true standards of excellence that the international community recognizes and follows. No one rebels against gravity and dismisses Newton's law of universal gravitation just because Isaac Newton (1643–1727) was European and a product of his era and education. Why do so many missionaries want to let indigenous Christians self-theologize devoid of the theology and historical resources that the Holy Spirit has graciously given the church throughout the last 2,000 years?

Again, the analogy works in the secular world; humanitarian volunteers who are able to feed sick people and perform play therapy with HIV orphans might indeed be offering a kind of therapeutic service to those in need. But no sane person would assume that the same untrained volunteers should try their hand at invasive surgery, let alone general medical practice. Only in the Christian world do we actually boast of not having formal theological training. This *laissez-faire*, carefree approach to missions, though dubbed as loving and empowering, is malpractice and negligence of the worst kind.

Lest we misunderstand that most Majority-World Christian leaders should have earned formal credentials and that those who have minimal formal education are illegitimate leaders, some of the most biblically faithful and fruitful Christian leaders in church history have been self-taught and not formally trained; they know the power of prayer and the authority of the Word of God. Nevertheless, when possible, earning a degree in formal theological education proves to be a great asset for most Majority-World ministry contexts. Stressing the sufficiency of Scripture for those who have no opportunity to study formally, many reputable ministries employ well-tested training for oral-based learners and a-literate (not illiterate) Christian leaders. Majority-World Christians are in numerous ways more intelligent and stronger-minded than many Westerners, though they might not inculcate information according to a formal Western educational style. Where Westerners rely on smart phones, Bible software, and technology for instantaneous references and resources, Majority World Christians often rely on their reinforced memorization skills and mnemonic devices.

A challenge for Western missionaries is that we have an immense surplus of information and teaching available to us, and we tend to turn training into a data dump. Majority-World Christian leaders need no mental download of all we have studied; they just need someone to give them the tools and training necessary to handle Scripture rightly. Prioritizing and emphasizing content in such training significantly depends upon the allotted opportunity. In other words, the trainer must prioritize what to teach based upon whether he has two weeks, two months, or two years, etc. This is one reason why the missionary should be a trained theologian at some level; a well-trained missionary should be competent to teach a topic or a biblical book in a few minutes, a few hours, or a few days, knowing how and what to prioritize and emphasize for his audience in the time available according to their capacity to learn.

Conclusion

Much of missionary service is spent undoing damage done by careless and negligent missionaries who have come in, preached a gospel-lite message, elicited a response, vaccinated them against the devil and hell with 'Jesus loves you and has a wonderful plan for your life', and left without training up leaders who are mighty in the Scriptures. The indigenous leaders are left to follow their cultural intuitions in church leadership. Why? Because it takes too long to stay and do the hard work of teaching. And frankly, the lifelong labor of slow Great Commission discipleship is not very attractive. Who wants to support the ten-year development of a single church and a few indigenous Christian leaders when you can support church planting movements that claim to easily plant ten churches in one month?

The most common request I hear from global church leaders is, 'Please, teach us the Bible.' Is it not worth the hard work of studying to be a missionary-theologian who is able to rightly handle the word of truth and train others to do the same (cf. 2 Tim. 2:2)? There is no mercy ministry platform, social justice endeavor, and church-planting method more loving than humbly coming alongside brothers and sisters around the world, partnering with them, teaching them, and training them to train others also. It is the only way to truly empower the global church—to leave the Bible alone in their blood.

CHAPTER 7

THE MISSIONARY AS PASTORAL MODEL AND CHURCH-PLANTER

'The greatest missionary is the Bible in the mother tongue. It never needs a furlough, is never considered a foreigner.'
—W. CAMERON TOWNSEND

'WHO'S your authority?', his ministry director asked. Unsure of the intended meaning, Sean replied, 'What kind of authority? Medical authority? Financial authority? Occupational authority? Scriptural authority?' The ministry director's question came after discussions with numerous supporting churches that each had missions pastors claiming unique spiritual authority over Sean's life and who each had a different idea of God's specific will for his next chapter of life and ministry. On individual occasions they said that they were speaking for God to Sean, but ironically they would each speak contrary words from God. These men would often be using similar vocabulary, but in effect they each had their own self-made dictionary. During this chaotic time, he heard these leaders make authoritarian claims such as:

- 'You are only to talk to me, and I talk to God on your behalf; and your wife is only to talk to you as you talk to me.'
- 'If you choose to pursue a particular ministry option without the permission of your spiritual authority, God's wrath will be poured out on you.'

- 'You must make as quick of a move as possible so that you can get under the covering of your new spiritual authority.'

- 'You are not to listen to your doctors because they aren't charged with authority over you. They don't know what you need because they are not pastors.'

- 'You need an umbrella of protection, because if you are not submitting to a chain of command, then you cannot experience God's blessings and you are in danger of His punishment.'

- 'It is dangerous not to know who your spiritual covering is because you can walk outside of God's protection and blessing and into the power of Satan and destruction.'

- 'You must obey me as you would blindly obey your parents, because I said so; even if what I choose for you is wrong or not the best, you must submit to me because I answer to God for you.'

- 'God has given me a list of 5 steps you must do before I will allow you to go back to the mission field. In order to reclaim success in ministry, you must remain under my umbrella of protection.'

- 'I have a check in my spirit; I can't let you go until God makes it clear.'

A crisis of control

There are many scenarios like this that missionaries have shared with me over the years. Sadly, when pastors do not understand the dynamics of life and work as a missionary, sometimes they can exert too much control, seeking to help when in fact they are muddying and complicating the process of trials and griefs common to the life cycle of long-term missions. Moreover, this is even a problem among mission agency leaders who should know better. Often missions directors are not theologically trained, and they know their Bibles at an elementary level. They lead from their experience, intuition, impressions, and sentimental ideas. And, to be sure, this is a global problem, not merely a socio-economic, cultural, or denominational problem. The stories I have heard from missionaries sent out by well-intended churches in the Global South are chilling—pastors telling them they cannot have children because it would slow down God's work; missions directors telling missionaries on the field that the support they raised is going to be reallocated to another project that is better for the mission; pastors shaming missionaries for not having a church planted in two years; and even some pastors and missionaries themselves falsely claiming apostolic authority that leave people in fear, wondering when they are going to break an arbitrary rule that would disqualify them from their spiritual authority's self-appointed 'umbrella of protection'.

This is not only a struggle between pastors and missionaries, sadly, it is even a problem among mission agencies and the team leaders, area directors, and home office personnel who serve in them—indeed a challenge for every person involved in missions. The mission field is a context of extremely low accountability and commensurately high trust. Because of the isolation, lack of proximity, and absence of presence in so many unreached mission contexts, we need to realize that it can get messy very quickly. That in brief written communications too often perception is reality, that we need to send our best to the mission field (which is why the elder and deacon qualifications of 1 Timothy 3 and Titus 1 should be reasonable expectations for missionaries), that all parties involved are probably doing the best they can with what they know, and that Jesus is ultimately in control of establishing His church through sinful servants in that people group.

Such a barrage of popish declarations and heavy-handed authority easily drives people to depressive self-evaluation, doubt, worry, and confusion. Many missionaries who have choked down the bitterness of authoritarian oversight have the choice set before them: to replicate a similar pastoral leadership model in their ministries or to rest in Jesus, sow the seed of His Word, and encourage people willingly and joyfully to look to Christ as their chief Shepherd.

The missionary's response to authoritarianism and borderline spiritual abuse should not be to impugn all authority and submit to no one. That could be even more destructive, though anger and sadness are understandable emotions under such tension. Many missionaries have a fiercely independent spirit that God seems to use for pioneering new ventures, yet oftentimes such energy and passion needs to be tempered, humbled, and made teachable through learning to trust and submit to wise pastors and veteran mission agency leaders. Indeed, at times God even uses unwise authoritarian pastors and leaders to break down the missionary and craft him into the Word-centered servant He desires. Zeal without knowledge (cf. Prov. 19:2) is common for most of us in the early stages of ministry, but the wise missionary will learn to respectfully listen to criticism and genuinely heed advice, even when it seems disagreeable. And the wise missionary will also tenderly acquiesce the Lord's mysterious providences through imperfect leaders, frustrating policies, and uncontrollable events. Missionaries, known for their stubborn dedication, should remember that their determination could easily become inflexible and unsubmissive when they disagree with coworkers, supporters, pastors, and superiors. We must consciously put on a mindset of kindness, deference, and compliance, trusting the Lord to work in spite of all of our weaknesses and imperfections.

In all the years I have been training pastors and leaders around the world, probably the most common questions I receive relate to pastoral authority and the offices of apostle and prophet. As missionary-theologians, whether or not we are functioning as a traditional pastor, we nevertheless have the opportunity to model for fearful, weary saints how good and tender Christ is, how sufficient His Word is, and how to influence others in a way that points beyond themselves to Jesus and His Word. This is one reason why I propose that missionaries should be at least deacon qualified, if not elder qualified. The most impressionable lessons on spiritual leadership are taught by example, in the way you respond to unforeseen inconveniences, to what extent you lead from the Bible when asked questions, and how you demonstrate making decisions.

An opportunity to model shepherding

I am especially convinced that church-planting missionaries need to understand deeply what the Bible says and does not say about shepherding. There are two extremes that should be avoided: (1) the rapid cycle church-planter who claims that he can plant a church in a week by just helping a family unit read the Bible and talk to Jesus, which inevitably fizzles out or spirals into a cult where the influence of the alpha personality (patriarchal or matriarchal) dominates the group; and (2) the missionary who amasses a group of new and young believers, establishes it into a church, but never proactively trains elders and relinquishes leadership to them because he fears what could happen if his fledglings were to try flying on their own.

One problem is that many missionaries, in their earnest preparation, do not take the time before going to the field to study or even practice biblical shepherding, and to be fair, many mission agencies assume their sending churches would have ensured they were prepared for pastoral leadership and church-planting. In the enthusiasm and momentum of making an international move, this is one essential area of preparation that is either assumed or forgotten, and, in some agencies, disparaged due to decades of hearing of the shameful history of transplanting Western models of church into non-Western contexts. Yet, to be honest, church history never records a pure cultureless transfer of church practice and tradition—Nigerian church-plants in London look and operate like churches in Nigeria; Chinese church-plants in Panama look and operate like churches in China; Filipino church-plants in Kuwait look and operate like churches in the Philippines; and Moravian church-plants among Alaska Natives looked and operated like those in Moravia and Pennsylvania. It is simply part of the historical growth cycle of polycentric missions—everyone to everywhere.

Teaching pastoral leadership

Over the years I have considered what the Bible says and does not say about biblical authority and leadership because of all the questions I receive from pastors and missionaries that I teach in Asia and Africa. They are under the authority of charismatic 'apostles' that make claims, like the above-mentioned examples, of hearing God's voice and knowing His perfect will for those under their charge. There is a lust in many leaders for power and control, which if they do not crucify those impulses, they will become little popes who claim to speak *ex cathedra*. The papal abuses that Luther raged against in the Reformation are multiplied many times over in ministries and churches where leaders shut their Bibles, wait for an impression, trust in their status or position, and enforce rules that God never inspired. Too many Christian leaders, though claiming to hail from a Protestant tradition of *sola scriptura* and the priesthood of all believers, lead and speak like functional popes.

The fact of the matter is this: a man of God leads spiritually insofar as he humbly teaches and wisely applies the Word of God from its intended context. Show me a man who is contrite of heart and who trembles at the Word of God, and I will show you a man upon whom God looks with favor (cf. Isa. 66:2). But who of us are sufficient for this? When have any of us expressed enough contrition and trembled deeply and long enough at the Word? Never forget there is one Man upon whom the favor of the Lord rests, who earned equal favor for those who rest in Him. So, through resting in Christ the Chief Shepherd, we seek to humbly imitate Him and point past ourselves to Him in His Word.

God honors the humble, but He opposes the arrogance of going beyond what is written as though the Bible were not sufficient. We do not preach *with* the Word, *by* the Word, *about* the Word; rather, we merely preach the Word—courageous to say everything it says, humble to say no more and no less.

Martin Luther on the written word

Martin Luther contended that the Bible should be our light. He was contending against the same false spirit, manifested in two different ways, not unlike our day: on the one hand, the pope, the Romish Church, and its councils claimed spiritual authority over the Scriptures, and on the other hand, the Anabaptists and Zwickau prophets claimed spiritual authority in addition to the Scriptures. He raged against both. Luther defied the pope and the pope's authoritarian speaking *ex cathedra*, and Luther did not tolerate mystic perspectives such as the 'inner light' and musings of the Anabaptists, as though they were just an alternative style of worship and spiritual experience. According to Luther, the Bible should color and flavor our souls as David demonstrates in Psalm 119: 'In this psalm David always says that he will speak, think, talk, hear, read, day and night constantly—but about nothing else than God's Word and Commandments. *For God wants to give you His Spirit only through the external Word.*[1] Elsewhere Luther argued, 'Let the man who would hear God speak, read Holy Scripture.'[2]

Luther did not just advise that ministers avoid the blasphemies of the pope and the ecstasies of Thomas Müntzer (1489–1525) and the Zwickau Prophets and the activism of the Waldensians,[3] he moreover called for a deeper knowledge of the Scriptures altogether. Consider his charge for ministers to know the Bible in its original languages to guard themselves from the error of Rome and the Anabaptists and in order to preserve themselves in the gospel. There is a degree of attentiveness to detail and specificity when ministers slow down and think hard over the original languages. Even if they are not proficient readers of Hebrew and Greek, accessing the myriad of linguistic tools can still aid a minister in meditating on and delighting in the text of Scripture. As we lighten up in our devotion to *sola scriptura*, we will eventually lose the gospel itself. He says in 'To the Councilmen of All Cities in Germany That They Establish and Maintain Christian Schools' (1524):[4]

- In proportion then as we value the gospel, let us zealously hold to the languages.

- 'And let us be sure of this: we will not long preserve the gospel without the languages. The languages are the sheath in which this

---

1. Martin Luther, *What Luther Says,* Ewald M. Plass, ed., 3 vols. in 1 (St. Louis: Concordia, 1959), p. 1359. Emphasis added.

2. Plass, *What Luther Says*, p. 62.

3. The Zwickau Prophets, under the influence of Nikolaus Storch (born pre-1500, died after 1536), believed that true authority originated in the 'inner light' in each person, not in a sacred Book. They also believed in the imminent end of the world. These ideas indelibly influenced Müntzer's theology and practice. Müntzer was a radical reformer who spearheaded the Anabaptist movement, which employed mysticism, socialism, apocaplyticism, and egalitarianism. In addition to the Zwickau Prophets and the Anabaptist movement, the Waldensians originated from the leadership of Peter Waldo (1140–1205), who had a reputation for strict asceticism, simplicity, and poverty.

4. Martin Luther, *Luther's Works,* W. Brandt and H. Lehman, eds. (Philadelphia: Muhlenberg Press, 1962), pp. 357-66.

sword of the Spirit is contained; they are the casket in which this jewel is enshrined; they are the vessel in which this wine is held; they are the larder in which this food is stored; and, as the gospel itself points out, they are the baskets in which are kept these loaves and fishes and fragments. If through our neglect we let the languages go (which God forbid!), we shall not only lose the gospel.

- It is inevitable that unless the languages remain, the gospel must finally perish.

- But where the preacher is versed in the languages, there is a freshness and vigor in his preaching, Scripture is treated in its entirety, and faith finds itself constantly renewed by a continual variety of words and illustrations.

- We should not be led astray because some boast of the Spirit and consider Scripture of little worth, and others, such as the Waldensian Brethren think the languages are unnecessary.

- So I can by no means commend the Waldensian Brethren for their neglect of the languages. For even though they may teach the truth, they inevitably often miss the true meaning of the text, and thus are neither equipped nor fit for defending the faith against error. Moreover, their teaching is so obscure and couched in such peculiar terms, differing from the language of Scripture, that I fear it is not or will not remain pure. For there is great danger in speaking of things of God in a different manner and in different terms than God himself employs. In short, they may lead saintly lives and teach sacred things among themselves, but so long as they remain without the languages they cannot but lack what all the rest lack, namely, the ability to treat Scripture with certainty and thoroughness and to be useful to other nations. Because they could do this, but will not, they have to figure out for themselves how they will answer for it to God.

Shepherding imagery

Missionaries who model pastoral leadership are delegated a huge responsibility in shepherding the flock of God, without a doubt. There is only a small vestige of respect left for ministers in some parts of the world where Christianity has historically taken root; the rest of our global society has not only abandoned respect for pastors but has denigrated them with suspicion as charlatans and hucksters. Nevertheless, the weightiness of the office and the disapproval of the culture at large does not dismiss the fact that pastors must meet a biblical standard, indeed a higher standard than the average layman.

It seems that in the twenty-first century, pastors, missionaries, and church leaders around the world aspire to be so many things, good things in their own right, but not biblical things. In God's common grace, is it a good thing to aspire to be an efficient organizational leader, a charismatic motivational speaker, or a strong visionary that can mobilize constituents and investors? Of course. Those are good things; they demonstrate a God-honoring hard-work ethic and fortitude. However, too many spiritual leaders, when under the stress of ministry, lead from muscle memory, as it were, doing what they have done in other occupations and making decisions that just seem to work best for the desired outcome. This is how leadership in missions and the church sometimes begins to look like leadership in the world. One challenge among global church leaders is that we do not often define terms biblically; we define them culturally, which can change in each context.

For example, the imagery of shepherding is a most common biblical metaphor for pastoring and biblical leadership. In the urbanized world of the twenty-first century, very few people have ever had exposure to ranching, shepherding, farming, and animal husbandry. Fewer and fewer people directly depend on caring for animals and harvesting animals for their subsistence. Christian leaders who, then, read passages about shepherding the flock of God (cf. 1 Pet. 5:2), must use their imaginations of what shepherding sheep might be like. Ideas like ownership, direction, protection, and provision certainly come to mind. But if we are only using our imaginations to fill in for what we do not understand by experience as most of the world has understood until the modern era of urbanization, we lose the color and flavor of the meaning of those metaphors with which the original audience would have doubtlessly been familiar.

Unless we have spent time with a chief shepherd as his apprentice (or under-shepherd) around a flock of sheep, we will not know intuitively that sheep tremble when they hear a different voice other than their chief shepherd. It takes them a while to get used to another's voice, and they only submit to the apprentice's voice as long as the chief shepherd's voice is the dominant voice. Sheep are the only animals in the world that cannot survive independent of people. Baby rams can get their horns caught in weeds and hang themselves; sheep see moving water and get scared and drown themselves; sheep are timid; sheep are tender; sheep are submissive both in their shearing and in their slaughter; sheep are easily lost, and it is very hard to find and rescue them; sheep are happy to stay near the shepherd because they feel vulnerable without him. The shepherd must speak gently to the sheep and treat them with tenderness. Moreover, the under-shepherd must be careful to imitate the chief shepherd by feeding the sheep with what the chief shepherd would use, by watching vigilantly for predators both on the perimeters and in the middle of the flock, and by speaking in a way that his rhythm of talking, tone, and inflection reflect the chief shepherd. The under-shepherd must imitate the chief shepherd like this so that the sheep are persuaded to fearlessly follow the apprentice's leadership knowing that he has been trained and set apart by the chief shepherd to guide, feed, and keep watch over the flock.

Goats, on the other hand, constantly do things that distract the shepherd and keep him preoccupied with fixing or cleaning what they break or ruin. Goats are loud and sloppy; they are belligerent and headstrong. They do not care about the voice of the shepherd as much as they care about following their stubborn animal instincts. They like to eat things that are not the cleanest and choicest food. They are rough and not gentle; they are boisterous and insensitive. Goats are in so many ways, unlike sheep, obstinate and thus exhausting.

Additionally, shepherds as described in the Bible are not only tender, patient, and attentive to their sheep; shepherding was a manly charge, a warrior's task.[5] Hazards and threats from predators, robbers, bandits, rocky crags, slippery slopes, unforgiving wilderness, flash floods, and

---

5. For an accessible and popular-level discussion of this warrior-shepherd motif, see Alastair Roberts, 'The Fighting Shepherd', *Alastair's Adversaria* (14 July 2012) https://alastairadversaria.com/2012/07/14/the-fighting-shepherd/, (accessed 1 December 2018).

waterless, barren plains all demanded that the shepherd be strong-minded and able-bodied, with a steely resolve to guide and watch over his flock, even at the cost of his own life. Yahweh, the warrior (Exod. 15:3), shepherded His flock by striking down and forcing out those who would harm them (Ps. 78:52-55, 70-72), and He safely led them to His holy mountain (Exod. 15:13-17). God shepherded His people through Moses (Ps. 77:19-20; cf. Isa. 63:11), and with Moses' shepherd staff God afflicted the Egyptians (Exod. 4:20; 7:7-10; 17:9; Num. 20:8-9) and divided the sea enabling the Hebrews to escape and brought the waters back to consume the Egyptian army (Exod. 14:16-31; cf. Ps. 78:5-55). Similarly, David was a warrior-shepherd, whose shepherding duty was partly hunting down and slaying bears and lions (1 Sam. 17:34-36). Shepherds in the Bible were more like gritty, protective ranchers and cowboys guiding and guarding their herds than they were the soft, serene portraits of the harp-playing boy David lounging with his sheep in an idyllic meadow. The biblical office of shepherd requires men of Bible-filled leadership, polemical abilities, theological conviction, uncompromising courage in the face of controversy, and sharpshooter vision amidst the fog of error, knowing how to competently lead and affectionately feed the sheep so as to honor the Chief Shepherd (cf. Ezek. 34:5-8; John 10:1-10)—tenacity with the Word tempered by tenderness of heart.

The Chief Shepherd leads His sheep

The church is called the 'flock of God' (1 Pet. 5:2), and Jesus is called the 'Chief Shepherd' (1 Pet. 5:4). When a missionary or pastor describes a congregation as 'my church' or 'my people', he should be careful that his words do not communicate more than he might intend, which is especially true for those who model pastoral priorities to young spiritual leaders. Of course, that can be an honest mistake to make in casual conversation just as a businessman might refer to his place of employment as 'my company'. But if a missionary/pastor were sensitive about his role under the Chief Shepherd, he would immediately correct himself because he knows the church is Christ's possession, and Christ is Lord over what He owns. Similarly, if a businessman always had the CEO standing right next to him, he would certainly refer to the company not as his but as 'the CEO's company'. Spiritual leadership should not to be confused with lordship. This spiritual leadership is not possessive, heavy-handed, parental, dictatorial, and authoritarian; it does not lead outside of its delegated authority. The sheep exist not to provide the under-shepherds with a sense of meaning and career satisfaction; the under-shepherds exist to provide the sheep with the guidance and care delegated to them from the Chief Shepherd.

Missionaries are rightfully jealous for the planted church they have labored for in a remote people group never before penetrated with the gospel. And as much as we love the flock, it is not our flock; Jesus is the Chief Shepherd. It is not our church; Jesus is Lord over the church, and His jealousy for His people is unrivaled. Be careful lest you function like a pope, speaking as though you were an indispensable mediator between the church and God. And beware lest you let your voice, your opinions, your persona, and your gifts/talents drown out the voice of the Chief Shepherd found in the Word. This inevitably happens, especially in a teaching ministry, when the pastor does not *regularly* and *humbly* remind people that Jesus is the Lord of the church and that He sanctifies His people through the Christ-centered Word. We are all prone to put our trust in what we can perceive with our physical senses, and we do not easily look to Jesus if we are not frequently reminded to look beyond the spiritual leader to the One to whom the Word points. The people of God, especially a young church that has emerged out of an unreached people group, do not make the connection by osmosis. They must be reminded to remember Jesus, *repeatedly*. This requires the missionary/pastor to remind himself of who he is and who he is not, *repeatedly*.

Pastoral wisdom v. scriptural authority

Some missionary leaders and pastors might argue that there is not a Bible verse for every situation, question, and crisis. True. The Bible is not a magic book that has an answer to everything scientific, medical, economic, political, psychiatric, biological, and dietary. So, what about those knotty extra-biblical issues? It helps to understand a distinction between pastoral wisdom and Scriptural authority. If we lack wisdom, the Bible tells us to ask for more (James 1:5). A whole book in the Old Testament (Proverbs) is devoted to the virtue of wisdom.

Author and pastor John MacArthur was once asked during a conference, 'To what extent is a member of a church required to obey his pastor? How much authority does a pastor have in the lives of his congregants?' MacArthur, renowned for an authoritative proclamation style and devotion to the Word of God, humbly and helpfully replied:

> None. No authority. I have no authority in this church, personally. My experience doesn't give me any authority. My knowledge doesn't give me any authority. My education doesn't give me any authority. I have no authority. My position doesn't give me any authority. My title doesn't give me any authority. That's why I don't like titles. Only the Word of God has authority. Christ is the Head of the church, and He mediates His rule in the church through His Word. I have no authority. I don't have authority beyond the Scriptures. I can never exceed what is written (1 Cor. 4:6). To do that, Paul says, is to become arrogant and to regard yourself as superior. I have nothing to say to you that puts any demand on you if it isn't from the Word of God. And you are probably talking out of some experience where you felt that some undue authority was exercised over you or somebody you know by a pastor. We need to be reminded that as pastors, even though the Lord has lifted us up and given us this kind of responsibility, we possess no personal authority. If I am telling you what God has said in His Word, that has authority, right? But I cannot exceed what is written. I can't tell you about your life. I can give you wisdom if you ask, but I may have no more wisdom than somebody else. You would get more wisdom on many issues out of my beloved Patricia than you would get out of me. She's not in the pulpit, but she has spiritual insight and spiritual wisdom. And if you ask for advice and wisdom, hers in many cases would exceed mine. So, the pastor in himself has no authority. Listen to what Paul says, 'Who is Paul? Who is Apollos? Who is Cephas?' We're nothing. It's all of Christ. It's all of the Holy Spirit. It's all of the Scripture.[6]

Mature Christian leaders and pastors must give counsel that emerges from biblically informed wisdom, and often there is counsel that has no chapter or verse. We must simply make a decision based upon the best wisdom we can discern and then trust God to work His good

---

6. John MacArthur, 'John MacArthur on a Pastor's Authority', published by Grace to You, 29 August 2017, https://youtu.be/X65vspiZLLA (accessed 1 October 2017).

purposes. The problem is if you counsel someone and they make a decision based upon your counsel *because you are their pastor and you said so*, then they are trusting in you primarily and not mainly in God.

Imagine communicating in a way that demonstrates you are submitting your every word to God's command, qualifying your words such as, 'Based upon how I perceive the situation and options, it seems to me that the first option would be a wiser and more prudent decision than the second option. From my imperfect perspective, it seems that both options would please God. Nevertheless, I have no chapter or verse that speaks directly to this situation, and as in anything, we must trust God's authority to superintend and lead. And we must equally trust that God is our benevolent eternal Father who causes all things to work together for the good of those who love Him and who are called according to His purpose; He is not a genie, a crystal ball, nor a source of good luck and karmic fortune.' They might still take your advice, but they would walk away more impressed in God's sovereignty than your advice.

To be sure, no one speaks authoritatively from God outside of the Bible. People will gravitate to your insight and advice if you counsel in a way that they think your opinion is what they should do *because* you are their spiritual authority (not because you can accurately point to Scripture to support your advice). Moreover, you function much like a pope to them if they do not do what you prescribe and then you insinuate or let them believe they are in danger of missing some measure of secret blessing that would have been theirs if they had submitted to your extra-biblical word. For most church-planters and pastors, control is their drug of choice. You can take away a man's money, a man's woman, but do not touch his control and power. Yet many are not self-aware enough to notice that they crave control because they justify it, calling it 'pastoral care'.

Since no missionary or pastor has personal authority over another person, he should be careful to formulate anything he says that is not biblically derived with a preface comment like, 'it seems to me', 'in my humble opinion', 'in my personal experience', etc. God cares about the specificity of our speech. As a man of God counsels, advises, guides, directs, challenges, and comforts with the Bible, so he imitates the voice and likeness of the Chief Shepherd. With all eyes watching his pastoral model, the missionary who courageously asserts no less than what the Bible claims and is meek enough to not exceed what is written, he will prove himself a trustworthy apprentice to the Chief Shepherd, through whom the flock of God delight to be led because it is the voice of Jesus they hear. And all those under-shepherds in training will watch carefully and take note. A Christian leader winsomely, courageously persuading others with an open Bible and a humble heart is precisely the kind of spiritual leader true sheep are inclined to follow.

Leading in a biblically persuasive way

A leader of a para-church ministry that promotes the health and centrality of the local church teaches elders-in-training to repeat aloud and meditate regularly on their responsibilities as indicated in the first part of Hebrews 13:17, which says: 'Obey your leaders and submit to them, for they are keeping watch over your souls, as those who will have to give an account.' Some pastors interpret these words to mean that church members should do whatever they say, and blindly at that. Questioning their spiritual authority is never permissible because they are God's anointed means of releasing blessing or judgment into the lives of church members. And in their mind, these verses claim that they are responsible as intermediaries and representatives to God for their parishioners' health and life. Submitting to their chain of command ensures unbroken blessing (meaning, life is enjoyable and pleasant) from God through them to the member. To not obey them blindly as a child would a parent is a surefire way to accrue God's judgment because the leader represents God and speaks for God in a mediatorial role. Does this sound popish? Cultic? Indeed, it shares a similar authoritarian and narcissistic spirit.

According to *Strong's Concordance*, the verb, 'obey' (*peithō*) usually suggests seeking to earn someone's favor or to win their approval through persuasion.[7] And in Hebrews 13:17, the verb in the passive/middle

---

7. See πείθω – *peithō*, 3982, *Olive Tree Enhanced Strong's Dictionary*: '1) persuade 1a) to persuade, i.e. to induce one by words to believe; 1b) to make friends of, to win one's favour, gain one's good will, or to seek to win one, strive to please one.' See also https://biblehub.com/greek/3982.htm (accessed 8 August 2018).

voice, suggests letting oneself be persuaded to trust a person.[8] *Mounce's Dictionary* demonstrates that whenever *peithō* is used in the passive and middle, it is translated thus: 'to be persuaded of, be confident of, Luke 20:6; Rom. 8:38; Heb. 6:9; to suffer one's self to be persuaded, yield to persuasion, to be induced, Acts 21:14; to be convinced, to believe, yield belief, Luke 16:31; Acts 17:4; to assent, listen to, obey, follow, Acts 5:36, 37, 40.'[9] According to W.E. Vine, in Hebrews 13:17: 'The *obedience* suggested is not by submission to authority, but resulting from persuasion. *Peithō* and *pisteuō*, "to trust," are closely related etymologically; the difference in meaning is that the former implies the obedience that is produced by the latter.'[10]

Moreover, the verb for 'submit' (*hupakouō*) that is frequently used in the New Testament (cf. Luke 8:25; 17:6; Eph. 6:1, 5; Col. 3:20, 22; Rom. 6:16; 1 Pet. 3:6; Heb. 5:9; Phil. 2:12), which means 'to obey, follow, be subject to' is not used in this verse. The verb, *hupeikō*, is used only here in the New Testament. According to BAGD, in other extra-biblical Greek literature, it is used as 'to yield to someone's authority, to yield, to give way.'[11]

The next verb in this passage, 'keep watch' (*agrupneō*), means 'to be vigilant in awareness of threatening peril, be alert, be on the alert' (cf. Mark 13:33; Luke 21:36). It connotes a shepherd watching after and protecting his sheep.[12] And the last verb, 'must give an account' (*apodidōmi*) suggests, 'to meet a contractual or other obligation, pay,

---

8. *Olive Tree Enhanced Strong's Dictionary*: '2) be persuaded 2a) to be persuaded, to suffer one's self to be persuaded; to be induced to believe: to have faith: in a thing 2a1) to believe 2a2) to be persuaded of a thing concerning a person 2b) to listen to, obey, yield to, comply with 3) to trust, have confidence, be confident.'

9. See [4275] πείθω *peithō* in William D. Mounce, *Mounce's Complete Expository Dictionary of Old and New Testaments Words* (Grand Rapids: Zondervan, 2006).

10. See πείθω *peithō* in W.E. Vine, M.A. Entry for 'Obedience, Obedient, Obey', *Vine's Expository Dictionary of New Testament Words*, https://www.studylight.org/dictionaries/ved/o/obedience-obedient-obey.html, 1940 (accessed 8 August 2018); see also https://www.blueletterbible.org/search/Dictionary/viewTopic.cfm?topic=VT000 1953, (accessed 8 August 2018).

11. Walter Bauer, *A Greek-English Lexicon of the New Testament and Other Early Christian Literature* (BAGD) revised and edited by Frederick William Danker, 3rd edition (Chicago: University of Chicago, 2000), p. 1030.

12. Bauer, *A Greek-English Lexicon*, p. 16.

pay out, fulfill' (cf. Matt. 12:36; 20:8; 21:41; 22:21; Mark 12:17; Luke 16:2; Acts 4:3; 19:40; Rom. 13:7; 14:12; 1 Cor. 7:3; 1 Pet. 4:5).[13] With all these nuances in mind, Hebrews 13:17 could be understood thought-for-thought as thus: *Let yourselves be persuaded by your leaders who guide you because they are watchfully caring for your souls as people who must fulfill their obligations. Let yourselves be persuaded in order that their work of vigilantly tending to your souls might be joyful and not burdensome, for that would be of no advantage to you.*[14]

It is a false and inflated claim for a pastor, missions leader, or missionary to say to a member of the flock, 'you are under my authority; the decisions I make for you, even if they are imperfect, are still God's will for you because I am like your parent. I answer to God for you, and God will bless you if you remain under my spiritual covering and umbrella of authority.' Luther and the Reformers stormed against this kind of rubbish in the Roman Catholic Church. The Puritan John Owen (1616–1683), in his commentary on Hebrews, rightly asserted:

> [The authority of the pastor] hath respect unto them in their office only. If those who suppose themselves in office do teach and enjoin things that belong not unto their office, there is no obedience due unto them by virtue of this command. So is it with the guides of the church of Rome, who, under a pretence of their office, give commands in secular things, no way belonging unto the ministry of the gospel.[15]

Furthermore, Matthew Henry (1662–1714) helpfully argued:

> It is not an implicit obedience, or absolute submission, that is here required, but only so far as is agreeable to the mind and will of

---

13. Bauer, *A Greek-English Lexicon*, p. 109-10.

14. For a similar attempt at paraphrasing this verse and taking into account the nuances of these words, see Steve Smith, 'Spiritual Authority's Most Abused Verse', *Liberty for Captives*, 24 August 2012, https://libertyforcaptives.com/2012/08/24/hebrews-1317-spiritual-authoritys-most-abused-verse/ (accessed March 8, 2017). Smith proposes thus: 'Allow yourselves to be persuaded by your leaders who guide you; they alertly care for your souls as people who must fulfill their responsibilities and give an account; allow yourselves to be persuaded so that their work might be a joy, not a burden; for that would be of no advantage to you.'

15. John Owen, *John Owen On Hebrews: A Classic Puritan Commentary* (Kindle Locations 76596-76598), Kindle Edition.

God revealed in his word. ... And, when they find that ministerial instructions are agreeable to the written word, they must obey them.[16]

Charging a church member or missions team member to submit to one's personal authority equal to or in place of the Word of Christ is not spiritual leadership according to the delegation of the Chief Shepherd. Intuition and gut instinct inevitably drive such so-called spiritual authority, calling it an umbrella of protection, inner guidance, impressions, spirit-leadings, prophetic words, inner peace, life experience, and a check in the spirit. Nevertheless, many missionaries and pastors who use such terminology undoubtedly mean well and overlook the limits of delegated biblical authority. Sadly, the enemy seems to use fear of losing control to deceive Christian leaders into asserting too much authority to the point of suppressing their followers' individuality and freedom in those areas where Scripture is silent. Spiritual leadership requires immense humility and self-forgetfulness under the Word of Christ, and spiritual followership likewise demands a submissive spirit that learns to trust and be confident in those who lead with the Word of Christ. We are all sinful and in need of grace and forgiveness. I have learned hard lessons in both areas of leadership and followership, and I wish I could go back and do better in some situations. Though the pain and humiliation can feel persistent, there is much peace and contentment in looking past our failures to Christ who leads his people by his Word through his fickle, fearful apprentices.

This is a worldwide phenomenon that I see in most places where I teach. As pastors and missionaries move away from just teaching the Bible and pointing people to rest in Christ, their public persona and sage-like wisdom inevitably fill the void. We are prone to speak in addition to Scripture and to relegate Jesus to a position of mascot, cheering us on when we get discouraged and celebrating our every achieved goal as though He were on the sidelines watching us coach, score, and receive the MVP award. But Christ invites us to a much

---

16. See M. Henry, 'Commentary on Hebrews 13 by Matthew Henry.' Blue Letter Bible. Last modified 1 March 1996. https://www.blueletterbible.org/Comm/mhc/Hbr/Hbr_013.cfm

more restful work—church-planting and pastoral leadership that makes it all about Jesus and is content to let the Word do the work.

Truth-teaching and faithful

Surveying the surrounding literary context of the debated passage in Hebrew 13:17 helps illuminate the implications for what kind of Christian leader is worthy of being obeyed and followed.

The two main qualities in this passage's expanded literary context that establish the persuasiveness of the leader's spiritual influence are his truth-teaching and faithfulness, his honor to teach the Word and his honorableness to personally live in light of that Word. Only ten verses before, the writer calls Christians to 'remember your leaders, those who spoke to you the word of God. Consider the outcome of their way of life, and imitate their faith' (Heb. 13:7), and then two verses later in Hebrews 13:9, the writer warns Christians: 'Do not be led away by diverse and strange teachings.' In other words, Christians should critically evaluate their leaders' teaching and life, which flies in the face of the interpretation of Hebrews 13:17 that suggests Christians should uncritically submit to their leaders simply because they hold an elevated position of spiritual authority.

Evident throughout his letters is Paul's application of his spiritual authority as persuasive influence based upon his devotion to teaching the Word and his faithfulness in conforming his life to the Word. He even combines these two features of spiritual leadership in a single charge to Timothy: 'Keep a close watch on yourself and on the teaching. Persist in this, for by so doing you will save both yourself and your hearers' (1 Tim. 4:16). Throughout his letters, Paul is careful not to invoke the authority of his office of apostle in order to punish or to mandate cold obedience. Instead, he seeks to influence believers by his life and teaching using words like, *appeal, plead*, and *encourage*.

Paul's personal example of leading with humble persuasiveness is on full display in the book of Philemon. Paul could have commanded Philemon to take back Onesimus, but he says, rather: 'Accordingly, though I am bold enough in Christ to command you to do what is required, yet for love's sake I prefer to appeal to you' (Philem. 8-9). And he later says: 'I preferred to do nothing without your consent in order that your goodness might not be by compulsion but of your own accord' (Philem. 14). Paul is not even talking about a non-biblical subjective impression he had about God's hidden perfect will for Philemon's life; Paul is talking about applying and obeying gospel-centered principles of forgiveness and reconciliation (cf. Philem. 17-19) as the recipients of the letter would have understood from the other prison epistles (cf. Eph. 5:32; Col. 3:13) and the apostolic teachings of Christ (cf. Matt 6:12-15; 18:21-35). Paul was trying to be as humbly persuasive as possible. These were not even extra-biblical issues about which Christians can freely agree to disagree. Paul could have wielded his apostolic authority and commanded Philemon to do what he says, but even here, in applying gospel-centered principles, Paul employs soft diplomacy and appeals sensitively to Philemon so as to persuade and influence him to choose benevolence on his own heart-felt accord and not by taciturn obligation.

In his first letter to Corinth, Paul explains how the church members should regard him: a slave of Christ and steward of the mysteries of God. God requires him to faithfully administer the mysteries of God (1 Cor. 4:1-2). Paul neither listens to the commendation nor the condemnation of others or of himself, since 'the Lord will bring to light the things now hidden in darkness and will disclose the purposes of the heart. Then each one will receive his commendation from God' (4:5). Paul so desires that Christians put their trust in the Word of God and that they do not succumb to boasting in themselves or their leaders. He is seeking to humbly lead by example as a trustworthy steward of God's truth in order to persuade them to be likewise trustworthy and truth filled. And he says: 'I have applied all these things to myself and Apollos for your benefit, brothers, that you may learn by us not to go beyond what is written, that none of you may be puffed up in favor of one against another' (4:6). Previously, Paul pointed to the power of Christ in his ministry as a means of boasting: 'What then is Apollos? What is Paul? Servants through whom you believed, as the Lord assigned to each. I planted, Apollos watered, but God gave the growth. So neither he who plants nor he who waters is anything, but only God who gives the growth' (3:5-7). Without a doubt, Paul demonstrates that faithful spiritual leadership is supremely concerned with persuasively leading according to the Book and humbly pointing to God's sufficiency, not drawing attention to the leader's credentials, achievements, position, or self-imposed authority.

In the subsequent epistle to Corinth, Paul commends himself as a minister of the New Covenant, but he bases it upon 'the open statement of the truth' (2 Cor. 4:2). Throughout 2 Corinthians, Paul seeks to defend his apostolic calling and legitimacy in the face of super-apostles who commend themselves based upon their power, position, and prestige. Though Paul could have claimed authority based upon heavenly revelations and experiences (12:1-10), throughout the letter he appeals to his own integrity (1:12-18) and he rests in the reality that God is the one who ultimately recommends and commends His servants (3:1-6). When Paul does commend himself, he highlights his Christ-like character and faithfulness to the gospel in the face of adversity (6:3-10). Paul points to his suffering as an apostle (11:1-33) and in his weakness in order to draw attention to the sufficiency and power of Christ alone (12:1-10). He is determined to exercise his authority as an apostle to build up and not break down or intimidate (10:8-9). In order to do this, Paul assumes a posture of meekness and gentleness in person (10:1), and he makes clear that he boasts in the Lord, not in himself, since no one is self-approved and self-appointed; God alone approves and commends His servants (10:17-18).

Wandering stars

God's people have always been plagued with leaders who do not lead with the Word of God. They come in many different forms. Some produce noticeable signs and wonders, and in contemporary terms, they employ methods that produce unbelievable results in impressive ways. But, if their teaching does not submit to and give honor to the God of the Bible, they are to be avoided. God is testing us whether we love Him and fear Him. Moses says:

> If a prophet or a dreamer of dreams arises among you and gives you a sign or a wonder, and the sign or wonder that he tells you comes to pass, and if he says, 'Let us go after other gods,' which you have not known, 'and let us serve them,' you shall not listen to the words of

> that prophet or that dreamer of dreams. For the LORD your God is testing you, to know whether you love the LORD your God with all your heart and with all your soul. You shall walk after the LORD your God and fear him and keep his commandments and obey his voice, and you shall serve him and hold fast to him (Deut. 13:1-4).

Or as Paul puts it in another way: 'If anyone thinks that he is a prophet, or spiritual, he should acknowledge that the things I am writing to you are a command of the Lord. If anyone does not recognize this, he is not recognized' (1 Cor. 14:37-38). In other words, spiritual leaders only speak with authority when they speak according to the Word of God. If they give commands devoid of the Bible, promote their own position and power, and produce results that detract from or add to the Scripture and God's honor, they should be marked and avoided (cf. Rom. 16:17).

Many spiritual leaders around the world go beyond what is written and seek to direct the flock in areas that the Bible does not address: who to marry, what job to take, whether to get involved in politics, what ministry to join, what house to buy, how much money to give, how to be successful and powerful, etc. These spiritual leaders might say, 'God laid it on my heart to tell you .... I don't have peace about it. ... You need to obey me because I am your authority. ... God has given me a sense that He will bless you if you do this.' Similarly, in Israel people sought mediums and necromancers for spiritual guidance and for power. The prophet Isaiah had some sharp words for this kind of divination:

> And when they say to you, 'Inquire of the mediums and the necromancers who chirp and mutter,' should not a people inquire of their God? Should they inquire of the dead on behalf of the living? To the teaching and to the testimony! If they will not speak according to this word, it is because they have no dawn. They will pass through the land, greatly distressed and hungry' (Isa. 8:19-21).

Even with the best intentions, if spiritual leaders claim any sort of unmediated direct channel to the Holy Spirit apart from the Word of God, they are listening to deceiving spirits. The only antidote to the poison of divination is to run to the Bible. If they will not speak according to the Word of God, they have no light, and they will languish as in a land of spiritual famine, going from one spiritual high to another, conference to conference, best-selling book to best-selling book, method to method. As Jude says, they are 'shepherds feeding themselves; waterless clouds, swept along by winds; fruitless trees in late autumn, twice dead, uprooted; wild waves of the sea, casting up the foam of their own shame; wandering stars, for whom the gloom of utter darkness has been reserved for ever' (Jude 12-13). Peter makes similar denouncements in 2 Peter 2:17, and then he says they speak 'swollen words' (v. 18). These people use language that is extravagant, flashy, imaginative, narcissistic, flamboyant, and spiritualized—the kind of language that more genteel evangelical leaders describe as creative, nuanced, provocative, and fresh.

Conclusion

The temptation to go beyond the Scriptures and speak in an authoritative way as though we have a direct connection to God outside of Scripture has been around since the Fall. In missions especially, there is a fascination with the novel and the innovative, because whether we admit it or not, we follow our creed: 'if it works, then it must be true'. And in our day of low devotion to written biblical propositions and objective truth and of high commitment to experientialism and unremitting narcissism, is it any wonder that spiritual leaders so effortlessly go beyond what is written? Not only do such people exceed what is written and pretend to speak authoritatively about unrevealed providences that only God knows, but they also disturb and trouble the lambs for whom Christ has died. Let us, then, follow the example of the Chief Shepherd as both trustworthy and truth-filled stewards of the mysteries of God, endeavoring never to go beyond the Scriptures, entrusting our souls to God who alone knows our hearts and will commend us accordingly. Let us not fall into the trap of providing unauthorized fire that neither gives true light nor lasting heat, but rather let us direct people to the eternal burning and shining light of God's Word. Jesus is the true Church-planter, and He uses His Word, through His Spirit to gather His people from all the *ethnē*. Let us rest in His work.

> *The Bible is the written Word of God,*
> *It tells about the living Word of God.*
> *On every page, on every line,*
> *You'll find the Son of God Divine.*
> *If you want to learn to know the King of kings,*
> *If you want to learn of all the heavenly things,*
> *Read the Book, learn the Book, let the Book teach you.*[17]

---

17. A children's chorus by the late Ruth H. Munce (1898–2001), a missionary and a Christian school teacher.

CHAPTER 8

THE MISSIONARY AS APOLOGIST

'Much that we call service to Christ is not such at all. If we are doing this for Christ, we shall not care for human reward or even recognition.'
—A.T. PIERSON

I ONCE was talking with a man who expressed concerns to me about his son-in-law who was moving with the man's daughter to Asia as missionaries. This father, an elder in his church, was thrilled that they were going to do the work of the Lord, but one time he asked his son-in-law, 'What are you going to do when you get there?' The young man, bright-eyed and exuding naïve optimism, said, 'I'm just going to love on them and say, "Jesus".' Stunned, the father-in-law thought, Really? Just the name 'Jesus'? What about learning the language and proclaiming the biblical gospel. Similarly, I personally know a self-styled missionary-theologian who has made an intellectual impact in the missions and theology world with his books and articles. One time I asked him directly, 'How would you simply explain the gospel to locals in your context?' He quickly replied, 'Jesus is King.' I inquired for more, but apparently that was enough for him. Again, though this is an improvement to the missionary who wants to merely 'love on people' and say the name of Jesus, is this adequate? Is that the sufficient gospel message found throughout the Bible? Certainly the name of Jesus and the fact that Jesus is King are key parts, but neither of those satisfactorily communicate good news and why it is good. They communicate words and information more than news. Contemporary Christianity's increasingly sloppy articulations of the gospel require the missionary-theologian to think, study, and teach like an apologist and polemicist, defending the faith against the onslaught of post-modern redefinitions, intellectual laziness, and evasive theological nuance.

Contending for the faith

I have met a handful of missionary leaders recently who teach that faith in the Bible does not mainly mean trust; it means covenant faithfulness and loyalty. Indeed, the Greek word sometimes translated as 'faith' can suggest those connotations in some contexts, but these leaders refuse to teach the young little churches scattered throughout the remote mountain terrains where they serve the Reformation doctrine of *sola fide* because they say it is a European construct from a bygone era that emphasized contractual law more than covenantal relationship. So, instead of teaching 'faith alone', they teach 'loyal faithfulness'. My question to them is, 'How do you know then if you have been faithful enough to secure your end of the bargain for salvation?' The reply I have heard is that there is really no doctrine that gives objective ground for assurance and that assurance is also an unbiblical construct that emerged out of Enlightenment thinking. They claim that the indigenous people groups they work with do not ask questions of assurance but questions of what steps they need to do to experience God. In other words, the missionary leaders are accommodating the indigenous peoples' merit-based worldviews and twisting Scripture and reimagining theology to suit the people group's worldview.

Many of these missionaries have studied enough of contrarian theologians and avant-garde culture warriors to appear to have mastered many talking-points and hot topics. Yet they often confuse 'grace' and 'faith' in their explanations, which indicates they are fairly undiscerning and are probably just parroting what they have read or heard from other sources. The gospel to them, then, is that anyone can have a life-giving relationship with God through loyal covenant faithfulness.

The *locus* of the purported 'gospel' is a life-giving relationship with God. Yes, that is an implication and consequence of the gospel, but is that truly *the* gospel? Does not the gospel require that we understand what the Bible says about God, mankind/sin, Christ, and the demand to respond in trust and repentance? True, there are many creative ways to start a gospel conversation, but if the indispensable features of the gospel are not adequately communicated, our hearers only have heard a portion of the good news, which is not finally good news.

What is wrong with the above-mentioned statement that the good news is we can have a life-giving relationship with God through our faithfulness? A few things. That is not truly good news; it is good advice. (And Buddhist-background believers, Hindu-background believers, and Muslim-background believers subconsciously latch on to anything that sounds meritorious, ritualistic, and formulaic). Sure, it might imply that part of the covenant faithfulness is God's doing; but it certainly, then, suggests that we must contribute our share of covenant faithfulness to make the relationship work. Historically, some aberrant versions of Christianity have promoted a partial works-based relationship with God, in principal and practice emphasizing one's best performance and then letting God do the rest (e.g., 40 per cent is our obedience and 60 per cent is God's grace). This is why the doctrine of trust *alone* is essential. Trust alone (not trustworthiness), faith alone (not faithfulness) is the instrumental cause of justification, in which we are irrevocably united to Christ and adopted permanently into the Father's house. For people groups that languish under the anxious weight of merit-based religions, the good news of salvation by grace *alone* through faith *alone* is breath-taking. Any gospel message that requires our own covenant faithfulness is bad news. It raises the question, 'How much is enough?' Well, it is never enough. Only Christ kept covenant enough, and He kept the covenant and secured its blessings for us who rest in His faithfulness alone, not in addition to our own attempts at faithfulness. Faith is a secure trust in objective truth, not mainly a subjective sense that comes and goes based upon our perceived performance.

A partial truth that becomes a whole truth is ultimately an untruth. And when eternity is on the line, people who trust in anything more or less than the gospel are not saved. God saves us from God alone, for

God's glory alone, by grace alone, through faith alone, in Christ alone, revealed in Scripture alone.

So many well-meaning missionaries want to spread the gospel to people who have never heard it before. This is noble and praiseworthy. Let their tribe increase. What happens is that they grow tired of the hostility and resistance. And they start looking for theological silver bullets. Incrementally their theological precision erodes as does their confidence in the apostolic Word they once received years ago. They go to great lengths to adopt the worldview in order to bridge the intellectual gap. From my own experience, this is very easy to do.

Here is the challenge: most normal-minded people around the world have no conceptual problems engaging and comprehending other worldviews. I have met illiterate yak herders at the highest lake in the world in Tibet who are on their smart phones listening to and singing word-for-word the lyrics of the latest American hip-hop songs in the entertainment media. Often, the challenge is not for lack of understanding, though that is initially a major part of it that we neglect to their peril. Obviously, we need to teach new concepts and define terms, but they are undeniably smart and capable people. However, the obstacle is mainly because they are dead in their sins and trespasses and do not desire the knowledge of the Holy One. The fallen human condition on this side of the Fall and this side of the New Heavens and New Earth suppresses the truth in unrighteousness.

Of course, we need to explain what we mean and mean what we say, but people are actually pretty sharp. Most people in the world have intuitively learned multiple languages at a young age, which means they automatically operate in and differentiate between different cultural/linguistic worldviews. In many ways they have a head-start on the average Westerner who only knows one main cultural/linguistic worldview. They know what to do when the power goes out for days and how to farm, raise crops, breed and train animals, among other life-or-death survival skills, unlike most monolingual digital natives in the West who know nothing of farming, hunting, and thriving without electricity and the Internet.

Paul's culture-confronting polemics and apologetics in Athens

In contemporary evangelicalism, Paul's sermon on Mars Hill (Acts 17) is one of the most popular and yet one of the most misunderstood and misused passages in the whole New Testament. It is truly an example of a frontline truth encounter. If you have ever been around a seeker-sensitive church, or if you have ever received training in missions and outreach, you would have likely heard Paul's sermon on Mars Hill commended as the premier example of contextualization and relevant cultural engagement. When church growth gurus look to Paul's speech as a prescription for how we are to engage culture in a relevant way, the whole thrust of this narrative malfunctions. And the term, 'engage culture', is a relatively new term. 'Engaging culture' has no standard definition, so since there is no universal definition, then it essentially could be everything we do.

Many Christian leaders claim that Paul was employing a postmodern method of attractional communication. But this completely misses the point. There was no mutually beneficial conversation where both parties walked away feeling enlightened and validated. Paul does not feign to be on a mystical quest in search of diverse spiritualities, nor does he try to build a bridge to non-Christian worldviews in order to win their approval. He preaches the gospel, in all its low-brow foolishness and absence of worldly sophistication. He specifically heralds the one doctrine that they would consider shockingly ridiculous—the resurrection of the dead. This is tremendously important because the main point of the text will not be as piercing if we misunderstand the context of Paul's audience. Paul's theology of God is the main point, not his methodology of communication. His theological potency fades away if we misinterpret his method. The main point of this passage is that the Sovereign God summons everyone to submit to His Son.

How did Paul communicate?
The first part of the account says:

> Now while Paul was waiting for them at Athens, his spirit was provoked within him as he saw that the city was full of idols. So he reasoned in the synagogue with the Jews and the devout persons, and in the marketplace every day with those who happened to be there.

> Some of the Epicurean and Stoic philosophers also conversed with him. And some said, 'What does this babbler wish to say?' Others said, 'He seems to be a preacher of foreign divinities'—because he was preaching Jesus and the resurrection. And they took him and brought him to the Areopagus, saying, 'May we know what this new teaching is that you are presenting? For you bring some strange things to our ears. We wish to know therefore what these things mean.' Now all the Athenians and the foreigners who lived there would spend their time in nothing except telling or hearing something new (Acts 17:16-21).

Earlier in Acts 17, Paul offended the Jewish populace in Thessalonica, and their leaders stirred up civil unrest. Because he could no longer do ministry there, he departed at night to Berea (17:10). When he arrived in Berea, he started preaching publicly. And the Jews from Thessalonica went there and forced him out again. From the context Paul was obviously not clandestinely trying to fit in to the culture and employ friendship evangelism, throwing out God-conversations as a passing comment every now and then. He was in the public square preaching the gospel. Obviously, he was not concerned with winning the respect of the culture by seeking to blend in with cordial discussions, which is evident because wherever he went, people opposed him nearly to the point of death.

So, Paul was brought to Athens, and he was waiting for a few weeks for Silas and Timothy to come join him. While waiting for them he explored the city and its culture and started preaching the gospel in the synagogue and public square, not wanting to waste that providential opportunity. It is critical to notice how Paul 'engaged the culture', so to speak. He showed no evidence of integrating or celebrating the culture; furthermore, the culture was nauseating to him, and he never attempted slick methods of charitably repackaging the gospel and redeeming the culture. His disgust for the culture's idols compelled him to reason in the synagogues. This word for 'reasoning' implies no multi-perspectival ecumenism or scholarly confab. It suggests a polemical debate. That Paul hosted no deferential dialogue neither means he was big-headed nor pugnacious; with loving truth he proclaimed the gospel without dulling the piercing points of its counter-cultural truths. He studied the culture to confront the biblical truths they would most likely reject, which is clear from the historical context of the beliefs of his hearers. Paul had been analyzing their culture distinctives so that he knew how to present the gospel so as to poke holes in their worldviews.

Who were Paul's hearers?

The Stoic philosophy was approximately three and a half centuries old by Paul's era. The Stoics were classic secularists who believed they could, through ascetic and unpretentious lives, numb to pain or pleasure, conquer their emotions and reach the apex of human enlightenment. Random fate determined all things, rendering everything meaningless.[1] Their worldview sounds strikingly similar to the halls of secular philosophy and humanistic religion departments in American universities.

Life's purpose, according to the Epicureans, was to binge on passion and pleasure, escaping pain at all costs. Denying an afterlife altogether, they feared no divine judgment and shamelessly welcomed excess and indulgence. They espoused a form of evolutionary theory long before Charles Darwin (1809–1882).[2] Their worldview and lifestyle seem to resemble today's Deists, evolutionists, or pleasure-seeking educated Urbanites in metropolitan America, living for the moment with no fear of God.

There was a third group, which Luke does not mention, but some scholars suggest were most likely present. They were the Cynics, the oldest and largest of the philosophical traditions. Their ideals had

---

1. For succinct summaries of the historical context, see Richard N. Longenecker, *Acts*, The Expositor's Bible Commentary, Kindle Edition (Grand Rapids: Zondervan Academic, 2017), Kindle Locations 10302-10305; F.F. Bruce, *The Book of the Acts*, New International Commentary (Grand Rapids: Eerdmans, 1988), pp. 328-31.

2. See Benjamin Wiker, *Moral Darwinism: How We Became Hedonists*, Christian Classics Bible Studies (Downers Grove, IL: IVP Academic, 2002), 59-74. See also M.E. Sadler, *The Acts of the Apostles* (London: George Bell & Sons, 1908), 329. For a useful evaluation of Paul's interaction with the Stoic and Epicurean worldviews and belief systems, see Ben Witherington, *The Acts of the Apostles: A Socio-Rhetorical Commentary*, New Testament Commentary (Grand Rapids: Eerdmans, 1997), 511-20. David G. Peterson provides an accessible commentary on the historical and cultural context, synthesizing many reputable sources; see David G. Peterson, *The Acts of the Apostles*, The Pillar New Testament Commentary (Grand Rapids: Eerdmans, 2009), pp. 486-505.

experienced something of a revival by the first century A.D.[3] They would have been pervasive throughout the general populace and undoubtedly represented in Paul's audience. The Cynics pursued true happiness by becoming one with nature and through liberating themselves from affluence, notoriety, and authority. Essentially the early naturalistic and hygiene-neglecting New Agers, the Cynics even abandoned cultural mores and social conventions like upholding familial and civic obligations, 'professing instead a cosmopolitan utopia and communal anarchism.'[4] So, when we understand that Paul's communication was actually confronting these major cultures, we can then see the convicting, penetrating force of his message and why it was not considered open-minded or politically correct.

What did Paul communicate?

What was the content of his message and how did he employ it so that it would convict its hearers? These are basic doctrines of God that would have been outrageous and offensive to the worldviews of the three above-mentioned groups. Before Paul could preach the *good news* of salvation, he had to first declare the culture-confronting *fearful news* that God is the Sovereign Creator, Universally Present, and the Righteous Judge.

God is Creator and Lord

The next part of the account says,

> So Paul, standing in the midst of the Areopagus, said: 'Men of Athens, I perceive that in every way you are very religious. For as I passed along and observed the objects of your worship, I found also an altar with this inscription, 'To the unknown god.' What therefore

---

3. See Donald R. Dudley, *A History of Cynicism: From Diogenes to the 6th Century A.D.* (London: Methuen & Co., 1937), p. 124.

4. Charilaos Platanakis, 'Cynic', in *Encyclopædia Britannica* (Encyclopædia Britannica, Inc., 4 February 2018), https://www.britannica.com/topic/Cynic-ancient-Greek-philosophy (accessed: 18 September 2018). For scrutinizing insights into Paul's methods and the nature of Paul's audience. See Phil Johnson, 'Paul and Culture', Pyromaniacs, https://teampyro.blogspot.com/2008/04/paul-and-culture.html 2 April 2008 (accessed: 23 March 2012).

you worship as unknown, this I proclaim to you. The God who made the world and everything in it, being Lord of heaven and earth, does not live in temples made by man, nor is he served by human hands, as though he needed anything, since he himself gives to all mankind life and breath and everything. And he made from one man every nation of mankind to live on all the face of the earth, having determined allotted periods and the boundaries of their dwelling place, that they should seek God, and perhaps feel their way toward him and find him (17:22-27a).

Paul is claiming that there is one God, and He made all things. God is. He is not just one of many other gods in the Greek Pantheon or in multi-cultural Western society. He is sovereign over everything and nothing happens apart from His will. This is wholesale defiance against every aspect of Greek philosophy and any other contemporary religion. Islam, Buddhism, Atheism, Evolution, Deism, American Civil Religion, Marxism, Mormonism, New Ageism—they are all shattered under the self-sufficiency of God's lordship. The God of the Bible has determined the allotted existence of every nation down to the second and not one more. When God says, 'enough', Rome falls, Constantinople falls, London falls, Moscow falls, Beijing falls, and Washington D.C. falls. This is true for every world ruler down to every citizen. Isaiah says:

> Who has measured the Spirit of the Lord, or what man shows him his counsel? Whom did he consult, and who made him understand? Who taught him the path of justice, and taught him knowledge, and showed him the way of understanding? Behold, the nations are like a drop from a bucket, and are accounted as the dust on the scales; behold, he takes up the coastlands like fine dust. ... All the nations are as nothing before him, they are accounted by him as less than nothing and emptiness (Isa. 40:13-15, 17).

America, Persia, China, Venezuela, Rome, Great Britain, Egypt, Greece, Germany—nothing.

Daniel says:

> His dominion is an everlasting dominion, and his kingdom endures from generation to generation; all the inhabitants of the earth are

accounted as nothing, and he does according to his will among the host of heaven and among the inhabitants of the earth; and none can stay his hand or say to him, 'What have you done?' (Dan. 4:34-35).

God is not served

This passage from Acts changed my life forever. I was wrestling through the truths of God's providence and lordship. It was a new concept for me, and I had this sense that God was summoning me to know Him in a whole different way. I decided to read through the Bible and mark every passage that spoke of the power and self-sufficiency of God. In the evenings after work, I would go out into the nearby forest and pray. One evening as the sun was setting, I was crying out to God to open my eyes to see Him for who He really is. And I laid on the ground and trembled under the heavy holiness of God when this verse came to mind with unbelievable force: (Acts 17:25) 'God is not served by human hands, as though he needed anything, since he himself gives to all mankind life and breath and everything.' The phrase, 'God is not served ... as though he needed anything', reverberated throughout my soul like a thousand thunderclaps, my chest heaving under His terrible force.

For the first time in my life, I was swept away in the ocean of God's sovereignty and self-sufficiency, and I was held hostage by the fear of God. I felt horribly insignificant. And I loved it! I realized I could neither bargain with God, nor give Him anything that He had not already given to me. The question was no longer, 'what is God's will for my life and what does He need from me?' The question was now, 'What is God's will?' Full stop. I realized I had been *using* God for *me* and *my* plans and *my* fulfillment, thinking I was actually giving to God something He *needed* from me. But God flattened me and showed me that He was going to use me for *Him* and *His* plans and *His* fulfillment. And when He is done with me, my breath will stop, and He will take me home. You and I are just a means to His end. God does not need you. The truth that God does not depend on you and that you cannot fail Him and frustrate His plans, that is unspeakably good news.

This is the penetrating truth of Paul's sermon. These verses obliterate self-autonomy, independence, and man-made religion. The Athenian philosophers were seeking for what God had written on their hearts, but they had suppressed it. They were looking for God in all their other gods and philosophies, and nothing was satisfying their intellectual quest. So, they built an altar to 'the unknown god', knowing they had not found Him, though He is not far from each one of us. What a sad statement: they built an altar to 'the unknown god'. Imagine going nearly mad in your conscience by the reality that there is some god out there that you intuitively sense needs to be appeased, so you devote yourself to building an altar that hopefully manages to placate this unknown god with unknown expectations and unknown rules. And at the end of the day, at the end of the year, and at the end of your life, how can you know if you have done enough? You cannot. The unknown god is just that, unknown. Distant. Aloof. Arbitrary. Imagine what a fearfully anxious existence that must have been.

God's universal presence

Additionally, in verses 27-29, Paul emphasizes God's immanence, or His universal presence. The next part of the account says:

> Yet he is actually not far from each one of us, for 'In him we live and move and have our being'; as even some of your own poets have said, 'For we are indeed his offspring.' Being then God's offspring, we ought not to think that the divine being is like gold or silver or stone, an image formed by the art and imagination of man (27b-29).

God is not locked into carved idols of gold or wood. He is everywhere. Paul underscored the point that the unknown god they were trying to pacify is closer and more real than they imagined. This would be like someone going to Seattle to experience its well-known beauty and magnificence. And they spend all their time slopping through the torrential downpours, looking at the tall buildings, the Space Needle, the art museum with all its bizarre art displays, and the whole time they are thinking, 'there must be more to Seattle's beauty and magnificence than this. Everyone who visits raves about the spectacular beauty of this area.' Then a sunny day breaks through. To their astonishment they see in the distance a most majestic, powerful volcano—10,000 times more beautiful than any Space Needle or post-modern art exhibit. Inside Mt. Rainier is more power than all the electricity and technology in Seattle, and it could blow and wipe out the whole city, leveling the empires of Jeff Bezos and Bill Gates. And that volcano was there thousands of years before Seattle was ever settled and will still be there thousands of years after Seattle is gone. That fearful discovery of mind-boggling greatness is what Paul is pushing them to see, and he could not have done that if he were just trying to contextualize and highlight similarities between Athenian religions and Christianity.

In verse 28, Paul quotes two poets. Many post-modern contextualizers will argue that Paul was quoting the philosophers' favorite poets to be culturally relevant. The first quote is by Epimenides, a poet from the sixth century B.C. (over 600 years prior), and the second quote is from Aratus, a poet from the third century B.C. (over 300 years prior).[5] Paul was not embracing contemporary culture by quoting these poets. These poets were not the equivalent of Paul Simon, Kurt Cobain, or Bono. Paul was quoting from their ancient literature, demonstrating that their ancient ancestors once acknowledged these general truths about God. The Athenian philosophers had suppressed the common grace that was once plain to their forefathers. He was using these quotes to shame his hearers for deviating from what their ancestors taught. This was cultural confrontation, not contextualized accommodation. Today, it would be like quoting Christian truths from poet William Shakespeare (1564–1616) and Deist intellectual Thomas Jefferson (1743–1826) to rebuke social liberals or evolutionary atheists, pointing out that a celebrated poet and a distinguished thinker of Western culture both recognized such biblical truths. Paul was demonstrating that God is universally pervasive; and their ancestors knew it.[6]

---

5. See Witherington, *The Acts of the Apostles*, pp. 521-34; Longenecker, *Acts*, Kindle Locations 10386-10402.

6. For a classic evangelical treatment of Paul's missionary skill displayed at Mars Hill, see John R.W. Stott, *The Message of Acts: The Spirit, the Church & the World*, The Bible Speaks Today (Downers Grove, IL: InterVarsity Press, 1994), pp. 276-91. For a penetrating treatment of Paul's contextualizing, see Phil Johnson, 'Paul and Contextualization', Pyromaniacs, 9 April 2008, https://teampyro.blogspot.com/2008/04/paul-and-contextualization.html (accessed 30 May 2011).

God's righteousness and the resurrection

Paul then proceeded to put the nail in the coffin, as it were, by preaching God's righteousness. He says:

> The times of ignorance God overlooked, but now he commands all people everywhere to repent, because he has fixed a day on which he will judge the world in righteousness by a man whom he has appointed; and of this he has given assurance to all by raising him from the dead.' Now when they heard of the resurrection of the dead, some mocked. But others said, 'We will hear you again about this' (vv. 30-32).

These people hardly thought of themselves as ignorant. And it would be rare today to find someone in our culture who willingly admits they are ignorant. Moreover, Paul says: 'God commands all people everywhere to repent.' This is the gospel call—a summons from the King, not an open-house invitation. People everywhere are born Adamic rebels in defiance of the King. God warns all people everywhere to repent because He will judge the world in righteousness, and that is certain because He raised His Son Jesus Christ from the dead and through Him God will judge the world. This is why the resurrection from the dead is such an offensive, controversial, laughable doctrine in every era, in every nation, in every culture.

All the philosophers were materialists, and even to those who believed in an afterlife, the thought of people having resurrected bodies either on the New Earth or in hell sounded like absolute nonsense. The lordship of God and the resurrection of the dead always bring mockery. Everyone knows that if the physical resurrection of Jesus Christ is historically true, that He is physically alive today in heaven, then they are undeniably doomed if they do not repent and trust in Jesus—an inescapable truth written on every heart.

When the lordship, creative power, universal presence, and righteousness of God and His Son's resurrection are rightly preached, people either balk at it or believe in it. God's Word will never be socially acceptable nor politically correct, so our gospel proclamation must hold the same counter-cultural edge. Fallen culture is meant to be confronted, not accommodated. The gospel is a command, not merely an invite.

A contextualized example: traitor to heir

Below is an example of a time when I made a concerted effort at entering the worldview of an Asian friend in order to communicate the gospel to him. The cognitive dissonance he was experiencing was not only because of my limited language ability but because my starting point was not connecting to him in the way that I had hoped.[7]

'In your culture, what is the greatest act of sin someone can commit?' This was a question I asked this young Asian man with whom I had been meeting for months to do evangelistic Bible studies. He was an enthusiastic pursuer of 'truth,' and he wanted to know about biblical truth. So, over some spicy lamb kebabs every Wednesday, we would go through biblical texts and his objections. As we met together weekly, I began to realize that his appreciation for the law and for the fact that all sinners have broken the law was not as personalized as it was for me. In his mind, everyone in his country breaks the law, even the police and politicians. Corruption is to be expected because that is how business is done. Corruption is only bad if you get caught and publicly humiliate someone. 'Rules are for fools'—a common statement flaunted even in highest levels of government. So, the reason transgression is bad is not because it misses the mark of transcendent perfection, *per se*, but because it transgresses a social code and consequently brings about shame and dishonor to yourself or, even worse, to someone you ought to honor. The losing of face because of shame motivates the morality of so many cultures, specifically the one in which I was ministering. This does not mean that there is no room for guilt/innocence and law/grace in a gospel explanation in this culture; it just means that it takes some theological aptitude, cultural nuance, and interpersonal *finesse* to work through many other layers of millennia-old worldviews in order to get to that point. Often the subjective starting point in a gospel conversation is through the relationship-controlling honor-shame worldview, but the ending point is the eventual realization that the person, in Adam as their representative ancestor, has dishonored God

---

7. A version of this account by the author was first posted here: 'From Traitor to Heir,' www.desiringGod.org. https://www.desiringgod.org/articles/from-traitor-to-heir, 29 August 2014.

through transgressing an objective standard of God's righteousness and therefore faces the consequence of shame and the penalty of death. Enter the good news of penal substitutionary atonement, propitiation, expiation, and imputation of Christ's righteousness.

My friend did answer my aforementioned question about the greatest sin. But first he explained that it was the worst sin because it brought the worst shame. The sin? Betrayal. Then I realized how I could start to explain the facets of the gospel more clearly.

I argued that all people have betrayed their Creator, choosing rather to honor themselves and their own creations, thus bringing unspeakable dishonor to Him. Instead of abandoning them because of their shameful acts, in order to honor the greatness of His name, God the Father sent His Son to become a Man and to live the life that perfectly honors the Father and to die the most inglorious death imaginable that only the worst of traitors deserve. In so doing, the Father's execution of the Son would take away His righteous anger and the shame of all who would bow the knee in humble trust, thus honoring Him. And in exchange, the Father would adopt them as sons and lavishly bestow upon them the eternal inheritance of His one faithful Son.

That hit a nerve. His face went from a frown when I told him that he had betrayed God to a jaw dropping expression when I explained that Christ endured the shame of the cross in the place of all who would turn from their dishonorable treason and trust in Him alone as their honor-earner, law-keeper, execution-bearer, and shame-taker. All treason committed against the Emperor of the universe would be eternally pardoned because of the slain Lamb. All dishonorable shame brought upon the Creator of the universe would be eternally expiated by the forsaken Scapegoat. All pleasure and privilege bestowed upon the honorable Son would be imputed to those who honor Him through their trust in the Son. Trust alone in Christ alone is what turns a shameful traitor into an honorable heir. Without trust it is impossible to honor Him.

Conclusion

Too many times mission agencies, missionary-sending churches, and missions teams settle for too little. A bleeding heart and warm body does not biblically qualify someone to cross a culture, open their mouth, and claim to speak on behalf of the Potentate of time. I am thankful for so many of the big-hearted missionaries I know, whose hearts can be sometimes bigger than their heads. I love them sincerely. They are my dearest friends and frontline comrades. And I even find myself often operating more with my heart than my head. But I am equally concerned that much of our spiritual legacy and fruitfulness will not last a day longer than we do, let alone into eternity, if we neglect contending for the apostolic gospel and the apostolic text.

The call to take the everlasting gospel to the nations is a sacred duty that requires a missionary to be much in prayer and mighty in Scripture. Fun-loving charisma, a love for exotic food, an emotive fascination with cultural beauty, a raging wanderlust, and an appetite for adventure do not suffice. The unreached people groups need no missionaries who aim to accommodate and appropriate the target culture so as to make the gospel more palatable and inoffensive. The missionary who cares little about theological precision and rightly dividing the word of truth, cares little about gospel communication, the eternal state of lost souls, and the honor of God in the salvation of the *ethnē*. Show me a missionary who cares about the salvation of lost souls and the discipleship of untrained believers, and I will show you a missionary who studies to show himself approved unto God, a workman who does not need to be ashamed, rightly handling the word of truth.

CHAPTER 9

ADONIRAM AND ANN JUDSON AS WORD-DRIVEN MISSIONARY-THEOLOGIANS[1]

'All missionary operations, to be permanently successful, must be based on the written Word. Where that Word is most regarded and honored, there will be the most pure and permanent success.'

—ADONIRAM JUDSON

THE first American Baptist missionaries to Burma, Adoniram Judson and Ann Hasseltine Judson, were equally devoted to spreading the good news of Jesus Christ to the Buddhists of Burma. The foundational source of the Judsons' perseverant mission was the supreme and sufficient Word. This chapter will seek to demonstrate that the Judsons' allegiance to the written Word dominated their evangelism and disciple-making strategies, and it will demonstrate Ann Judson's contribution to the mission, though cut short by her untimely death. Moreover, it will paint a historical portrait of a missionary-theologian extraordinaire. Much of the Judson legacy credits Adoniram for his ministry, which lasted twenty-four years longer after Ann's death, primarily due to the decades of records and volumes of sources available related to Adoniram. This chapter will consequently reflect their legacy as mostly witnessed in the accounts

---

1. The content of this chapter chiefly derives from E.D. Burns, *A Supreme Desire to Please Him: The Spirituality of Adoniram Judson* (Eugene, OR: Pickwick, 2016), pp. 64-93, 188-212. Additionally, an abbreviated version of this chapter is included in E.D. Burns, '"The Golden Lamp Hung Out of Heaven": Adoniram and Ann Judson's Bibliocentric Strategy for Reaching the Buddhists of Burma', *Emerging Faith: Lessons from Mission History in Asia* (Littleton, CO: William Carey Publishing, 2020).

of Adoniram. Much of Adoniram's lifelong devotion and bibliocentric ministry philosophy stemmed from the foundation laid with Ann in the first years of ministry together. This chapter will illustrate the Judsons' bibliocentric strategies for reaching the Buddhists of Burma.

To issue a missiological synthesis and analysis of Adoniram and Ann Judson's missionary-theologian strategies, academic responsibility and historical judiciousness requires us to remember that their theological and historical contexts were much different to ours. Merely critiquing their strategies through the filters of modern-day priorities and sentiments would prove to be historically myopic. If the chief end of the Judsons' engagement of Buddhism was so that both parties could have a mutually affirming interfaith dialogue, as though they were serving in the globalized twenty-first century, then Adoniram and Ann Judson's strategies might seem intolerant and antiquated. But since their *telos* for engaging Burmese Buddhists was to make Buddhist-background believers trust in Jesus Christ's work alone as their atonement and righteousness and who went on to independently plant and shepherd their own indigenous churches, then the Judsons' Bible-centered strategy was a dynamic success, the spirit of which all Bible-centered missiologists should heed and seek to emulate.

Methodology is always derivative of theology; simply put, what Christians truly believe about God, sin, salvation, humanity, and the Bible will directly determine how they conceive and execute ministry strategy. For the Judsons, the work of sowing gospel seed was slow and not as socially acceptable as other humanitarian efforts, but Adoniram and Ann were certain that the written Word required proclamation through publication and preaching. They were not dreadfully depressed when growth was slow, because the overriding purpose of their Bible-proclamation was for the glory of God. They were generally hesitant to grant assurance to new 'professing believers' until those believers had showed a degree of submission to Scripture.

Similar to the articles of agreement adopted by Judson and two other missionary companions,[2] the Judsons' missiological convictions and practices were: the importance of personal faith and believer's

---

2 Wayland, *A Memoir*, 1:184.

baptism, evangelism and contextualization, linguistic and cultural acquisition, and the establishment of self-supporting indigenous churches.[3] Or stated another way, the Judsons' methods were learning the language and culture proficiently, publicly preaching the gospel, translating the Bible and distributing tracts, planting churches, and training indigenous pastors.[4] 'Literate and civilized as they were',[5] the Burmese were ready for the written Word of God, thought Judson initially. Though their literacy was high compared to other parts of Asia, because their literacy level was insufficient for reading the Scriptures, the Judsons 'opened a school for teaching adults to read.'[6] Adoniram later said it was his 'intention to place [three Karen] men in the adult school, and qualify them to read and interpret the Scriptures to their countrymen.'[7]

We must note that in light of all that history celebrates of the Judson legacy, his motivation was not for acclamation or reputation. He insisted that his name should 'live in oblivion or disgrace till the great day.'[8] Hence, Judson would assert that all study and admiration of his Bible-centered missionary labor should look finally to the glory of Christ Himself, whose redeeming love is 'a beautiful study for eternity!'[9] Judson appealed:

---

3 Keith E. Eitel, 'The Enduring Legacy of Adoniram Judson's Missiological Precepts and Practices', in Jason G. Duesing, ed., *Adoniram Judson: A Bicentennial Appreciation of the Pioneer American Missionary*. Studies in Baptist Life and Thought, ed. Michael A.G. Haykin (Nashville: B&H Academic, 2012), pp. 129-48.

4 Stephen Neill, *A History of Christian Missions*, 2nd ed., The Penguin History of the Church, vol. 6 (Harmondsworth, England: Penguin Books, 1986), p. 249.

5 Courtney Anderson, *To the Golden Shore: The Life of Adoniram Judson*, 2nd ed. (Valley Forge, PA: Judson Press, 1987), p. 56.

6 Wayland, *A Memoir*, 2:11.

7 Wayland, *A Memoir*, 2:12.

8 Adoniram Judson, 'Letter from the Rev. Adoniram Judson, Jun. to Dr Baldwin, Dated Rangoon, December 9, 1819', *The Baptist Missionary Magazine* (1819), p. 2:380. See also Robert T. Middleditch, *Burmah's Great Missionary: Records of the Life, Character, and Achievements of Adoniram Judson* (New York: E.H. Fletcher, 1854), pp. 97-8, quoted in Burns, *A Supreme Desire to Please Him*, p. 212.

9 Emily Chubbuck Judson, 'Closing Scenes in Dr. Judson's Life, Maulmain, Sept. 20, 1850', *The Baptist Missionary Magazine* (1850), p. 31:36., quoted in Burns, *A Supreme Desire to Please Him*, p. 212.

> Brethren, look to Jesus. This sight will fill you with the greatest consolation and delight. Look to Him on the cross; so great is His love that, if He had a thousand lives, He would lay them all down for your redemption. Look to Him on the throne; His blessed countenance fills all heaven with delight and felicity. Look to Him in affliction; He will succor you. Look to Him in death; He will sustain you. Look to Him in the judgment; He will save you.[10]

In a sermon on Colossians 1:27, entitled, 'Christ in you, the hope of glory', Judson said that Christ indwells the hearts of His people by faith in Him, by love to Him, and by His love conveyed to them. He said that the evidence of Christ's 'character stamped on our souls' is love for God and love for people. This indwelling Christ loves His people 'to the end', and Christ will fill up His indwelling in their future glorification. The inferences of such truths, Judson maintained, are that 'the indwelling of Christ is the greatest of all blessings.' Therefore, he said, it is the 'first thing ... to which we ought to attend.' If communion with the indwelling Christ is experienced to some degree, he urged, 'How careful we ought to be to improve the blessing! It is necessary to peace of mind, usefulness, future eminence.'[11]

Judson affectionately longed to please Christ more than any other duty. His spirituality was oriented around his consuming devotion to obey Christ's command to preach the gospel to the nations, in order that he might please Christ and enjoy eternity in Christ's happy presence. Obedience to the Great Commission was not an option for any Christian, and especially for those Christians whom God had called specifically to go as missionaries. Judson counted it a high honor and a high duty to lovingly deny himself and in imitation of Christ, labor to translate the Word and proclaim the good news of salvation in Christ. He would often say, 'If we only please Christ, no matter for the

---

10 Judson was speaking to students at Madison University in Hamilton, New York, in 1846. Edward Judson, *The Life of Adoniram Judson, By His Son, Edward Judson* (New York: Randolph, 1883), p. 474. See also Middleditch, *Burmah's Great Missionary*, p. 373, quoted in Burns, *A Supreme Desire to Please Him*, p. 212.

11 Wayland, *Memoir*, 2:498, quoted in Burns, *A Supreme Desire to Please Him*, p. 188.

rest!'[12] The Judsons' Bible-centered missionary strategies emerged out of a vibrant enjoyment of Christ through trusting in their unbreakable union with Christ. This cannot be overlooked because if we forget that Adoniram and Ann Judson's fruitful endurance was because of their faith in Christ's work for them, we will be tempted to look mainly to their *faithfulness* and emulate their techniques and methods in order to manufacture similar results. The point is that they modeled for contemporary missionary-theologians a life devoted to pleasing and loving Christ through Word-centered translation, evangelism, and discipleship, all because of Christ's righteous life and loving death in their place for their eternal enjoyment of God.

Strategic Model 1: The Judsons practiced Bible-centered conversionism

Judson's theology of baptism greatly influenced his view of Christian conversion. His passion for the conversion of the heathen was not satisfied with mere tract distribution or immediate professions of faith. Judson recorded that when a Buddhist would begin considering Christianity, all his relatives and acquaintances would rise up to prevent him. It would have been tempting to soften the exclusivity of the gospel and thus promote religious multi-perspectivalism and ecumenical dialogue, but Judson's adherence to biblical convictions prevented him from settling for inoffensive and socially acceptable theological minimalism. In a journal entry in February 1820, Judson recorded a conversation he had with the Buddhist teacher, Moung Shwa-gnong, which illustrates his convictions. Moung Shwa-gnong insisted that he held to the fundamentals of the Christian religion, but Judson was not convinced that he was a genuine convert. Moung Shwa-gnong said, 'I believe in the eternal God, in his Son Jesus Christ, in the atonement which Christ has made, and in the writings of the apostles, as the true and only Word of God.' Yet, Moung Shwa-gnong claimed he tried avoiding persecution by going along with people to the pagoda for worship so that he did not look out of place, but he was

---

12 Wayland, *Memoir*, 2:372, quoted in Burns, *A Supreme Desire to Please Him*, p. 185.

sincerely not in agreement with his former ways of worship. Judson observed that Moung Shwa-gnong was progressing in the direction of discipleship, but he contended that Moung Shwa-gnong still lacked full devotion to Christ's commands in Scripture. Judson said, 'Teacher, you may be a disciple of Christ in heart, but you are not a full disciple. You have not faith and resolution enough to keep all the commands of Christ, particularly that which requires you to be baptized, though in the face of persecution and death.'[13] Moung Shwa-gnong consequently left without pursuing baptism any further. But five months later, Moung Shwa-gnong found Judson and confessed his desire to be baptized, convincing Judson of his submission to Christ's written command to be baptized and corresponding evidence of spiritual life.

Strategic Model 2: The Judsons made disciples with the Word

Judson sought to train up the church through the regular teaching of the Word. When he was not translating, he was teaching and training. Judson developed biblical/theological education for the Burmese ministers-in-training. The Bible courses covered both the Old and New Testaments, but the teachers prioritized the New Testament, teaching 'verse by verse, with comparison of parallel passages made in the recitation room. It was the constant aim of the teacher not only to unfold the sense of the Scriptures, but also to show the pupils practically how to make the bible [sic] its own interpreter.'[14]

Ann played an indispensable role in discipling young believers. Where Judson was a linguistic genius, mastering grammar and syntax, Ann was a social magnet, as it were, that attracted language skills. Her language acquisition emerged from her dynamic intuition and lively personality. Other than being the source of their home's warm hospitality, Ann contributed significantly to translating Judson's first tract—*A View of the Christian Religion*[15]—

---

13 Wayland, *A Memoir*, 1:263.

14 'Intelligence from the Missions, Theological Training of Native Pastors', *The Baptist Missionary Magazine* 34 (1854), p. 8.

15 Adoniram Judson, *A View of the Christian Religion in Three Parts: Historic, Didactic, and Preceptive*, 15th ed. (Maulmain: American Baptist Mission Press, 1860).

and her own evangelistic/discipleship tract—The Catechism[16]—into Siamese. Ann's *Catechism* also underwent translations into Talaing (Mon) and Karen. Within eleven years after Ann's death, by 1837, the Judsons' mission station had distributed a copy of the *Catechism* to every family in Rangoon. By 1890, the printing press had printed 273,000 copies of it.

Just as Judson saw the dictionary as indispensable for the ongoing propagation of the Scriptures, he also viewed Bible-based discipleship as the vehicle for the ongoing sustenance and maturity of the indigenous church. Two of his main works for Bible-centered discipleship illustrate his ability to synthesize doctrine for the sake of discipleship: 'A Burman Liturgy' and *A Digest of Scripture*.[17]

Judson's 'A Burman Liturgy' provided doctrines useful for discipleship. Judson prepared this liturgy in 1829 for new missionaries who had not yet learned the language and for his Burmese assistants whom he trained for ministry. Judson's copious devotion to biblical detail influenced his commitment to systematize the biblical commands for the sake of obeying Scripture rightly.

More extensive than his liturgy, Judson's *A Digest of Scripture* is a compendium of doctrinal assertions using the language of Scripture in order to teach the basic doctrines of the Bible. Judson did not write a thorough systematic theology textbook, but he compiled the Scriptural evidence necessary for producing such a larger work. Grounded in the infallibility and sufficiency of the Bible, Judson sought to use the Bible's own language to explain its doctrine. *A Digest of Scripture* exemplifies his conviction of the perspicuity of Scripture and its power to convert and revive the soul. In nearly two hundred pages of biblical text upon text, Judson outlined what he saw as the whole of Scriptural doctrine for the sake of training the church to think and live biblically.[18]

---

16 Ann Judson, *The Catechism* (Rangoon: American Baptist Mission Press, 1909).

17 Wayland, *A Memoir*, pp. 2:467-75; and Adoniram Judson, *A Digest of Scripture, Consisting of Extracts from the Old and New Testaments: On the Plan of 'Brown's Selection of Scripture Passages'* (Maulmain: American Baptist Mission Press, 1838).

18 Judson, *A Digest*, p. i-iv.

Strategic Model 3: The Judsons prioritized proclaiming the Word

Judson contended that gospel proclamation is not comprised only of oral communication, though proclamation is certainly not less than oral communication. Proclamation, moreover, essentially involves distribution of the Scriptures. Judson scolded those who were indifferent to the universal dissemination of the Bible. At the ninth annual meeting of the American and Foreign Bible Society, held May 15, 1846, in New York, Judson gave an address[19] that unpacked his theology of gospel proclamation and his Word-centered piety. Judson argued that the Greek word for *proclaim* has the idea of oral preaching and literature distribution, just as a king's ambassador could proclaim a pardon to the inhabitants of a city through both oral declaration and printed publication, and just as Paul could equally proclaim the gospel through both preaching in the synagogues and publishing gospel truth through his Epistles. Judson's intention was not to demote the power of preaching, but to promote the efficacy of the biblical text.

Judson further explained that when a missionary first goes to a heathen people, the missionary's communication is largely oral; however, 'he will have very imperfectly fulfilled his commission if he leaves them without the written Word.' Judson maintained that such neglect results in the kind of 'mischievous consequences' that are evident in mission stations 'conducted by the Man of Sin,' that is, Roman Catholic missions. He went on to caution that among some Protestant mission stations, there had recently been 'a tendency to promote the oral communication of the gospel, not, indeed, to an undue pre-eminence, but in such a manner as to throw a shade over the written communication by means of tracts and Scriptures.' He argued that though the initial indiscriminate, evangelistic preaching of the gospel and tract distribution might initially seem more successful, 'all missionary operations, to be permanently successful, must be based on the written Word. Where that Word is most regarded and honored, there will be the most pure and permanent success.' He illustrated

---

19 E. Judson, *The Life*, p. 468-76.

that the written 'Word of God is the golden lamp hung out of heaven to enlighten the nations that sit in darkness, and to show them the path that leads from the confines of hell to the gates of paradise.' Judson upheld the Bible, in its original languages, as comprehensively containing all existing revelation from God to the world. The written Word is 'just *the book*, the one book, which Infinite Wisdom saw best adapted to answer the end of a written revelation.' He charged that God entrusted His perfect Word as 'the sacred deposit in the hands of the church.' Judson issued woes to those who deny others to partake in such a treasure and to those who seek to snuff out the light of the gospel of heaven. Judson wished to see the Bible translated and broadcast in every language and to be 'deposited in every palace, and house, and hut inhabited by man.'[20]

Eight years earlier, Judson had uttered similar sentiments in a letter to the American Baptist Board. He said that he had hoped to complete the Bible and deposit it in every village and township across Burma. Though it would require great endurance and much expenditure, once Bibles were positioned in the places of influence and prominence in each town, the seed sown 'would spring up in abundant fruit to his [God's] glory.' He observed that the townspeople would often gather at the houses of the educated leader, whether it be a priest or principal, in each village for the purpose of listening to the leader read from a religious book. Consequently, he said that he sought to introduce and leave the Bible at the chief location in every town in order that the light of the gospel would efficaciously pervade the dark corners of the Burman empire where no missionary could reside.[21]

In the letter, Judson went on to say that Protestant missions of his era differed from Roman Catholic missions by 'honoring and sounding out the Word of God.' He asserted that those missionaries who esteem the proclamation of Scripture higher than any other charitable venture would 'be most owned of God, and blessed with the influence of the Holy Spirit.' Seeking to contextualize by donning priestly garments of a monk, he would refer to an analogy he used

---

20 Wayland, *A Memoir*, 2:235-8. Emphasis in original.
21 E. Judson, *The Life*, pp. 410-11.

for contextualization in evangelism: He likened the Bible to 'only one golden lamp which God has suspended from heaven' to guide sinners heavenward. He warned that missionaries dare not obscure its light by preventing its indiscriminate and universal circulation. He cautioned against perceiving this goal as somehow devaluing the role of gospel preaching, because preaching is 'the grand means instituted by Christ for the conversion of the world.' However, he explained that all evangelism and discipleship 'must be based on the written Word.' Even if the preacher were to move on from a village, the gospel witness would not depart with him, since 'the inspired Word may still remain to convert and to edify.' From his bibliocentric perspective, preaching the gospel and the written Word were inseparable. Together they are, Judson contended, 'the two arms which are to pull down the kingdom of darkness, and build up the Redeemer's. Let us not cut off one of these arms, for the other will by itself be comparatively powerless.' He was convinced that the history of the church testified to the fact that one of these arms alone is powerless without the other.[22]

Publishing the Word

Two very important events marked the year 1816: the arrival of a printing press and the appointment of a professional printer from Philadelphia, George H. Hough (1757–1830), to operate the press. As the strategies and capacity of the mission station developed, their most productive and intensive years were from 1836–1837, during which the mission station, under Judson's visionary leadership, and with the enthusiastic assistance of six indigenous preachers, disseminated over ten million copies of tracts and evangelistic literature in three different languages. The tract distribution teams blanketed Rangoon and the vicinity three times to ensure every family received the literature. Judson would meet every morning with his indigenous evangelists to pray and debrief on the previous day's work, which provided opportunity for constructive feedback and encouragement. By 1839, because of this broad-sowing initiative, several hundred

---

22 Wayland, *A Memoir*, 2:126-7.

were seeking baptism, and only a few years later, the Rangoon mission station recorded 774 Burmese members. Seven years after Judson's death, one village chief said that the study of the Scriptures and tracts, received twenty-two years earlier from Judson himself, had led his whole village to forsake their idolatry.[23]

For Judson, the work of translation, Bible distribution, and proclamation were the chief work of missions, and if a door were shut in one region, he did not agree with employing some other socially acceptable platform for the purpose of staying in that region. Rather, he contended that the missionary ought to continue trying to enter other locations in order to broadcast the Bible to as many people in as many nations as the Lord wills.

Regarding the possibility of expanding translation and literature distribution into China after he had finished his Bible translation, for example, Judson wrote of his passion to see the Bible dispensed in other languages for the conversion of the nations. From his activistic evangelical perspective, there was no other alternative to such missionary work. Because of the indomitability of the proclaimed Word, he said his duty was to scatter gospel seed, letting the Scripture do all the work. He charged: 'But we must all go forward, preaching the gospel, and distributing bibles and tracts in every possible way, and in every language under heaven. If one door is shut up, we must push in at another.'[24]

Translating the Word

Judson admitted that he had a different translation philosophy than many missionaries: 'to ascertain the exact meaning of the *original text*, and to express that meaning as exactly as the nature of the language into which they shall translate.'[25] The labor of many missionaries, he said, had been 'dreadfully misdirected'. He said that it was the duty of

---

[23] Jack McElroy, *Adoniram Judson's Soul Winning Secrets Revealed: An Inspiring Look at the Tools Used by 'Jesus Christ's Man' in Burma* (Shirley, MA: McElroy Publishing, 2013), p. 21-2.

[24] Middleditch, *Burmah's Great Missionary*, p. 312.

[25] Wayland, *A Memoir*, 2:146. Emphasis in original.

a man to spend his whole life to produce 'a *really good* translation', and this required working '*slow* and *sure,* and to see to it that whatever we do, in regard to the inspired Word, is *well done.*'[26] His third and last wife, Emily C. Judson (1817–1854), described him as 'very strenuous about his Burmese version, and would no doubt have persevered in his translation if the whole world had been against him.'[27]

Regarding his work ethic and duty of translation, Judson wanted to express the biblical meaning in a way so accurate and understandable that his translation would need little revision in the future.[28] His eminent biographer, Francis Wayland (1796–1865), claimed that he mastered the Burmese language 'to a degree never before attained by a foreigner.'[29] Though Judson availed himself of the best of exegetical commentaries and scholarship,[30] he would not let the publications of scholars do the work for him. He ever insisted on going to the original biblical texts themselves and only using the critical commentaries as references. Thus, he would not canonize an interpreted verse until he was certain of its meaning in the original language and in the Burmese language.[31] Wayland recorded that a distinguished linguist in India who was an expert in Burmese said of Judson's translation: 'We honor Wycliffe and Luther for their labors in their respective mother tongues; but what meed [sic] of praise is due to Judson for a translation of the Bible, *perfect as a literary work*, in a language so foreign to him as the Burmese?'[32]

Approximately one hundred years after Judson's death, the Burma Christian Council invited the Prime Minister of Burma, U Nu (1907–1965), to attend a tea. The Christian leaders were discussing whether to publish a new Burmese Bible translation. U Nu, though a devout Buddhist, was quite familiar with the Christian Scriptures (i.e., Judson's

---

26 E. Judson, *The Life,* pp. 405-6. Emphasis in original.

27 E. Judson, *The Life,* p. 408.

28 Wayland, *A Memoir,* 2:165.

29 Wayland, *A Memoir,* 2:165.

30 Wayland, *A Memoir,* 2:166.

31 Wayland, *A Memoir,* 2:161-3.

32 Wayland, *A Memoir,* 2:167.

translation), and he retorted, 'Oh, no, a new translation of the Bible is not necessary. Judson's translation captures the language and idiom of Burmese perfectly and is very clear and understandable.'[33]

Preaching the Word

Adoniram and Ann were at times tempted to despair for lack of noticeable 'success' in their proclamation and translation efforts. Francis Wayland established how Adoniram and Ann valued the preaching of the gospel in missions as opposed to doing other 'fruitful' ministries, albeit good ones, which seemed to bring in more immediate 'fruit'. Wayland said that the letters of the Judsons never suggested regrets or doubts about the seeming fruitlessness of their labor. They did, however, indicate their concern that their friends in the States would grow weary of their lack of perceived success. Wayland said that Adoniram and Ann's letters expressed 'entire certainty' about the ultimate success of their work, though they might not see it till glory. He commented: 'Their confidence rested solely and exclusively on the Word of God ... relying not at all on what they could do, but wholly on what God had promised to do for them.'[34]

Though famous for his labor of love in translation, Judson was a preacher at heart. His desire to see the gospel preached drove him to translate the Bible from which the missionary must preach. For Judson, preaching the gospel was ultimately 'the great business of his life'.[35] He gave himself to translation because he believed God's providence ordained such a responsibility to him and because the American Baptist Board requested it.[36] Wayland recorded that whenever Judson's translation work intermitted, he would go to the *zayat* and preach heartily,[37] which one colleague, Justus Vinton (1806–1858), described

---

33 Russell E. Brown, 'The Life and Work of Adoniram Judson', *Andover Newton Quarterly* 2, no. 3 (1962): p. 24.

34 Wayland, *A Memoir*, 1:205-6.

35 Wayland, *A Memoir*, 2:97.

36 Wayland, *A Memoir*, 2:122.

37 Wayland, *A Memoir*, 2:97. Judson's biographer, Robert Middleditch (1825–1907), described the *zayat* as follows: 'It was divided in three parts. The first division, which was one third of the whole, was open to the road, and set apart for occupancy

thus: 'Every tone, every look, every sentence, spoke out in the most emphatic language, to tell us that the man was seriously in earnest, and himself believed the truths he uttered.'[38]

At the close of 1827, Judson's journal entries describe the mission's proclamation efforts under his leadership. He recorded a few strategies 'for the spread of truth': First, they met for public worship every Sunday at 10:30 in the morning, and the assembly numbered between twenty and seventy. Attendees included the missionaries, Buddhist scholars, native converts, truth-seekers, and occasional travelers. During the public meeting, they would sing songs of adoration and praise, followed by a casual extemporaneous homily, which depended upon the nature of those gathered each time. Then the assembly would finally close in prayer. Though some would leave right afterwards, many would remain and engage in religious discussions for a significant amount of time. Second, they would practice regular evening worship. This was more of a gathering for the mission families, the scholars, and the local Christians. Approximately twenty people gathered for the daily evening worship. They would begin by reading Scripture, and an explanation and exhortation would follow. After concluding in prayer, Judson would spend the remainder of the evening with the new converts and host 'instructive and profitable' conversations based on the Scripture. The next day he would reason from the Scriptures in the *zayat* with any truth-seekers who had attended the night before.[39]

Strategic Model 4: The Judsons rested in the infallible Word

Adoniram and Ann were convinced that the Bible, whether printed or preached, was an infallible evangelist. As such, they believed that the most faithful missionary strategy had to pattern itself after the model of the apostles in Acts who went about scattering the seed of

---

by Mr. Judson, for conversation with passers-by. The more central division was made entirely of boards, being intended for worship on the Sabbath, and for a school conducted by Mrs. Judson during the week. The third division was a sort of entry-way to the mission-house, situated in the rear and facing on another road.' Middleditch, *Burmah's Great Missionary*, p. 122.

38 Wayland, *A Memoir*, 2:388-9.

39 Middleditch, *Burmah's Great Missionary*, pp. 240-1.

the Word. In order to see the power of God in missionary activity, the missionary must heed this pattern. Consequently, the Judsons sought to seize every opportunity in conversations with individuals to implore them to be reconciled to God in light of the love of Christ.[40] Since God blessed the apostles' obedience to Christ's final command, the Judsons devoted themselves to keep the proclamation of the Word central to their missionary activity.[41]

Many missionaries considered the Burmese men too impenetrable to reach with the gospel, so they opened schools for the native children in order to educate them from a civilized Western worldview. They started with proclaiming the gospel, but after many setbacks, they opted for more humanitarian ministries and social work.[42] Adoniram, however, spent himself to evangelize instead of using other reputable social and educational platforms because he believed in the transforming power of the Word. Moreover, Judson was adamantly 'opposed to large missionary stations'[43] because he believed they became self-absorbed and unfruitful. Mission stations would distract missionaries from their devotion to God's work, and they would inevitably spend themselves on 'indirect, subsidiary, and questionable modes of effort, such as indoor labor, school teaching, English preaching, bookmaking—things in themselves good, but not distinctively missionary.'[44] Even further illustrating the Judsons' convictions, in one of her early letters in August 1817 to a friend, Ann Judson described the depravity of the Burmese hearts and illustrated how the Judsons viewed human depravity, which led them to the conviction that gospel proclamation is fundamental for conversion.[45] Even in his last year of life, Adoniram's commitment remained to

---

40 Wayland, *A Memoir*, 1:206-7.

41 Wayland, *A Memoir*, 2:167.

42 Wayland, *A Memoir*, 1:205-8.

43 Wayland, *A Memoir*, 2:96.

44 Wayland, *A Memoir*, 2:96-7.

45 Ann Hasseltine Judson, *An Account of the American Baptist Mission to the Burman Empire: In a Series of Letters, Addressed to a Gentleman in London* (London: J. Butterworth & Son and T. Clark, 1823), pp. 97-102.

preaching the gospel instead of educating natives in English schools and teaching English civility.'[46]

Strategic Model 5: The Judsons employed Bible-centered apologetics

Judson resolutely upheld the Bible as the supreme fountain of truth in evangelism and discipleship. A Buddhist teacher, Moung Shwa-gnong, was debating with Judson about the validity of the Christian gospel, and he told Judson that he could not adhere to a religion whose king would allow his son to undergo such humiliation. Judson's account of the controversy exemplifies his unswerving allegiance to the Bible, and it illustrates his own evangelistic method of Bible-based apologetics. After much debate over some tracts and the Gospel of Matthew, Judson said in direct terms that the Buddhist teacher was not a true disciple of Christ. Judson reasoned: 'A true disciple inquires not whether a fact is agreeable to his own reason, but, whether it is in the book. His pride has yielded to divine testimony. Teacher, your pride is still unbroken. Break down your pride, and yield to the Word of God.' Subsequently, the teacher later replied that he saw the error of trusting in his reason alone. He confessed his belief in Christ's crucifixion 'because it is contained in the Scripture.'[47] To Judson, this was a sign of new life because it demonstrated spiritual awakening to the revelation of the Scriptures.

Judson valued the written Word so much that he refused to 'waste' tracts by just handing them out without the recipients demonstrating interest. In 1831, he had given away ten thousand tracts, but only to those who requested them. People traveled for three months from Siam and China and from a hundred miles north of the capitol because they had heard that Judson was the man who gave away writings about how to escape the eternal hell. They asked him, 'Are you Jesus Christ's man? Give us a writing that tells about Jesus Christ.'[48]

---

46 Wayland, *A Memoir*, 2:317-19.

47 Jesse Clement, *Memoir of Adoniram Judson, Being a Sketch of His Life and Missionary Labors* (Auburn, NY: Derby and Miller, 1851), pp. 83-4.

48 Middleditch, *Burmah's Great Missionary*, pp. 273-4.

Of all Judson's tracts and literature, *The Golden Balance* interacted the most with the Buddhist worldview.[49] In this tract he compared and contrasted Christianity and Buddhism, demonstrating which religion is true based upon the most excellent aspects of each religion. For instance, he would ask and then answer some questions such as these: Which religion has the more excellent God? Is not Jesus Christ more excellent than Gautama? Which religion has the more excellent law? Which religion has the more excellent Scriptures? He would say that the most excellent and most supreme of each category would underscore which religion is true, for both cannot be true because they are mutually exclusive.[50] The distribution of this tract (100,000 copies) during 1836–1837 by Judson's Burmese disciples proved to be pivotal for their mission efforts, arousing interest among hundreds of Burmese to regularly visit the mission station to hear Judson and his Burmese protégés preach.

Concluding missiological applications for Missionary-Theologians

In the twenty-first century when more people are educated and yet more are simultaneously distracted by social media than ever before, our remaining task of proclaiming the written Word and making disciples of all *ethnē* is daunting. Though we have the providential blessings of immunizations, vaccinations, jet travel, and instantaneous communication, the geopolitical and cultural shifts in our day are just as unpredictable and volatile as nineteenth-century Burma. The Judsons never knew when a fever might claim their lives or a xenophobic monarch might imprison them on false charges, so they sought to impress upon the Burmese people that the written Word is the golden lamp from heaven, which indeed would serve as the timeless source of eternal truth for the people even after the Judsons were gone.

In terms of missiological strategies, we might differ in how we adapt culturally, learn languages, and establish relationships, but

---

49 Adoniram Judson, *The Golden Balance*, 6th ed. (Maulmain: American Baptist Mission Press, 1836).

50 Judson, *The Golden Balance*.

the long-lasting, life-producing power is neither in our pragmatic methods nor our unique strategies. As the Judsons would contend, the life-creating power is in the seed, the written Word; when we uphold the dissemination of the Word—whether through speaking or writing—as sufficient and central, then we can rest, knowing that the Vinedresser is in control and will cultivate His vineyard in His time, in His way.

Let us consider, finally, the witness of Adoniram Judson to the faithful work of God through His written Word. The Judsons knew that the planting of the seed of the Word of God would prove to be a slow growth, and they were not naïve to the gradual cultivation of that seed. Sensing dissatisfaction among supporters back home because of the Judsons' perceived lack of results, Adoniram pushed back in a letter and defended the slow growth of sowing the Word: 'If they ask again, what prospect of ultimate success is there?—tell them, as much as there is an Almighty and faithful God who will perform his promises, and no more.'[51]

This chapter has shown that the supreme and sufficient Word was the burning and shining golden lamp from heaven that guided the Judsons' mission strategies. For Adoniram and Ann, the biblical message was a summons from the King that demanded earnest proclamation through oral preaching, translation, publication, and dissemination. Allegiance to Christ's command to be baptized was the first step of assurance of genuine conversion. Seeking to honor the Word of Christ, the Judsons went 'forward, preaching the gospel, and distributing bibles [sic] and tracts in every possible way, and in every language under heaven.'[52]

---

51 Adoniram Judson, 'Extract of a Letter from Mr Judson to Mr. Rice, Rangoon, August 3d, 1816', *The Baptist Missionary Magazine* 1 (1817): p. 184.

52 Middleditch, *Burmah's Great Missionary*, p. 312.

CONCLUSION

THIS book has sought to argue for the happy union between the discipline of theology and the practice of missions, yet always expressed out of gratitude for the sovereign grace of God in the person and work of Christ alone to save us and commission us for such an honorable task. I have argued that, because of our righteous standing and union with Christ and because of His reign over the nations, when the Holy Spirit propels Bible-centrality that mobilizes the heart, instructs the mind, and consecrates the life of the missionary to Christ, fruit-bearing in mission will inevitably result. Out of a trusting gratitude to Christ for His substitutionary, redeeming grace alone, received by faith alone, *to the degree that missionaries lead with the Christ-centered Word, are directed by the Christ-centered Word, experience God through the Christ-centered Word, and impress upon people the sufficiency of the Christ-centered Word, to that degree are they faithfully following Christ as He establishes His church among all the nations. Jesus is the true Missionary; proclaiming His Word is the method, through the means of His Spirit.*

The first chapter made a case for the doctrine of Christian righteousness being the source of strength and sanctifying power of the missionary. The second chapter grounded the missionary mandate and subjective/objective missionary call in the Word of God; the third chapter outlined the centrality of prayer and the pursuit of Word-centered godliness for the missionary; the fourth chapter argued that the missionary should devoutly immerse himself in the biblical text so that his ministry philosophy and methods are theologically sound; the fifth chapter highlighted how to theologically consider the challenges and opportunities of partnering with sending churches;

the sixth chapter made a case for leading, serving, and partnering with the global church in a way that is biblically faithful, theologically helpful, and relationally sensitive; the seventh chapter discussed how a missionary-theologian should consider modeling the role of a Bible-centered shepherd and not overstepping his authority; the eighth chapter demonstrated how the missionary should and can be a courageous apologist that neither compromises the gospel nor unnecessarily accommodates the worldviews of the target culture; and the ninth chapter is a historical and academic synthesis of Adoniram and Ann Judson's Word-centered missionary models.

The Pauline example set forth throughout his doctrinal writings and in his persistent missionary lifestyle should challenge missionaries and missionary-senders to evaluate the degree to which the Bible and theology actively control their minds, motives, and methods. As Paul exemplified in writing Romans as a kind of missionary support letter for going to Spain, missiology and theology are true friends that could do more together than apart.

A true missionary burns with passion for the nations because of the revelation he sees in the pages of Scripture, not merely because of an experience or an impression he once had; a true theologian rejoices in the unbreakable promises of God littered across the pages of the Bible and thus longs for God to be worshiped among all the *ethnē*, and he does not merely find the Bible stimulating for study and intriguing as a literary masterpiece. A theologian that cares little for the gospel to run and triumph among the nations is out of touch with the God of the Bible whom he claims to know and study; a missionary who belittles theology because he claims it quenches the Holy Spirit and limits God is dangerous to the souls of men and should not be entrusted with the sacred gospel and the missionary mantle. Show me a man with grit, who rests in Christ's work, abides in Christ's Word, set apart by his church, with a Bible open in hand, on his knees in prayer, with the nations in his sights, and the honor of Christ pulsing through his desires; then I will show you a missionary who is consecrated, competent, trustworthy, rightly handling the Word of truth, approved unto God, and has no need to be ashamed.

If our chief aim, as missionary-theologians, is to honor Christ, out of gratitude for the gospel, would it not be appropriate to remind

CONCLUSION

ourselves what is most pleasing to Him? Adoniram Judson said it this way:

> If any of you enter the Gospel ministry in this or other lands, let not your object be so much to 'do your duty,' or even to 'save souls,' though these should have a place in your motives, as to *please the Lord Jesus*. Let this be your ruling motive in all that you do. Now, do you ask, *how* you shall please Him? How, indeed, shall we know what will please Him but by *His commands*? Obey these commands and you will not fail to please Him. And there is that 'last command,' given just before He ascended to the Father, 'Go ye into all the World, and preach the Gospel to every creature.'[1] It is not yet obeyed as it should be. Fulfill that, and you will please the Saviour.[2]

Since pleasing Christ is heeding His final departing words, namely, the Great Commission, and since making disciples who are students of Christ is core to the Great Commission, the work of missions requires missionaries who are sold out, never-turning-back, and self-denying in their pursuit of the Word of God, out of gratitude for the grace of God. We must immerse ourselves in the Word in order to teach it accurately and compellingly to the nations yet undiscipled.

May God be pleased to raise up a new generation passionate for the Book, devoted to the Great Commission, in happy submission to the sovereignty of Christ, and ready to go wherever and whenever and do the next thing. May we be soldiers of the cross and heralds of the Book, courageous to say all that it says and humble to say no more. Sent into the world. Sanctified by the Word.

> *'For a long time I felt much depressed after preaching the unsearchable riches of Christ to apparently insensible hearts; but now I like to dwell on the love of the great Mediator, for it always warms my heart, and I know that the gospel is the power of God—the great means which he employs for the regeneration of our ruined world.'*
>
> —DAVID LIVINGSTONE

---

1. Mark 16:15 (KJV).

2. Edward Judson, *The Life of Adoniram Judson, By His Son, Edward Judson* (New York: A.D.F. Randolph & Co., 1883), pp. 473-4; Wayland, *A Memoir*, 2:234-5. Emphases in original.

APPENDIX 1

THE MISSIONARY LIFE: NO SHORTCUTS[1]

By E.D. Burns

WHAT would you say to a budding missionary candidate? I have a close friend who is a veteran pastor, missionary, and now a member care director in the city in which I serve. He says there has been a surge of young adults in recent years who have landed on the field, enthusiastic to redeem the city and bring justice to the oppressed, but they do not stay longer than two years due to exhaustion, dejection, and even loss of faith. The member care workers call this the 'radical effect'—young adults, with bleeding hearts, seeking to do something radical for Jesus and the world, who do not follow through with their initial impulse. Often the prospects of formal theological training prior to going to the field seem so irrelevant and demotivating. Shortcutting formal training is easier.

Recently I thought of a number of words of advice that I would give a missionary candidate, knowing what I know now about the missionary life. Here are two of the points that I would share. They are basic; or at least, they *should* be basic:

Doctrine Matters

First, little did I suspect that some of the greatest battles for biblical truth would not only be with Muslims, Atheists, and Buddhists, but

---

1. This article was originally published by the author on 5 December 2014 at The Gospel Coalition: 'The Missionary Life: No Shortcuts', *The Gospel Coalition* (5 December 2014), https://www.thegospelcoalition.org/article/the-missionary-life-no-shortcuts/

with others who claimed to be serving Christ alongside me. In my experience of many years overseas, the battle lines have been drawn on issues such as the inerrancy and sufficiency of Scripture, the extent and the intent of God's special revelation, the nature and the mission of the church, the message and the means of gospel proclamation, the biblical qualifications of elders, the sovereignty of God and the lordship of Christ, and the nature of the unregenerate and regenerate heart. I began to observe an unspoken a-theological *ethos* in the missions world, and indeed, in many cases, theological minimalism reigns. Mobilization efforts of would-be missionaries often focus on the prospects of exciting cultures, idealistic passions, immediate needs, and creative platforms; whole mission teams commonly unite around such emphases. The doctrine of choice is often pragmatism: 'if it works, then it must be true.' Doctrinal distinctives are usually the least common denominator. In our urgency, there is an impatience for the slow work of sowing seed and the even slower work of training up biblically qualified indigenous elders. The need-for-speed and result-driven methods commonly shortcut the tiresome labor of training local pastors to be mighty in the Scriptures. Yet, our missionary methodology always reveals our theology, or lack thereof. For instance, a deficient view of Scripture leaves it unused and/or misused in evangelism and discipleship; defective views of depravity and regeneration employ methods of 'reaching' people that do not command repentance and submission to Christ's kingship; and, errant ecclesiology leads to teaching professing converts that they neither have to leave their religious structures nor forsake their religious texts.

Eckhard Schnabel helpfully explains:

> Missionaries, evangelists and teachers who have understood both the scandal of the cross and the irreplaceable and foundational significance of the news of Jesus the crucified and risen Messiah and Savior will not rely on strategies, models, methods or techniques. They rely on the presence of God when they proclaim Jesus Christ, and on the effective power of the Holy Spirit. This dependence on God rather than on methods liberates them from following every new fad, from using only one particular method, from using always the same

techniques, and from copying methods and techniques from others whose ministry is deemed successful.[2]

We must heed the appeal 'to contend for the faith that was once for all delivered to the saints' (Jude 3). One of the enemy's oldest tricks is to coax us to let our guard down and assume the gospel. When the hard edges of gospel doctrine are assumed, they are quickly forgotten; the mission, then, is aborted.

Pain is Part of the Plan

Second, I grew up with a health disability that would have prevented me from ever going to college, obtaining a job, or living a long, normal life. Before God mercifully delivered me from it, he graciously delivered me through it. Many days and nights, I lay in the darkness of my room in much pain and nausea, praying in the silence that God would give me the sustaining grace to preach the gospel to the nations. I started pre-seminary at the age of five when God sent me my wisest and most influential teacher: Affliction. Through his loving discipline, God taught me about his sovereign goodness and inscrutable wisdom.

Having grown up facing much affliction, and having learned well the theology of suffering under a sovereign God, I still was naïve to how unrelenting and inexplicable are the trials of the missionary life. If it were not for the doctrine of God's wise sovereignty in suffering, I would never have made it. Long-term missions can indeed be a place of excitement and adventure; however, it is inescapably a place of adversity and barrenness. It is moreover the land of self-emptying: learning to laugh at yourself; learning to think, feel, dream, and reason in a foreign language; learning to enjoy the adopted family of Christ in light of distant relationships back home; learning to keep silent in the face of stiff criticism from those who once supported you; learning to eat the Word of God as your daily food; learning to pray for your wife and children because their lives literally depend upon it; and learning to navigate wisely on the path of self-denial amidst a global culture immersed in self-indulgence, self-promotion, and self-preservation.

---

2. Eckhard Schnabel, *Paul the Missionary: Realities, Strategies and Methods* (Downers Grove, IL: InterVarsity Press, 2008), p. 404.

I would soberly admonish any missionary candidate that the mission field is not all romance and radical adventure; it is also mingled with heartbreak, loss, and self-denial. But therein we discover God's boundless love and wise providence. C.S. Lewis said, 'The pains You give me are more precious than all other gains.'[3] God loves his servants so much that he allows them to suffer, so that his grace would sustain them in order to make his glory known. Our weakness is the God-ordained instrument through which the Holy Spirit fills us with the power of Christ. When we embrace our weakness and inadequacy, then we know that any good that comes from us is because of Christ.

D.A. Carson says it best:

> The more the leaders are afflicted with weakness, suffering, perplexity, and persecution, the more it is evident that their vitality is nothing other than the life of Jesus. This has enormously positive spiritual effects on the rest of the church. The leaders' death means the church's life. This is why the best Christian leadership cannot simply be appointed. It is forged by God himself in the fires of suffering, taught in the school of tears. There are no shortcuts.[4]

---

3. C.S. Lewis, 'As the Ruin Falls', in *Poems* (1st pub., 1964), p. 110.

4. D.A. Carson, *How Long, O Lord?: Reflections on Suffering and Evil* (Grand Rapids: Baker Academic, 2006), p. 81.

APPENDIX 2

ADVICE TO MISSIONARY CANDIDATES[1]
By Adoniram Judson

To the Foreign Missionary Association of the
Hamilton Literary and Theological Institution, N.Y.

DEAR BRETHREN: Yours of November last, from the pen of your Corresponding Secretary, Mr. William Dean, is before me. It is one of the few letters that I feel called upon to answer, for you ask my advice on several important points. There is, also, in the sentiments you express, something so congenial to my own, that I feel my heart knit to the members of your association, and instead of commonplace reply, am desirous of setting down a few items which may be profitable to you in your future course. Brief items they must be, for want of time forbids my expatiating.

In commencing my remarks, I take you as you are. You are contemplating a missionary life.

First, then, let it be a missionary *life*; that is, come out for life, and not for a limited term. Do not fancy that you have a true missionary spirit, while you are intending all along to leave the heathen soon after acquiring their language. Leave them! for what? To spend the rest of your days in enjoying the ease and plenty of your native land?

Secondly. In choosing a companion for life, have particular regard to a good constitution, and not wantonly, or without good cause, bring a burden on yourselves and the mission.

---

1. E. Judson, *The Life*, Appendix D.

Thirdly. Be not ravenous to do good on board ship. Missionaries have frequently done more hurt than good, by injudicious zeal, during their passage out.

Fourthly. Take care that the attention you receive at home, the unfavorable circumstances in which you will be placed on board ship, and the unmissionary examples you may possibly meet with at some missionary stations, do not transform you from living missionaries to mere skeletons before you reach the place of your destination. It may be profitable to bear in mind, that a large proportion of those who come out on a mission to the East die within five years after leaving their native land. Walk softly, therefore; death is narrowly watching your steps.

Fifthly. Beware of the reaction which will take place soon after reaching your field of labor. There you will perhaps find native Christians, of whose merits or demerits you can not judge correctly without some familiar acquaintance with their language. Some appearances will combine to disappoint and disgust you. You will meet with disappointments and discouragements, of which it is impossible to form a correct idea from written accounts, and which will lead you, at first, almost to regret that you have embarked in the cause. You will see men and women whom you have been accustomed to view through a telescope some thousands of miles long. Such an instrument is apt to magnify. Beware, therefore, of the reaction you will experience from a combination of all these causes, lest you become disheartened at commencing your work, or take up a prejudice against some persons and places, which will embitter all your future lives.

Sixthly. Beware of the greater reaction which will take place after you have acquired the language, and become fatigued and worn out with preaching the gospel to a disobedient and gainsaying people. You will sometimes long for a quiet retreat, where you can find a respite from the tug of toiling at native work—the incessant, intolerable friction of the missionary grindstone. And Satan will sympathize with you in this matter; and he will present some chapel of ease, in which to officiate in your native tongue, some government situation, some professorship or editorship, some literary or scientific pursuit, some supernumerary translation, or, at least, some system of schools;

anything, in a word, that will help you, without much surrender of character, to slip out of real missionary work. Such a temptation will form the crisis of your disease. If your spiritual constitution can sustain it, you recover; if not, you die.

Seventhly. Beware of pride; not the pride of proud men, but the pride of humble men—that secret pride which is apt to grow out of the consciousness that we are esteemed by the great and good. This pride sometimes eats out the vitals of religion before its existence is suspected. In order to check its operations, it may be well to remember how we appear in the sight of God, and how we should appear in the sight of our fellow-men, if all were known. Endeavor to let all be known. Confess your faults freely, and as publicly as circumstances will require or admit. When you have done something of which you are ashamed, and by which, perhaps, some person has been injured (and what man is exempt?), be glad not only to make reparation, but improve the opportunity for subduing your pride.

Eighthly. Never lay up money for yourselves or your families. Trust in God from day to day, and verily you shall be fed.

Ninthly. Beware of that indolence which leads to a neglect of bodily exercise. The poor health and premature death of most Europeans in the East must be eminently ascribed to the most wanton neglect of bodily exercise.

Tenthly. Beware of genteel living. Maintain as little intercourse as possible with fashionable European society. The mode of living adopted by many missionaries in the East is quite inconsistent with that familiar intercourse with the natives which is essential to a missionary.

There are many points of self-denial that I should like to touch upon; but a consciousness of my own deficiency constrains me to be silent. I have also left untouched several topics of vital importance, it having been my aim to select such only as appear to me to have been not much noticed or enforced. I hope you will excuse the monitorial style that I have accidentally adopted.

I assure you, I mean no harm.

In regard to your inquiries concerning studies, qualifications, etc., nothing occurs that I think would be particularly useful, except the simple remark, that I fear too much stress begins to be laid on what is termed a thorough classical education.

Praying that you may be guided in all your deliberations, and that I may yet have the pleasure of welcoming some of you to these heathen shores, I remain

>Your affectionate brother,
>
>A. JUDSON
>Maulmain, June 25, 1832

APPENDIX 3

THE MISSIONARIES' CHARGE AND CHARTER

NO. 383

A SERMON DELIVERED ON SUNDAY MORNING,
APRIL 21, 1861

BY REV. C.H. SPURGEON

AT THE METROPOLITAN TABERNACLE, NEWINGTON.[1]

> 'And Jesus came and spake unto them, saying,
> All power is given unto me in heaven and in earth;
> go ye, therefore, and teach all nations, baptizing them in
> the name of the Father, and of the Son, and of the Holy Ghost.'
> MATTHEW 28:18-19 (KJV).

WHILE I was meditating in private upon this text, I felt myself carried away by its power. I was quite unable to calmly consider its terms or to investigate its argument. The *command* with which the text concludes repeated itself again, and again, and again in my ears, till I found it impossible to study, for my thoughts were running hither and thither, asking a thousand questions, all of them intended to help me in answering for myself the solemn inquiry, 'How am *I* to go, and teach *all* nations, baptizing them in the name of the Father, and of the Son, and of the Holy Ghost?'

---

1. See Charles Spurgeon, Sermon #383, *Metropolitan Tabernacle Pulpit*, Volume 7, http://www.spurgeongems.org/vols7-9/chs383.pdf.

The practical lesson seemed to me to overwhelm in my mind the argument of which that lesson is but a conclusion, 'Go ye and teach all nations.' My ears seemed to hear it as if Christ were then speaking it *to me*. I could realize His presence by my side. I thought I could see Him lift His pierced hands, and hear Him speak, as He was known to speak, with authority, blended with meekness, 'Go ye and teach all nations, baptizing them in the name of the All-glorious God.'

Oh, I would that the church could hear the Savior addressing these words to her now, for the words of Christ are living words, not having power in them yesterday alone, but today also. The injunctions of the Savior are perpetual in their obligation, they were not binding upon merely apostles, but upon *us* also, and upon every Christian does this yoke fall, 'Go ye therefore, and teach all nations, baptizing them in the name of the Father, and of the Son, and of the Holy Ghost.' We are not exempt today from the service of the first followers of the Lamb, our marching orders are the same as theirs, and our Captain requires from us obedience as prompt and perfect as from them. Oh, that His message may not fall upon deaf ears, or be heard by uninterested souls!

Brethren, the heathen are perishing, shall we *let* them perish? *His* name is blasphemed, shall we be quiet and still? The honor of Christ is cast into the dust, and His foes revile His person and resist His throne, shall we His soldiers suffer this, and not find our hands feeling for the hilt of our sword, the sword of the Spirit, which is the Word of God? Our Lord delays His coming, shall we begin to sleep, or to eat, or to be drunken? Shall we not rather gird up the loins of our mind, and cry unto Him, 'Come, Lord Jesus, come quickly'?

The scoffing skeptics of these last days have said that the anticipated conquest of the world for Christ is but a dream, or an ambitious thought, which crossed our leader's mind, but which never is to be accomplished. It is asserted by some that the superstitions of the heathen are too strong to be battered down by our teachings, and that the strongholds of Satan are utterly impregnable against our attacks. Shall it be so? Shall we be content to foolishly sit still?

Nay, rather let us work out the problem, let us prove the promise of God to be true, let us prove the words of Jesus to be words of soberness, let us show the efficacy of His blood, and the invincibility of His Spirit by going in the spirit of faith, teaching all nations, and winning them to the obedience of Christ our Lord.

I do not know how to begin to preach this morning, but still it seems to me, standing here, as if *I* heard that voice saying, 'Go ye therefore, and teach all nations.' And my soul sometimes pants and longs for the liberty to preach Christ where He was never preached before, not to build upon another man's foundation, but to go to some untrodden land, some waste where the foot of Christ's minister was never seen, that there 'the solitary place might be glad for us, and the wilderness rejoice and blossom as the rose.'

I have made it a solemn question whether I might not testify in China or India the grace of Jesus, and in the sight of God I have answered it. I solemnly feel that my position in England will not permit my leaving the sphere in which I now am, or else tomorrow I would offer myself as a missionary. Oh, do none of you hear the call this morning?

You who are free from so great a work as that which is cast upon me—you who have talents as yet undevoted to any special end, and powers of being as yet unconsecrated to any given purpose, and unconfined to any one sphere? Do you not hear my Master saying, in tones of plaintive sorrow, blended with an authority which is not to be denied, 'Go ye therefore, and teach all nations, baptizing them in the name of the Father, and of the Son, and of the Holy Ghost'?

Oh, that I could preach like Peter the Hermit—a better crusade than he! Oh, that there were might in some human lips to move the thousands of our Israel to advance at once, unanimously and irresistibly to the world's conquest, like one tremendous tide rising from the depths of the ocean, to sweep over the sands, the barren sands which are now given up to desolation and death! Oh, that once again the voice of thunder could be heard, and the lightning spirit could penetrate each heart, that as one man the entire church might take the marching orders of her Lord, and go teach all nations, baptizing them in the name of Israel's God!

O Lord, if *we* fail to speak, fail not You to speak. And if we know not how to bear Your burden, or express Your amazing thoughts, yet speak You with that all-constraining silent voice which well-trained ears can hear, and make Your servants obedient to You now, for Christ's sake!

THE MISSIONARY-THEOLOGIAN

'Awake, Thou Spirit, who of old
Didst fire the watchman of the church's youth,
Who faced the foe, unshrinking, bold,
Who witness'd day and night the eternal truth,
Whose voices through the world are ringing still,
And bringing hosts to know and do Thy will.

Oh, that Thy fire were kindled soon,
That swift from land to land its flame might leap!
Lord, give us but this priceless boon
Of faithful servants, fit for Thee to reap.
The harvest of the soul; look down and view
How great the harvest, yet the laborers few.

Oh, haste to help ere we are lost!
Send forth evangelists, in spirit strong,
Arm'd with Thy Word, a dauntless host,
Bold to attack the rule of ancient wrong;
And let them all the earth for Thee reclaim,
To be Thy kingdom and to know Thy name.'

This morning, we shall first dwell a little while upon the *command*, and then secondly, we shall enlarge upon the *argument*. There is an argument, as you will perceive, 'Go ye *therefore* , and teach all nations.'

I. First, my brethren and very briefly indeed, a few things about the COMMAND.

And we must remark, first, what a singularly loving one it is. Imagine Mohammed on his dying bed saying to his disciples, 'All power is given unto me in heaven and in earth,' what would be his command? 'Go ye, therefore, with sharp scimitars, and propound faith in the prophet, or death as the dread alternative, avenge me of the men who threw stones at the prophet, make their houses a dunghill, and cut them in pieces, for vengeance is mine, and God's prophet *must* be avenged of his enemies.'

But Christ, though far more despised and persecuted of men, and having a real power which that pretended prophet never had, says to

His disciples, as He is about to ascend to heaven, 'All power is given unto me in heaven and in earth. Go ye therefore, and teach all nations, baptizing them in the name of the Father, and of the Son, and of the Holy Ghost.' It is the voice of love, not of wrath. 'Go and teach them the power of My blood to cleanse, the willingness of My arms to embrace, the yearning of My heart to save!

'*Go and teach them.* Teach them no more to despise Me, no more to think My Father an angry and implacable Deity. Teach them to "bow the knee, and kiss the Son," and find peace for all their troubles, and a balm for all their woes in Me. Go speak as I have spoken, weep as I have wept, invite as I have invited, exhort, entreat, beseech and pray, as I have done before you. Tell them to come unto Me, if they be weary and heavy laden, and *I* will give them rest. And say unto them, "I have no pleasure in the death of him that dies, but had rather that he should turn unto me and live." What a generous and gracious command is that of the text, "Go ye, therefore, and teach all nations, baptizing them in the name of the Father, and of the Son, and of the Holy Ghost."'

Note, too, how exceedingly plain is the command 'Go ye, *teach* all nations.' The Romish church has misunderstood this. She says, 'Go ye, mystify all nations, sound in their ears a language once living, but now dead, take to them the Latin tongue, and let that be sounded with all the harmony of sweet music, and they will be converted. Erect the sumptuous altar, clothe the priest in mystic garments, celebrate mysterious rites, and make the heathen wonder, dazzle them with splendor, amaze them with mystery.'

But 'Nay,' says Christ, 'nay, go ye and *teach.*' Why, it is the mother's work with her child. It is the tutor's work with the boy and with the girl, 'Go ye, and teach.' How simple! Illustrate, explain, expound, tell, inform, narrate. Take from them the darkness of ignorance, reveal to them the light of revelation. Teach! Be content to sit down, and tell them the very plainest and most common things. It is not your eloquence that shall convert them, it is not your gaudy language or your polished periods that shall sway their intellects. Go and teach them.

Teach them! Why, my hearer, I say again, this is a word which has to do with the rudiments of knowledge. We do not preach to children, we teach them, and we are not so much to preach to nations, that word seems too big and great for the uncivilized and childish people. Go ye, and teach them first the very simplicities of the cross of Christ.

And note how He puts it next. Who are to be taught? 'Go ye and teach *all nations*.' The Greek has his philosophers, teach *him*, he is but a child, he is a fool, though he thinks himself to be wise. There be polite nations which have a literature of their own, far larger and more extensive than the literature of the Christian, teach them, nevertheless, they are to be *taught*, and unless they are willing to take the learner's place, and to become as little children, they can in no wise enter into the kingdom of heaven.

Do not debate and argue with them, put not yourself with them upon their level as a combatant concerning certain dogmas, insist upon it that *I* have sent you—sent you to teach the most erudite and profoundly learned, and when you shall claim it, I am with you always to back your claim, and men shall be willing to sit at your feet to be taught the name of Jesus.

I do not know whether *all* our missionaries have caught the idea of Christ, 'Go ye and *teach* all nations,' but many of them have, and these have been honored with many conversions. The more fully they have been simple teachers, not philosophers of the Western philosophy, not eager disputants concerning some English dogma, I say the more plainly they have gone forth as teachers sent from God to teach the world, the more successful have they been. 'Go ye, therefore, and teach.'

Some may think, perhaps, there is less difficulty in teaching the learned than in teaching the uncivilized and barbarous. There is the same duty to the one as to the other, 'Go and teach.' 'But they brandish the tomahawk.' Teach them, and lie down and sleep in their hut, and they shall marvel at your fearlessness and spare your life. 'But they feed on the blood of their fellows, they make a bloody feast about the cauldron in which a man's body is the horrible menu.' *Teach* them, and they shall empty their war kettle, and they shall bury their swords, and bow before you, and acknowledge King Jesus. 'But they are brutalized, they scarcely have a language—a few clicking sounds make up all that they can say.' Teach them, and they shall speak the language of Canaan, and sing the songs of heaven.

APPENDIX 3

The fact has been proved, brethren, that there are no nations incapable of being taught, nay, that there are no nations incapable afterwards of teaching others. The Negro slave has perished under the lash, rather than dishonor his Master. The Eskimo has climbed his barren steeps, and borne his toil, while he has recollected the burden which Jesus bore. The Hindu has patiently submitted to the loss of all things, because he loved Christ better than all. Feeble Malagasy women have been prepared to suffer and to die, and have taken joyfully suffering for Christ's sake.

There has been heroism in every land for Christ, men of every color and of every race have died for *Him*, upon His altar has been found the blood of all kindreds who are upon the face of the earth. Oh! tell me not they cannot be taught. Sirs, they can be taught to die for Christ, and this is more than some of you have learned. They can rehearse the very highest lesson of the Christian religion—that self-sacrifice which knows not itself, but gives up all for Him.

At this day, there are Karen missionaries preaching among the Karens with as fervid an eloquence as ever was known by Whitefield. There are Chinese teaching in Borneo, Sumatra, and Australia, with as much earnestness as Morison or Milne first taught in China. There are Hindu evangelists who are not ashamed to have given up the Brahmian thread, and to eat with the Pariah, and to preach with him the riches of Christ. There have been men found of every class and kind, not only able to be taught, but able to become teachers themselves, and the most mighty teachers too, of the grace of the Lord Jesus Christ. Well was that command warranted by future facts, when Christ said, 'Go ye, teach all nations.'

But brethren, the text says, *'Baptizing them.'* They are to be taught, and afterwards they are to be baptized. I know not why it is that we yield to the superstitions of our Christian brethren, so much as to use the word *baptize* at all. It is not an English, but a Greek word. It has but one meaning, and cannot bear another. Throughout all the classics, without exception, it is not possible to translate it correctly, except with the idea of immersion, and believing this, and knowing this, if the translation is not complete, we will complete it this morning. 'Go ye, therefore, and teach all nations, *immersing* them in the name of the Father, and of the Son, and of the Holy Ghost.'

Now, I think that our Missionary Society, while it may take precedence in matters of time—for it was the first that was ever commenced with the exception of the Moravians—ought also to take precedence in matters of purity, because we *can* carry out this text in every country, teaching first and baptizing afterwards. We do not understand the philosophy of baptizing, and afterwards teaching. We hold that we must teach first, and then, when men are disciples, we are to baptize them. Not the nations. The Greek does not bear that interpretation, but those who have been discipled, we are to baptize into the Sacred Name.

We think that our brethren do serious damage to the Gospel by baptizing children. We do not think their error a little one. We know it does not touch a vital point, but we do believe that infant baptism is the prop and pillar of Popery, and it being removed, Popery and Puseyism become at once impossible. You have taken away all idea of a national godliness, and a national religion when you have cut away all liberty to administer Christian ordinances to unconverted persons. We cannot see any evil which would follow if our brethren would renounce their mistake, but we can see abundant mischief which their mistake has caused, and in all kindness, but with all fidelity, we again enter our solemn protest against their giving baptism to any but disciples, to any but those who are the followers of the Lamb.

Throw down her hedges? Give her supper and her baptism to those who are not Christ's people? Break down her walls? Remove her barricades? God forbid! Except a man be renewed in heart, we dare not allow him to participate in the ordinances which belong to Christ's church. Oh! it is a disastrous thing to call unconverted children Christians, or to do anything which may weaken their apprehension of the great fact, that until they are converted, they have no part or lot in this matter.

Brethren, if you differ from me on this point, bear with me, for my conscience will not let me conceal this solemn truth. To you who agree with me I say, while our other friends can do in some things more than we can—and we rejoice in their efforts, and would heartily bless God that they have shown more activity than ourselves—yet we ought to be ashamed of ourselves if we are a whit behind.

We are a body of Christians who can fairly and purely teach and baptize, we can obey this command of Christ abroad, as well as at home, without running counter to our practice in one place by our practice in the other. We ought to be first and foremost, and if we be not, shame shall cover us for our unfaithfulness. Again, I say, I hear that voice ringing in the Baptist's ear, above that of any other man, 'Go ye, therefore, and teach all nations, baptizing them in the name of the Father, and of the Son, and of the Holy Ghost.'

I have endeavored to be brief, but I find I have been long, and therefore pass at once to the argument with which the text commences.

II. The ARGUMENT is this, 'All power is given unto me in heaven and in earth. Go ye, *therefore*, and teach all nations.'

Three things here. Christ had suffered, bled and died, He had now risen from the dead. As the effect of His finished work, He had as Mediator received all power in heaven and in earth. There is no allusion here to His inherent power that is not given to Him, that is His native right. He has, as God, all power in heaven and in earth. The text relates to Him as Mediator. As Mediator, He had not this power once. He was weak, He was despised, He was forsaken, even of His God. But now, having finished the work which was given Him to do, His Father honors Him. He is about to lift Him to His right hand and gives Him, as the result of resurrection, all power in heaven and in earth. Three things, then. First, this is the picture of the church's history, and *therefore*, she should teach all nations. Secondly, this is the church's right. Thirdly, it is the church's might, and for all these reasons she ought to teach all nations.

1. First, this is the church's *picture*. Christ suffers, bleeds, dies. Do you give up His cause? Do you look upon it as forlorn and desolate? He is nailed to the tree, the world abhors Him, fools gaze, and sinners laugh. Do you lay down your weapons and say, 'It is idle to defend such a man as this'? It is all over now, He bows His head upon the cross. 'It is finished,' says He, and do your unbelieving hearts say, 'Ay, indeed, it is finished. His career is over, His hopes are blighted, His prospects withered'?

Ah! little do you know that His shame was the mother of His future glory, that the stooping was the rising, that the crown of thorns was in fact the fruitful root out of which sprang the eternal crown of glory. He is put into the grave do you say that there is the grave of all your faith could believe, or your hope could suggest? He rises, brethren, and His resurrection takes effect, and fruit from the fact that He died and was buried. Do you not see the picture?

We have been sending out heralds of the cross these eighteen hundred years. They have landed upon many a shore to die. Fever has taken off its hundreds, cruel men have slain their scores, from the first day until now, the record of the mission is written in blood. Somewhere or other there always must be martyrs for Christ. It seems as if the church never could plow a wave without a spray of gore. She is still in Madagascar persecuted, afflicted, tormented, still are her ministers hunted about like partridges upon the mountains, and her blood is dying the shambles of her slayers.

Do you give up all hope? Shall we, as we look upon the tombs of our missionaries, say that Christ's cause is dead? Brethren, as you turn over the long roll, and read the names of one after another who sleeps in Jesus, shall you say, 'Let us close the doors of the mission house, let us cease our contributions, it is clear the case is hopeless, and the cause can never have success'? Nay, rather, the church must suffer that she may reign. She must die that she may live. She must be stained with blood, that she may be robed in purple. She must go down into the earth, and seem to be buried and forgotten, that the earth may help the woman, that she may be delivered of the man child.

Courage! Courage! Courage! The past is hopeful, because to the eye it seems hopeless. The cause is glorious, because it has been put to shame. Now, now let us gather the fruits of the bloody sowing, let us now reap the harvest of the deep plowing of agony and suffering which our ancestors have endured.

I think that no true-hearted Christian will ever give up any enterprise which God has laid upon him, because he fears its ultimate success. 'Difficult,' said Napoleon, 'is not a French word.' 'Doubtful,' is not a Christian word. We are *sure* to succeed, the Gospel *must* conquer. It is possible for heaven and earth to pass away, but it is not possible for God's Word to fail, and therefore it is utterly impossible that any nation, or kindred, or tongue should to the end stand out against the attacks of love, against the invasion of the armies of King Jesus.

Thus, you see a fair argument can be built upon the text. Inasmuch as Christ is to His people a picture of what they are to be, inasmuch as by His suffering all power was given to Him in heaven and in earth, so after the sufferings of the church, the wounds of her martyrs, and the deaths of her confessors, power shall be given to her in heaven and in earth, and she shall reign with Christ over the nations gloriously.

2. We now take a second view of the argument. This is the church's *right*. All power is given to Christ in heaven and in earth. What then? Why this? Kings and princes, potentates and powers, are you aware that your thrones have been given away? Do you know it, you crowned heads, that your crowns have been given—given away from you to one who claims to be King of kings, and Lord of lords?

Do you pass decrees forbidding the Gospel to be preached? We laugh at you. You have no power to prevent it, for all power is given unto Christ in heaven and in earth. Do you say that the missionary has no right upon your shores? The virgin daughter of Zion shakes her head at you, and laughs you to scorn. She has right anywhere and everywhere, she has rights in heaven without limit, and rights in earth without bound, for all power is given to her Head in heaven and in earth, and she therefore has a patent, a claim which is not to be disputed to take to herself all countries and all kingdoms, because the power above is given unto Christ.

What is that man doing on yonder shore? He has landed on an island in the South Seas. He is an intruder, banish him at once! Sirs, mind what you do, for surely you fight against God. But the man is sent away, he comes back again, or if not he, another. A severer edict is passed this time, 'Let us slay him, that the inheritance may still be ours.' But another comes, and another, and another. Why do you stand up and take counsel together against the Lord, and against His anointed? These men are not intruders, they are ambassadors come to make peace. Nay, more, they are delegates from heaven, come to claim the rightful heritage of King Jesus. You, in putting them away as intruders, have denied the rights of Christ, but to deny is one thing, and to disprove another. He has still a right to you, and therefore has the missionary still a right to come whithersoever he will, preaching the unsearchable riches of Christ.

Once or twice in my life I have met with some miserable little ministers, who, when I have gone into a village to preach, have questioned my right to preach in the village, because I ought to have asked them first, or to have consulted them. And can Christian men look on a district as their own dominion, and reckon God's servant as a poacher on their estates, or a brigand in their territories? Is there any place on this earth that belongs to any man so that he can shut out God's ministers?

We once for all put our foot upon any claim so ridiculous. Wherever there is found a man, there is the minister free to preach. The whole world is our parish. We know of no fetter upon our feet, and no gag upon our lips. Though kings should pass laws, the servants of Christ can bear the penalty, but they cannot disobey their Master. Though the Emperor should say the Gospel should not be preached by any unauthorized denomination in France, as I have heard he has said of late, we care not for him. What cares the church for a thousand Emperors? Their resolutions are mockery, their laws waste paper. The church never was yet vassal to the State, or servile slave to municipalities, and powers, and she neither can nor will be. At all the laws of states, she laughs and utterly defies them, if they come in the way of the law of Christ which says, 'Teach the Gospel to every creature.'

Brethren, I say, the church has a right anywhere and everywhere—a right, not because she is tolerated, the word is insult—not because the law permits, the law permitting or not permitting, tolerated or untolerated, everywhere beneath the arch of God's heaven, God's servants have a right to preach. Oh, that they would claim the right, and in every place teach and preach Jesus Christ continually.

3. But now, lastly, it seems to me that the argument of the text contains the church's *might*. 'All power is given unto me in heaven, and in earth; go ye, therefore, and teach all nations, baptizing them in the name of the Father, and of the Son, and of the Holy Ghost.' You have power to teach, fear not. Let this be your encouragement, you must succeed, you shall prevail. There never lived another man save Christ, who could say, 'All power is given me on earth.'

Canute puts his throne by the side of the sea, but the waves wet his person, and prove to his flattering courtiers that he is but a man. What power have kings over the lightning or the rushing winds? Can they control the tides, or bid the moon stand still? Power is not given unto man, even upon earth. Much less could any man say, all power in heaven belonged to him. This is a singular expression, one which only could be used by Christ. And if any other should attempt to use it, it were an imposition and a blasphemy. But the Lord Jesus Christ can say today, as He said then, 'All power is given unto me in heaven and in earth.'

Let us think, then, all power is given to Christ in providence. Over common daily events He has supreme authority. You have launched upon the sea, upon a mission voyage. He rules the waves, and wings the winds. Fear not, for tempest is His trembling slave. You have come near the shore, but there are hidden reefs, and sunken rocks. Fear not, for all power is given to Him in the lowest deep to guide you safely, and to bring you to your desired haven.

A band of men meet you upon the shore, brandishing their weapons. You are unarmed, you have nothing but the Word. You shall now prove that, 'More is He who is with you than all they who are with them.' Go, in this your might. All power is given to Christ—power over the wills of men, as well as over the waves of the sea. But political occurrences prevent your landing on a certain country, through treaties, or a lack of treaties, there is no room for the missionary in such-and-such an empire.

Pray and the gates shall be opened. *Plead* and the bars of brass shall be cut in two. Christ has power over politics. He can make wars, and create peace with a view to the propagation of His Word. He can change the hearts of princes, and preside in the counsels of senates. He can cause nations that have long been shut up to be opened to the truth.

And indeed, what a wonderful proof we have had of late, that all power belongs unto Christ, for human skill has been yoked to the chariot of the Gospel. How wondrously, my brethren, have the inventions of man of late years progressed! How could we have preached the Gospel to all nations—how could we have even known that America existed, if it had not been that the Lord put it into the mind of Columbus to discover the New World! And how wearisome our life, if with the ordinary slow navigation of the ancient times, we had to journey among all nations! But now we are carried across the waves so rapidly that distance is annihilated, and time forgotten. Truly God has opened up the world, and brought it to our threshold. If He has not made a smaller world, at least He has made it more convenient, and nearer to our hand.

And then, see how countries which once could not be reached, have been opened to us. The Celestial King of China, the rebel prince, invites us to come and preach. He does not merely permit—he invites. He builds places of worship, he is prepared, he says, that his brethren should come and teach him, and teach all his subjects, for they are imperfectly taught in the things of God. And the Imperial Sovereign of China too, though he does not invite, permits the missionaries to go among his millions. There is perfect liberty for us to preach to four hundred millions of persons who before had never seen the light of Calvary.

And there is India too, given up to our dominion, and the old Company, which always impeded us, rolled up in its shroud, and laid in its grave. And there are other lands and other places which once seemed to be environed by impassable mountains, into which we have now a road. Oh, for the will to dash through that road riding upon the white horses of salvation! Oh, for the heart, the spirit, and the soul to avail ourselves of the golden opportunity, and to preach Christ where He has never been preached before! All power, then, we can clearly see, over everything in this world has been given to Christ, and has been used for the propagation of His truth.

But brethren, let us recollect that power is given to Christ in heaven as well as on earth. All angels bow before Him, and the cherubim and seraphim are ready to obey His high behests. Power is given to Him over the plenitude of the Holy Spirit. He can pour out the mysterious energy in such abundance that nations can be born in a day. He can clothe His ministers with salvation, and make His priests shout aloud for joy. He has power to intercede with God, and He shall presently send out men to preach, presently give the people the mind to hear, and give the hearers the will to obey.

We have in the midst of us today our Leader. He is not gone from us. If His flesh and blood be absent, yet in body as well as spirit He still lives, adorned with the dew and beauty of His youth. As for the Mohammedan, *his* leader has long ago rotted in his coffin, but ours lives, and because He lives, His truth and His cause live also. We have with us today a Leader whose power is not diminished, whose influence in the highest heavens has suffered no impairing. He is universal Lord. Oh, let our efforts be worthy of the power which He has promised, let our zeal be in some respect akin to His zeal, and let our energy prove that the divine energy has not been withdrawn.

I wish that I could preach this morning, but the more earnest I feel, the more scant are my words with which to express my emotions. I have prayed to God, and it is a prayer I shall repeat till I die—I have prayed that out of this church there may go many missionaries. I will never be content with a congregation, or with a church, or even with ministers, many of whom have already gone out of our midst. We must have missionaries from this church. God's people everywhere will, I trust, aid me in training young soldiers for my Master's army. God will send the men, and faith will find the means, and we will ourselves send out our own men to proclaim the name of Jesus.

Brethren, it is a singular thing there are some young men who get the idea into their minds that they would like to go into foreign lands, but these are frequently the most unfit men, and have not the power and ability. Now, I would that the divine call would come to some gifted men. You who have, perhaps, some wealth of your own, what could be a better object in life than to devote yourself and your substance to the Redeemer's cause?

You young men who have brilliant prospects before you, but who as yet have not the anxieties of a family to maintain, why, would it not be a noble thing to surrender your brilliant prospects, that you may become a humble preacher of Christ? The greater the sacrifice, the more honor to yourself, and the more acceptable to Him. I have questioned my own conscience, and I do not think I could be in the path of duty if I should go abroad to preach the Word, leaving this field of labor.

But I think many of my brethren now laboring at home might with the greatest advantage surrender their charges, and leave a land where they would scarce be missed, to go where their presence would be as valuable as the presence of a thousand such as they are here. And oh! I long that we may see young men out of the universities, and students in our grammar schools—that we may see our physicians, advocates, tradesmen, and educated mechanics, when God has touched their hearts giving up all they have, that they may teach and preach Christ.

We want Vanderkists. We want Judsons, and Brainerds over again. It will never do to send out to the heathen men who are of no use at home. We cannot send men of third and tenth-class abilities, we must send the highest and best. The bravest men must lead the van. O God, anoint Your servants, we beseech You. Put the fire into their hearts that never can be quenched. Make it so hot within their bones that they must die or preach, that they must lie down with broken hearts, or else be free to preach where Christ was never heard.

Brethren, I envy anyone among you—I say again with truth, I envy you if it shall be your lot to go to China, the country so lately opened to us. I would gladly change places with you. I would renounce the partial case of a settlement in this country, and renounce the responsibilities of so large a congregation as this with pleasure, if I might have your honors. I think sometimes that missionaries in the field—if it be right to compare great things with such small ones—might say to you, as our English king did to his soldiers at the battle of Agincourt, changing the word for a moment—

> 'Ministers in England, now a bed,
> Might think themselves accurs'd they were not here,
> And hold their manhood's cheap, while any speak
> Who fought with us upon this glorious day.'

Have we none out of our sixteen hundred members—have we none out of this congregation of six thousand—who can say, 'Here am I, send me'? Jesus! Is there not one? Must heathens perish? Must the gods of the heathen hold their thrones? Must Your kingdom fail? Are there none to own You, none to maintain Your righteous cause? If there be none, let us weep, each one of us, because such a calamity has fallen on us.

But if there are any who are willing to give all for Christ, let us who are compelled to stay at home do our best to help them. Let us see to it that they lack nothing, for we cannot send them out without purse or scrip. Let us fill the purse of the men whose hearts God has filled, and take care of them temporally, leaving it for God to preserve them spiritually.

May the Lord, the divine Master, add His blessing to the feeble words that I have uttered, and let me not conclude till I have said, *I* must teach *you* too, and this is the teaching of God, 'Believe in the Lord Jesus Christ, and you shall be saved.' Trust Him with your soul, and He will save you. For 'He that believes and is baptized shall be saved; he that believes not shall be damned.'

SOURCES

Books

Anderson, Courtney. *To the Golden Shore: The Life of Adoniram Judson*. 2nd Edition. Valley Forge, PA: Judson Press, 1987.

Augustine. *Galatians, Ephesians, Philippians, Ancient Christian Commentary on Scripture, NT*. Volume 8. Edited by Mark J. Edwards. Downers Grove, IL: Inter Varsity Press, 1999.

Bauer, Walter. *A Greek-English Lexicon of the New Testament and Other Early Christian Literature* (BAGD). Revised and Edited by Frederick William Danker. 3rd Edition. Chicago: University of Chicago, 2000.

Bebbington, David W. *Evangelicalism in Modern Britain: A History from the 1730s to the 1980s*. Oxfordshire, UK: Routledge, 1989.

Bergler, Thomas. *The Juvenilization of American Christianity*. Grand Rapids: Eerdmans, 2012.

Boyarin, Daniel. *The Jewish Gospels: The Story of the Jewish Christ*. New York: The New Press, 2012.

Brainerd, David. *The Life and Diary of David Brainerd: With Notes and Reflections*. Edited by Jonathan Edwards. ReadaClassic.com, 2010.

Brandt W. and H. Lehman, Editors. *Luther's Works*. Philadelphia: Muhlenberg Press, 1962.

Bruce, F.F. *The Book of the Acts*. New International Commentary. Grand Rapids: Eerdmans, 1988.

Bruce, F.F. *The Epistle to the Galatians: A Commentary on the Greek Text*. The New International Greek Testament Commentary. Grand Rapids: Eerdmans, 1982.

Bryant, David. *Concerts of Prayer: For Spiritual Awakening and World Evangelization*. Grand Rapids: Baker Publishing Group, 1988.

Burns, E.D. *A Supreme Desire to Please Him: The Spirituality of Adoniram Judson*. Eugene, OR: Pickwick, 2016.

Carson, D.A. *The Gospel of John*. The Pillar New Testament Commentary. Grand Rapids: Eerdmans, 1991.

Carson, D.A. *How Long, O Lord?: Reflections on Suffering and Evil*. Grand Rapids: Baker Academic, 2006.

Cate, Patrick O. *Through God's Eyes*. Pasadena, CA: William Carey Library, 2003.

Clark, R. Scott. *Recovering the Reformed Confession: Our Theology, Piety, and Practice*. Phillipsburg, NJ: P&R Publishing, 2008.

Clement, Jesse. *Memoir of Adoniram Judson, Being a Sketch of His Life and Missionary Labors*. Auburn, NY: Derby and Miller, 1851.

DeYoung, Kevin and Greg Gilbert. *What is the Mission of the Church?: Making Sense of Social Justice, Shalom, and the Great Commission*. Wheaton: Crossway, 2011.

Dudley, Donald R. *A History of Cynicism: From Diogenes to the 6th Century A.D.* London: Methuen & Co., 1937.

Elmer, Duane. *Cross-Cultural Conflict: Building Relationships for Effective Ministry*. Downers Grove, IL: InterVarsity Press, 1993.

George, Timothy. *Galatians*. The New American Commentary. Volume 30. Edited by E. Ray Clendenen. Nashville: Broadman Holman, 1994.

Gleason, Michael F. *When God Walked on Campus*. Dundas, Ontario: Joshua Press, 2002.

Griffiths, Michael. *Give Up Your Small Ambitions*. Nashville: Accelerated Christian Education, 1993.

Hesselgrave, David J. *Planting Churches Cross-Culturally: North America and Beyond*. 2nd Edition. Grand Rapids: Baker Academic, 2000.

Holy Bible, *English Standard Version*. Wheaton: Crossway, 2011.

Judson, Adoniram. *A Digest of Scripture, Consisting of Extracts from the Old and New Testaments: On the Plan of 'Brown's Selection of Scripture Passages'*. Maulmain: American Baptist Mission Press, 1838.

Judson, Adoniram. *The Golden Balance*. 6th Edition. Maulmain: American Baptist Mission Press, 1836.

Judson, Adoniram. *A View of the Christian Religion in Three Parts: Historic, Didactic, and Preceptive*. 15th Edition. Maulmain: American Baptist Mission Press, 1860.

Judson, Ann. *The Catechism*. Rangoon: American Baptist Mission Press, 1909.

Judson, Ann Hasseltine. *An Account of the American Baptist Mission to the Burman Empire: In a Series of Letters, Addressed to a Gentleman in London*. London: J. Butterworth & Son and T. Clark, 1823.

Judson, Edward. *The Life of Adoniram Judson, By His Son, Edward Judson*. New York: Randolph, 1883.

Kane, J. Herbert. *Life and Work on the Mission Field*. Grand Rapids: Baker, 1990.

Kane, J. Herbert. *Understanding Christian Missions*. Grand Rapids: Baker, 1974.

Lewis, C.S. *Mere Christianity*. San Francisco: Harper, 2001.

Lewis, C.S. *The Screwtape Letters*. San Francisco: HarperOne, 2017.

Lewis, Peter. *The Genius of Puritanism*. Morgan, PA: Soli Deo Gloria, 1995.

Longenecker, Richard N. *Acts*. The Expositor's Bible Commentary. Kindle Edition. Grand Rapids: Zondervan Academic, 2017.

Lovett, Richard. *James Gilmour of Mongolia*. London: Religious Tract Society, 1892.

Lloyd-Jones, D.M. *What Is an Evangelical?* Carlisle, PA: The Banner of Truth Trust, 2002.

Lull, Timothy. *Martin Luther's Basic Theological Writings.* 2nd Edition. Minneapolis: Fortress Press, 2005.

Luther, Martin. *A Commentary on St Paul's Epistle to the Galatians.* Philadelphia: Quaker City Publishing, 1872.

Luther, Martin. *What Luther Says.* Edited by Ewald M. Plass. 3 Volumes in 1. St. Louis: Concordia, 1959.

Machen, J. Gresham. *Christianity and Liberalism.* Grand Rapids: Eerdmans, 2009.

Marsden, George M. *Fundamentalism and American Culture.* Oxford University, 2006.

McElroy, Jack. *Adoniram Judson's Soul Winning Secrets Revealed: An Inspiring Look at the Tools Used by 'Jesus Christ's Man' in Burma.* Shirley, MA: McElroy Publishing, 2013.

Morris, Leon. *Galatians.* Downers Grove, IL: Inter Varsity Press, 1996.

Mounce, William D. *Mounce's Complete Expository Dictionary of Old and New Testaments Words.* Grand Rapids: Zondervan, 2006.

Müller, George. *A Narrative of Some of the Lord's Dealing with George Müller, Written by Himself, Jehovah Magnified. Addresses by George Müller Complete and Unabridged.* 2 Volumes. Muskegon, MI: Dust and Ashes, 2003.

Murray, Iain H. *Pentecost—Today?: The Biblical Basis for Understanding Revival.* Reprint Edition. Carlisle, PA: Banner of Truth Trust, 2015.

Neill, Stephen. *A History of Christian Missions.* 2nd Edition. The Penguin History of the Church. Volume 6. Harmondsworth, England: Penguin Books, 1986.

Noll, Mark A. *The Rise of Evangelicalism: The Age of Edwards, Whitefield, and the Wesleys.* Downers Grove, IL: IVP Academic, 2018.

Noll, Mark A., David W. Bebbington, and George M. Marsden. *Evangelicals: Who They Have Been, Are Now, and Could Be.* Grand Rapids: Eerdmans, 2019.

Olson, C. Gordon. *What in the World is God Doing?* Cedar Knolls, NJ: Global Gospel Publishers, 2003.

Ott, Craig, Stephen Strauss, with Timothy C. Tennent. *Encountering Theology of Mission: Biblical Foundations, Historical Developments, and Contemporary Issues.* Encountering Mission. Grand Rapids: Baker Academic, 2010.

Owen, John. *John Owen on Hebrews: A Classic Puritan Commentary.* Kindle Edition.

Packer, J.I. *God in Our Midst: Seeking and Receiving Ongoing Revival.* UK: Authentic Publishing, 1987.

Packer, J.I. *A Quest for Godliness: The Puritan vision of the Christian Life.* Reprint Edition. Wheaton: Crossway, 2010.

Peterson, David G. *The Acts of the Apostles.* The Pillar New Testament Commentary. Grand Rapids: Eerdmans, 2009.

Pierson, A.T. *George Müller of Bristol and His Witness to a Prayer-Hearing God.* New York: Fleming H. Revell, 1899.

Piper, John. *A Peculiar Glory: How the Christian Scriptures Reveal Their Complete Truthfulness.* Wheaton, IL: Crossway, 2016.

Pratt, Zane, et al. *Introduction to Global Missions.* Nashville: B&H Publishing Group, 2014.

Ryle, J.C. *Holiness: Its Nature, Hindrances, Difficulties, and Roots.* Moscow, ID: Charles Nolan Publishers, 2001.

Ryle, J.C. *Principles for Churchmen.* 2nd Edition. London: William Hunt, 1884.

Sadler, M.E. *The Acts of the Apostles.* London: George Bell & Sons, 1908.

Schnabel, Eckhard. *Early Christian Mission.* Volume 1. Downers Grove, IL: IVP Academic, 2004.

Schnabel, Eckhard. *Paul the Missionary: Realities, Strategies and Methods.* Downers Grove, IL: InterVarsity Press, 2008.

Schreiner, Patrick. *Matthew, Disciple and Scribe.* Grand Rapids: Baker, 2019.

Silva, Moises. *Interpreting Galatians.* 2nd Edition. Grand Rapids: Baker Academic, 2001.

Spitters, Denny and Matthew Ellison. *When Everything Is Missions.* Orlando, FL: BottomLine Media, 2017.

Sproul, R.C. *Knowing Scripture.* Downers Grove, IL: InterVarsity Press, 2009.

Stanley, Brian. *The Global Diffusion of Evangelicalism: The Age of Billy Graham and John Stott.* Downers Grove, IL: 2018.

Steer, Roger. *George Müller: Delighted in God.* Scotland. UK: Christian Focus Publications, 1997.

Stott, John R.W. *The Message of Acts: The Spirit, the Church & the World.* The Bible Speaks Today. Downers Grove, IL: InterVarsity Press, 1994.

Strong, James. *Olive Tree Enhanced Strong's Dictionary.* Olive Tree Bible Software.

Sweeney, Douglas A. *The American Evangelical Story: A History of the Movement.* Grand Rapids: Baker Academic, 2005.

Talman, Harley and John Jay Travis, Editors. *Understanding Insider Movements: Disciples of Jesus within Diverse Religious Communities.* Pasadena: William Carey Library, 2015.

Trueman, Carl R. *The Creedal Imperative.* Wheaton: Crossway, 2012.

Waltke, Bruce. *Finding the Will of God: A Pagan Notion?* Grand Rapids: Eerdmans, 1995.

Wayland, Francis. *A Memoir of the Life and Labors of the Rev. Adoniram Judson, D.D.* 2 Volumes. Boston: Phillips, Samson and Company, 1853.

Wiker, Benjamin. *Moral Darwinism: How We Became Hedonists.* Christian Classics Bible Studies. Downers Grove, IL: IVP Academic, 2002.

Witherington, Ben. *The Acts of the Apostles: A Socio-Rhetorical Commentary.* New Testament Commentary. Grand Rapids: Eerdmans, 1997.

Articles

Brown, Russel E. 'The Life and Work of Adoniram Judson'. *Andover Newton Quarterly* 2, No. 3 (1962).

Burns, E.D. '"The Golden Lamp Hung Out of Heaven": Adoniram and Ann Judson's Bibliocentric Strategy for Reaching the Buddhists of Burma'. In Paul H. De Neui, Editor. *Emerging Faith: Lessons from Mission History in Asia.* Littleton, CO: William Carey Publishing, 2020.

Burns, E.D. 'Twelve Leadership Principles for Cross-Cultural Ministries'. *The Seminarian.* Toronto Baptist Seminary (March 2015).

Eitel, Keith E. 'The Enduring Legacy of Adoniram Judson's Missiological Precepts and Practices'. In Jason G. Duesing, Editor. *Adoniram Judson: A Bicentennial Appreciation of the Pioneer American Missionary.* Studies in Baptist Life and Thought. Edited by Michael A.G. Haykin. Nashville: B&H Academic, 2012.

Fernando, Ajith. 'Getting Back on Course'. *Christianity Today* 51 (November 2007).

'Intelligence from the Missions, Theological Training of Native Pastors'. *The Baptist Missionary Magazine* 34 (1854).

Judson, Adoniram. 'Extract of a Letter from Mr. Judson to Mr. Rice, Rangoon, August 3d, 1816'. *The Baptist Missionary Magazine* 1 (1817).

Judson, Adoniram. 'Letter from the Rev. Adoniram Judson, Jun. to Dr. Baldwin, Dated Rangoon, December 9, 1819'. *The Baptist Missionary Magazine* 2 (1819).

Judson, Emily Chubbuck. 'Closing Scenes in Dr. Judson's Life'. *The Baptist Missionary Magazine* 31 (1851).

Kolb, Robert. *The Theology of Martin Luther.* 'Lecture Notes'. Grand Rapids: The Institute of Theological Studies, 1994.

Lewis, C.S. 'As the Ruin Falls'. In *Poems*. 1st Published 1964.

Merrill, William P. 'Rise Up O Men of God!'. In *Hymns for a Pilgrim People*. Chicago: GIA Publications, 2000.

Patterson, Ben. 'Heart and Soul'. *Leadership Journal* (Winter 2000).

Smart, Robert Davis. 'Introduction'. In *Pentecostal Outpourings: Revival and the Reformed Tradition*. Grand Rapids: Reformation Heritage Books, 2016.

Webpages

Burns, E.D. 'From Traitor to Heir'. *www.desiringGod.org*. 29 August 2014. https://www.desiringgod.org/articles/from-traitor-to-heir.

Burns, E.D. 'The Missionary Life: No Shortcuts'. *The Gospel Coalition*. 5 December 2014. https://www.thegospelcoalition.org/article/the-missionary-life-no-shortcuts/.

Burns, E.D. 'Seven Things to Pray for Missionaries'. *Southern Equip*. http://equip.sbts.edu/article/7-things-topray-for-missionaries/.

Carter, Joe. 'Factchecker: Misquoting Francis of Assisi'. *The Gospel Coalition*. 11 July 2012. http://thegospelcoalition.org/blogs/tgc/2012/07/11/factchecker-misquoting-francis-of-assisi/.

Henry, M. 'Commentary on Hebrews 13 by Matthew Henry'. *Blue Letter Bible*. Last Modified 1 March 1996. https://www.blueletterbible.org/Comm/mhc/Hbr/Hbr_013.cfm.

Johnson, Phil. 'Paul and Contextualization'. *Pyromaniacs*. 9 April 2008. https://teampyro.blogspot.com/2008/04/paul-and-contextualization.html.

Johnson, Phil. 'Paul and Culture'. *Pyromaniacs*. 2 April 2008. https://teampyro.blogspot.com/2008/04/paul-and-culture.html.

Klett, Leah MarieAnn. 'Americans Spend More Money on Pet Halloween Costumes Than Reaching Lost: Missions Expert'. *The Christian Post*. 28 October 2018. https://www.christianpost.com/news/americans-spend-more-money-pet-halloweencostumes-than-reaching-lost-missions-andrew-scott.html.

MacArthur, John. 'John MacArthur on a Pastor's Authority'. *Grace to You.* 29 August 2017. https://youtu.be/X65vspiZLLA.

Piper, John. 'Ask Whatever You Wish'. *www.desiringGod.org.* Minneapolis: Desiring God Foundation, 1993. http://www.desiringgod.org/messages/ask-whatever-you-wish.

Platanakis, Charilaos. 'Cynic'. In *Encyclopadia Britannica.* Encyclopædia Britannica, Inc. 4 February 2018. https://www.britannica.com/topic/Cynic-ancient-Greek-philosophy.

Roberts, Alastair. 'The Fighting Shepherd'. *Alastair's Adversaria.* 14 July 2012. https://alastairadversaria.com/2012/07/14/the-fighting-shepherd.

Smith, Steve. 'Spiritual Authority's Most Abused Verse'. *Liberty for Captives.* 24 August 2012. https://libertyforcaptives.com/2012/08/24/hebrews-1317-spiritual-authoritys-most-abused-verse/.

Spurgeon, Charles. 'Sermon #383'. *Metropolitan Tabernacle Pulpit.* Volume 7. http://www.spurgeongems.org/vols7-9/chs383.pdf.

Spurgeon, Charles H. 'A Sermon and a Reminiscence'. *Sword and the Trowel* (March 1873). http://www.spurgeon.org/s_and_t/srmn1873.htm.

Vine, W.E. *Vine's Expository Dictionary of New Testament Words.* 1940. https://www.studylight.org/dictionaries/ved/o/obedience-obedient-obey.html.

Christian Focus Publications

Our mission statement –

STAYING FAITHFUL

In dependence upon God we seek to impact the world through literature faithful to His infallible Word, the Bible. Our aim is to ensure that the Lord Jesus Christ is presented as the only hope to obtain forgiveness of sin, live a useful life and look forward to heaven with Him.

Our books are published in four imprints:

CHRISTIAN FOCUS

Popular works including biographies, commentaries, basic doctrine and Christian living.

CHRISTIAN HERITAGE

Books representing some of the best material from the rich heritage of the church.

MENTOR

Books written at a level suitable for Bible College and seminary students, pastors, and other serious readers. The imprint includes commentaries, doctrinal studies, examination of current issues and church history.

CF4·K

Children's books for quality Bible teaching and for all age groups: Sunday school curriculum, puzzle and activity books; personal and family devotional titles, biographies and inspirational stories – because you are never too young to know Jesus!

Christian Focus Publications Ltd,
Geanies House, Fearn, Ross-shire,
IV20 1TW, Scotland, United Kingdom.
www.christianfocus.com